No Stress Tech Guide To
What's New In Crystal Reports 2008

Also Includes What's New In Crystal Reports XI

By Dr. Indera E. Murphy

Tolana Publishing
Teaneck, New Jersey

No Stress Tech Guide To What's New In Crystal Reports 2008: Also Includes What's New In Crystal Reports XI

Published By:
Tolana Publishing
PO Box 719
Teaneck, NJ 07666 USA

Find us online at www.tolanapublishing.com
Inquiries may be sent to the publisher: tolanapub@yahoo.com

Our books are available online at www.amazon.com, www.barnesandnoble.com, www.alibris.com and www.biblio.com. They can also be ordered from Ingram.

Copyright © 2008 Dr. Indera E. Murphy

All rights reserved. No part of this book may be reproduced or transmitted in any form or by any means, electronic or mechanical, including photocopying, recording, storage in an information retrieval system, or otherwise, without prior written permission from the publisher.

ISBN-10: 1-935208-01-2
ISBN-13: 978-1-935208-01-3

Library of Congress Control Number: 2008906888

Printed and bound in the United States Of America

Notice of Liability
Every effort has been made to ensure that this book contains accurate and current information. However, the publisher and author shall not be liable to any person or entity with respect to any loss or damage caused or alleged to be caused directly or indirectly, as a result of any information contained herein or by the computer software and hardware products described in it.

Trademarks
All companies and product names are trademarks or registered trademarks of their respective companies. They are used in this book in an editorial fashion only. No use of any trademark is intended to convey endorsement or other affiliation with this book.

Cover designed by Mary Kramer, Milkweed Graphics, www.milkweedgraphics.com

Quantity Discounts
Quantity discounts are available for corporations, non-profit organizations, corporations and educational institutions for educational purposes, fundraising or resale. See www.tolanapublishing.com/wholesale.html

Discount On Future Books
To be notified when new titles are released, send an email with the subject "New Book Release". This will entitle you to a pre-publish discount for new titles that are released.

V1.0

Who The Book Is For
This book is primarily for end-users and developers that have used a prior version of Crystal Reports and want to learn about the new features in Crystal Reports 2008, Crystal Reports XI or Crystal Reports XI Release 2 (R2). If you want in-depth coverage, see our Crystal Reports books below.

About The No Stress Tech Guide Series
The No Stress Tech Guide To What's New In Crystal Reports 2008, is part of a growing series of computer software training books that are designed to be used in a classroom setting, an online class or as a self-paced learning tool. This book can also be used as a textbook supplement or reference guide. The books in this series contain an abundance of screen shots to help reduce the "stress" often associated with learning new software.

Tolana Publishing believes that the following principals are important when it comes to computer software training books:

⇒ The text should be large enough that the reader does not have to squint.
⇒ The step-by-step instructions should really work and not leave something out.
⇒ Features or options that do not work as intended should be pointed out, not to bash the software company, but so that you don't think that you are crazy <smile>.
⇒ That there should be a realistic mix of theory, real world examples and hands-on exercises. It is important to know the past, because it helps you transition into the future with ease and dignity.

Other Titles In The No Stress Tech Guide Series

Microsoft Works 7	ISBN-10: 0977391221	ISBN-13: 978-0-9773912-2-6
Microsoft Works 8 & 8.5	ISBN-10: 0977391213	ISBN-13: 978-0-9773912-1-9
Windows XP	ISBN-10: 0977391205	ISBN-13: 978-0-9773912-0-2
Crystal Reports XI (Out of print)	ISBN-10: 097739123X	ISBN-13: 978-0-9773912-3-3
Crystal Reports XI For Beginners (2nd Edition)	ISBN-10: 1935208004	ISBN-13: 978-1-935208-00-6
OpenOffice.org Writer 2	ISBN-10: 0977391248	ISBN-13: 978-0-9773912-4-0
ACT! 2007	ISBN-10: 0977391256	ISBN-13: 978-0-9773912-5-7
Microsoft Works 9	ISBN-10: 0977391272	ISBN-13: 978-0-9773912-7-1
Crystal Reports For Visual Studio 2005	ISBN-10: 0977391264	ISBN-13: 978-0-9773912-6-4
Crystal Reports Basic For Visual Studio 2008	ISBN-10: 0977391280	ISBN-13: 978-0-9773912-8-8
Crystal Reports 2008	ISBN-10: 0977391299	ISBN-13: 978-0-9773912-9-5

Forthcoming Titles
Joomla!

About The Author

Dr. Indera Murphy is an author, educator and IT professional that has over 18 years of experience in the Information Technology field. She has held a variety of positions including, programmer, consultant, technical writer, web designer, course developer and project leader. Indera has designed and developed software applications and web sites, as well as, manage IT Projects. In addition to being an Executive Director and consultant, Indera is also an online adjunct professor. She teaches courses in a variety of areas including technical writing, information processing, Access, HTML, Windows, project management, spreadsheets, Dreamweaver and critical thinking.

Why A Book On What's New In Crystal Reports 2008?

With each new version of a software package comes brand new features, changes to existing features and features that have been removed. When a new version of software is promoted, only the new features are discussed. When most people upgrade to a new version of a software package, they probably do not want to pay the cost of and sift through a 600+ page book just to find out about the new features. That is the primary goal of this book - to point out the differences.

When you start using the latest version of a software package, you may or may not notice all of the changes from the previous version. It is possible that I have missed a few changes. That is another goal of this book, to point out everything that I noticed that is new, changed or removed.

It also dawned on me that a lot of people that buy Crystal Reports 2008 may be upgrading from a version prior to Crystal Reports XI. If so, having information on what's new in Crystal Reports XI and Crystal Reports XI (R2) will make the transition to Crystal Reports 2008 easier. I also wanted to cover some topics that are asked about, but are not new.

How This Book Is Organized

Section 1 Crystal Reports XI
- Chapter 1   Interface changes and new features in Crystal Reports XI.
- Chapter 2   Report design option changes in Crystal Reports XI.
- Chapter 3   Crystal Reports Release 2 (R2) changes.

Section 2 Crystal Reports 2008
- Chapter 4   Changes and new features in Crystal Reports 2008.
- Chapter 5   Report design option changes in Crystal Reports 2008.

TABLE OF CONTENTS

SECTION 1 CRYSTAL REPORTS XI

WHAT'S NEW IN CRYSTAL REPORTS XI 1-1
   Conventions Used In This Book 1-2
   Interactive Messages 1-4
   What's New In Crystal Reports XI? 1-4
      New Patch Installation 1-4
      Hierarchical Group Reports 1-4
      Single Sign-On 1-4
      Workbench 1-5
      Report Export Configuration 1-5
      RTF Export Format 1-5
      Updated Repository Explorer 1-5
      HTML Preview 1-5
      Enhanced Report Viewer 1-5
      N Value For Top N Style Reports 1-5
      Dependency Checker 1-5
      Drop And Drag Charts And Cross-Tabs 1-6
      Dynamic Graphic Location 1-6
      Dynamic And Cascading Prompts 1-6
      Updated Data Drivers 1-6
      Other New Features 1-6
   What Else Is Covered? 1-6
   Differences Between The Standard And Professional Editions 1-6
   Start Page Overview 1-8
      New Reports 1-9
      Recent Reports 1-10
      Resources Online 1-10
   Checking For Software Updates 1-10
   Table Linking Change 1-13
   Toolbar Changes 1-13
      Navigation Tools Toolbar 1-14
      Report Navigation Toolbar 1-15
   View Menu Options 1-16
   The Workbench 1-18
      Workbench Toolbar 1-18
      Report Packages 1-19
      How To Create A Folder In The Workbench 1-19
      Adding Reports To The Workbench 1-20
      Deleting Projects And Reports From The Workbench 1-20
      Maintaining The Workbench 1-21
   Repository Explorer 1-21
   The Repository 1-22
   Formula Editor 1-23
      Customizing The Formula Editor 1-24
   The Workshop Tree 1-24

Formula Expert 1-25
Exercise 1.1: Create A Formula Field 1-26
Dynamic Graphic Location 1-30
The Dependency Checker 1-31
Report Options 1-33
CrystalReports.com 1-34

REPORT DESIGN OPTION CHANGES IN CRYSTAL REPORTS XI 2-1
Cross-Tab Reports 2-2
Exercise 2.1: Create A Cross-Tab Product Report 2-6
The Chart Expert 2-7
   Type Tab 2-8
Chart Layout Options 2-8
Exercise 2.2: Create Charts From Cross-Tab Data 2-10
Cross-Tab Expert Overview 2-13
   Cross-Tab Tab 2-14
   Style Tab 2-15
   Customize Style Tab 2-15
Formatting Formulas 2-18
Exercise 2.3: Use The Cross-Tab Expert 2-18
Exercise 2.4: Create Conditional Formatting In Cross-Tabs 2-21
Cross-Tab Shortcut Menu 2-22
Report Viewers 2-22
New Report Export Options 2-22
Exercise 2.5: Create A Word Editable (RTF) Export File 2-22
Exercise 2.6: Creating Default Export Options 2-23
Exercise 2.7: Create A Histogram Chart 2-24
Parameter Fields 2-25
   Importing Values 2-25
The Create New Parameter Dialog Box 2-26
Exercise 2.8: Create A Static List Of Values Manually 2-28
   How To Sort The Entire Value List At One Time 2-31
Dynamic List Of Values 2-31
Exercise 2.9: Create A Dynamic Region List Of Values 2-32
   Cascading Prompts And List Of Values 2-33
Exercise 2.10: Create Cascading Prompts For Countries And Regions 2-33
Exercise 2.11: Create Cascading Prompts For Customers And Their Orders 2-34
Allow Range Values And Allow Multiple Values Options 2-36
Top N Reports With Parameter Fields 2-37
Exercise 2.12: Create A Parameter Field For A Top N Report 2-37
Exercise 2.13: Show The Bottom 20% Of Orders 2-40
Using Parameter Fields To Select The Sorting And Grouping Options 2-41
Exercise 2.14: Create A Parameter Field To Sort The Records 2-42
Exercise 2.15: Create A Parameter Field To Group Data 2-43
Adding Parameter Field Criteria To A Report 2-45
   Printing Parameter Range Fields 2-45
Exercise 2.16: Print Parameter Range Fields 2-46
Printing Multi Value Parameter Fields Using The Join Function 2-46
Exercise 2.17: Print Multi Value Parameter Fields 2-46
Exercise 2.18: Create A Hierarchical Group Report 2-48

CRYSTAL REPORTS XI RELEASE 2 (R2) 3-1
Crystal Reports XI Release 2 Overview 3-2
Adding Reports To The Workbench 3-2
   Workbench Toolbar 3-2
Field Explorer 3-3
Sort Fields In The Field Explorer 3-4
Object Size And Position Dialog Box 3-4
Custom Colors 3-5
Insert Summary Dialog Box 3-6
Find In Formulas Option 3-8
Exercise 3.1: Swapping Fields 3-8
Formula Workshop Changes 3-9
Auto Complete Option For Functions 3-9
Auto Complete Option For Tables And Fields 3-10
Export Options 3-10
Exercise 3.2: Create An Adobe Acrobat PDF Export File 3-10
Exercise 3.3: Create A Separated Values (CSV) Export File 3-12
Exercise 3.4: Create An Excel Data Only Export File 3-14

SECTION 2 CRYSTAL REPORTS 2008

WHAT'S NEW IN CRYSTAL REPORTS 2008 4-1
What's New In Crystal Reports 2008? 4-2
   Single Edition 4-2
   Reduced Installation File Size 4-2
   New Interface 4-2
   Parameter Panel 4-2
   Sort Control 4-2
   Built-In Bar Code Support 4-2
   Enhanced Cross-Tabs 4-2
   Save Reports Directly To CrystalReports.com 4-2
   Locale Settings 4-2
   Adobe Flash & Flex Integration 4-3
   Xcelsius Integration 4-3
   Flexible Pagination 4-3
   Other New Features 4-3
Start Page Changes 4-3
Download The Sample Reports And Database 4-4
Status Bar 4-6
Workbench Change 4-7
Preview Panel 4-7
Menu Changes 4-8
   View Menu Options 4-8
   Insert Menu Options 4-9
   Format Menu Options 4-10
   Database Menu Options 4-11
   Report Menu Options 4-12
   Help Menu Options 4-12
Toolbar Changes 4-13
   Standard Toolbar 4-13
   Insert Tools Toolbar 4-15
   Expert Tools Toolbar 4-16

External Command Toolbar	4-17
Data Source Connections	4-19
Create A Connection To The Data Source	4-19
Selecting A Data Source	4-21
Connecting To An Excel Spreadsheet	4-22
Shortcut Menus	4-24
Format Editor Number Tab Change	4-25
Special Fields	4-26
The Select Expert	4-27
Printing Change	4-29
Page Setup Options	4-30
Change The Paper Size	4-32
The Section Expert	4-32
Formula Workshop Changes	4-37
Workshop Tree	4-38
New Button Drop-Down List Options	4-38
Expression Editor Toolbar	4-39
REPORT DESIGN OPTION CHANGES IN CRYSTAL REPORTS 2008	**5-1**
Exercise 5.1: Create Page Breaks	5-2
Exercise 5.2: Use The Change Group Dialog Box Options	5-2
Chart Expert	5-3
The Create New Parameter Dialog Box	5-3
Parameter Panel	5-4
Long List Of Values Options	5-5
Predefined Templates	5-6
OLAP Reports	5-6
Exercise 5.3: Create An OLAP Report	5-6
Step 1: Create An OLAP Connection	5-7
Step 2: Select Options On The Rows/Columns Screen	5-10
Step 3: Modify The OLAP Report	5-12
XML Export Format	5-13
Basic XML Export	5-15
Find In Field Explorer Option	5-15
Bar Codes	5-16
Exercise 5.4: Bind Sort Control	5-16
How To Remove A Bind Control From A Report	5-18
Adding A Flash File To A Report	5-18
Formatting A Flash File	5-20
Exporting A Report With An Xcelsius File To A PDF File	5-20

WHAT'S NEW IN CRYSTAL REPORTS XI

Overview

Crystal Reports XI has a large amount of changes, both in the interface and in the creation and editing of reports. This chapter covers the interface changes.

You will learn about the following interface changes:

- ☑ Start Page
- ☑ Toolbars
- ☑ Menu
- ☑ Workbench
- ☑ Repository Explorer
- ☑ Formula Editor
- ☑ Workshop Tree
- ☑ Dependency Checker

Conventions Used In This Book

I designed the following conventions to make it easier for you to follow the instructions in this book.

- ☑ The `Courier font` is used to indicate what you should type.
- ☑ **Drag** means to hold down the left mouse button while moving the mouse.
- ☑ **Click** means to press the left mouse button once, then release it immediately.
- ☑ **Double-click** means to quickly press the left mouse button twice, then release it.
- ☑ **Right-click** means to press the right mouse button once to open a shortcut menu.
- ☑ Click **OK** means to click the OK button on the dialog box.
- ☑ Press **Enter** means to press the Enter key on your keyboard.
- ☑ Press **Tab** means to press the Tab key on your keyboard.
- ☑ Click **Save** means to click the Save button on the dialog box.
- ☑ Click **Finish** means to click the Finish button on the dialog box.
- ☑ SMALL CAPS are used to indicate an option to click on or to bring something to your attention.
- ☑ This icon indicates a tip or additional information about the topic that is being discussed.
- ☑ This icon indicates a shortcut or another way to complete the task being discussed.
- ☑ This icon indicates a warning that you need to be aware of or a feature that has been removed.
- ☑ NEW This icon is used to indicate the new items or options in a group of items or options.
- ☑ Press CTRL + V means to press and hold down the Ctrl key, then press the V key.
- ☑ The blinking cursor is the marker that is in the document and appears to the right of where you are typing. This is also known as the INSERTION POINT or KEYBOARD CURSOR. This is different then the pointer that is controlled by the mouse. The MOUSE POINTER looks like an I-beam when not in use.
- ☑ When you see "YOUR SCREEN SHOULD LOOK LIKE THE ONE SHOWN IN FIGURE X.X", or something similar in the exercises, check to make sure that your screen does look like the figure. If it does, continue with the next set of instructions. If your screen does not look like the figure, redo the steps that you just completed so that your screen does match the figure. Not doing so may cause you problems when trying to complete exercises later in the book.
- ☑ The instruction "Right-click on a field" means to right-click on the field in the details section of the report, unless noted otherwise.
- ☑ The section heading EXERCISE X.Y: (where x equals the chapter number and y equals the exercise number) represents exercises that have step-by-step instructions that you should complete. You will also see sections that have step-by-step instructions that are not an exercise. Completing them as you go through the book is optional, but recommended.

Chapter 1

- ☑ [See Chapter 2, Figure 2-8] refers to a screen shot that you can use as a reference for the current topic that is being discussed.
- ☑ [See Chapter 2, Database Concepts] refers to a section that you can use as a reference for the topic that is being discussed.
- ☑ "Clear the (name of option) option" means to remove the check mark from the option specified in the instruction.
- ☑ "E2.1 Report Name" is the naming convention for the reports discussed in this book. E2.1 stands for Chapter 2, Exercise 1. You may consider some of the report file names to be long. I did this on purpose, so that it is easier to know what topic the report covers. If you do not like to type or do not want to type the full report name, you can just type the first part as the file name. That way when you have to find a report to complete another exercise, you will be able to find the correct report. For example, if the report name is E5.5 Orders shipped between 4-1-2001 and 6-30-2001, you can save the report as E5.5.
- ☑ "Save the CH4.5 report as" means to open the CH4.5 report and save it with the new report name that is specified in the instructions. Doing this lets you keep the original report.
- ☑ **FILE** ⇒ **NEW** ⇒ **CROSS-TAB REPORT** means to open the **FILE** menu, select the option **NEW**, then select the option **CROSS-TAB REPORT**, as illustrated in Figure 1-1.

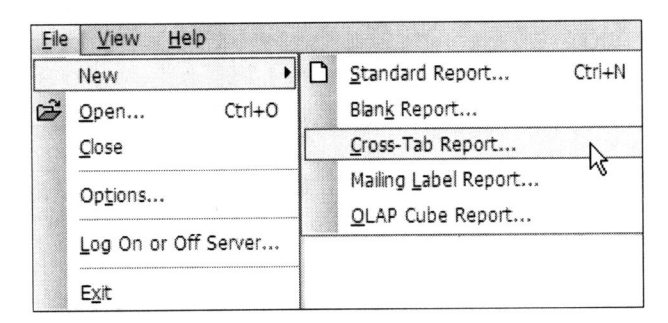

Figure 1-1 Menu navigation technique illustrated

Assumptions

(Yes, I know one should never assume anything, but the following assumptions have been made.) It is assumed that . . . .

- ☑ You know that the operating system used to write this book is Windows XP. If you are using a different version of Windows, some of the screen shots may have a slightly different look.
- ☑ You are familiar with the Windows environment including Windows Explorer and are comfortable using a mouse.
- ☑ You know that this button will minimize the open window and place an icon for it on the Windows taskbar. When you want to view the window again, click the button on the taskbar and the window will reappear.
- ☑ You know that this button will open the current window to the full size of your computer screen.

What's New In Crystal Reports XI

- ☑ ❌ You know that this button will close the window that is open.
- ☑ You have access to the Internet to download the practice files needed to complete the exercises in this book and to download any updates to Crystal Reports that are available.
- ☑ Optional: That you have access to a printer, if you want to print any of the reports that you will create.
- ☑ Optional: That you have Microsoft Word and Excel installed if you want to view the reports that will be exported to these formats. If you don't have either of these software packages, other options are covered in Chapter 2.

Interactive Messages

Like many other software packages, Crystal Reports will display interactive messages that require a response from you to confirm an action. Table 1-1 explains the three types of interactive message symbols and what they mean.

Symbol	Name	This interactive message type . . . . .
🛈	Information	Provides information about an action that you just performed.
⚠	Warning	Usually requires you to make a decision.
⊗	Critical	Requires you to make a decision before moving on to the next step.

Table 1-1 Interactive message types explained

What's New In Crystal Reports XI?

What you will notice that's new, depends on the previous version of Crystal Reports that you used, if any. The older the version of Crystal Reports that you are upgrading from, the more new features you will notice. I think that you will find the new interface more user friendly than previous versions.

New Patch Installation

This feature will allow you to easily download and install any updates that are available for Crystal Reports XI.

Hierarchical Group Reports

There are now more options that will allow you more control over how the data is indented on this type of report.

Single Sign-On

This feature allows Crystal Reports to be integrated into an existing security system, which means that multiple sign-ons are no longer a requirement.

Workbench

The Workbench allows you to keep projects organized and lets you group reports in folders based on your preference. You can store reports from different hard drive and server locations in the same folder. You can keep the Workbench open in the workspace so that you can easily access the reports that you need.

Report Export Configuration

This feature allows the export configuration options to be saved with the report, which means that the people that run the reports that you create do not have to set up the export options each time the report needs to be exported.

RTF Export Format

A second RTF export format has been added. The new RTF export format allows end users to edit a report without assistance from the person that actually created the report. This export format has been optimized for forms processing and accuracy. This means that you can select between the two RTF export formats depending on the needs of the report: the ability to edit the report or exact formatting, which is what the original RTF export format handles.

Updated Repository Explorer

This feature makes is easier to navigate in the Business Objects Enterprise System. You can share reports and other items with end-users and other report designers through the repository.

HTML Preview

This viewing option will let you see how reports will look when they are published to the Web. You can view the report on the Web while you are designing it. You no longer have to publish a report to the Web before you are able to view it.

Enhanced Report Viewer

The report viewer toolbar has been modified to be more consistent. The resizable Group Tree improves report viewing for long group names.

N Value For Top N Style Reports

You can add parameter input options for these types of reports. This will allow one report to meet the needs of several users, which could reduce the number of reports that you have to create and maintain.

Dependency Checker

This tool checks formula syntax in reports. It also checks for the following types of errors: database connections, fields, hyperlinks and subreports.

Drop And Drag Charts And Cross-Tabs

Crystal Reports can now automatically create a chart or Cross-Tab based on the data in the report. The charts are automatically updated when new data or variables are added to the report.

Dynamic Graphic Location

With this new feature, it is no longer necessary to store images (graphic files) that are needed for a report in the database. Images and pictures can now be placed on a report through a link in the database. This allows all of the images to be stored outside of the database. The reference to the image is stored in the database, which helps keep the database size smaller.

Dynamic And Cascading Prompts

With this feature, you are no longer restricted to using static value lists for parameter fields. Dynamic lists are populated from a database or from data stored in the repository each time the report is run. This means that the data in the drop-down list is always current. You can also create cascading prompts. This means that the options in one drop-down list control what you will see in another drop-down list.

Updated Data Drivers

The following data drivers have been updated - DB2, IBM, JDBC and XML. This means that you can connect to more types of databases.

Other New Features

Report Application Server (RAS)
Report Designer Component (RDC)
Integration with Business Objects Enterprise XI

What Else Is Covered?

In addition to covering the new features, functionality that may not be obvious is also covered. I decided to do this based on questions that I have been asked and because I have seen the same or similar questions posted on forums, over and over.

Differences Between The Standard And Professional Editions

Chapters 1 to 3 were written using the professional edition of Crystal Reports XI.
Each edition of Crystal Reports XI has slightly different features. Table 1-2 shows the differences between the standard and professional editions. This table is a condensed version of the "Crystal Reports XI Feature Comparison By Version and Edition" document that is on the Business Objects web site. The table below only includes features that are different between the editions.

Chapter 1

Feature	Standard	Professional
OLAP Reports	N	Y
Repository for component reuse	(1)	Y
HTML Preview	N	Y
Enhanced support for Business Objects Universes	N	Y
Ad hoc SQL query tool	N	Y
Languages other than English	N	Y
Dynamic and Cascading Prompts	(2)	Y

Table 1-2 Differences between the editions of Crystal Reports XI

(1) This feature requires the Crystal Reports Server software, which does not come with the standard edition. The Crystal Reports Server software installation CD comes in the box with the professional and developer editions.
(2) This feature can be viewed in the standard edition, but not created.

As you can see, there are not many features in the professional edition that are not in the standard edition. If you have the standard edition you will be able to complete almost all of the exercises in Chapters 1-3. If you have the developer edition you have all of the features shown in the table and can complete all of the exercises in Chapters 1-3, just like you can with the professional edition.

Create A Folder For Your Reports

You will create and modify reports in this book. It would be a good idea to store all of them in the same folder on your hard drive so that you can find them easily. I will refer to this as "Your folder". You will create the folder at the root of the C drive to store the reports in that you create. You also create two folders under your folder for the sample files that you can download. Some of these reports are used as the basis for reports that you create and others are used to demonstrate a concept.

All of the reports created in this book are located on this page of our web site in two zip files named new_in_crxi.zip and new_in_2008.zip.
(http://www.tolana.com/d/newin2008/crfiles.html)

While not recommended, some people want to jump around or skip some exercises. If that's you, you can use these files to complete the exercises of your choice.

1. Open Windows Explorer and click on the C drive.

2. File ⇒ New ⇒ Folder.

3. Type `Crystal Reports Book` as the folder name, then press Enter.

1-7

What's New In Crystal Reports XI

4. Click on the folder that you just created and create the two folders shown. When you are finished, your folder structure should look like the one shown in Figure 1-2.

```
Crystal Reports Book
    Crystal 2008
    Crystal XI
```

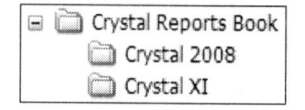

Figure 1-2 Folder structure

5. Go to the web page listed above and download the two zip files into the folder with the same name.

6. In Windows Explorer open the Crystal XI folder that you created. Right-click on the new_in_crxi.zip file and select **EXTRACT TO HERE** as shown in Figure 1-3.

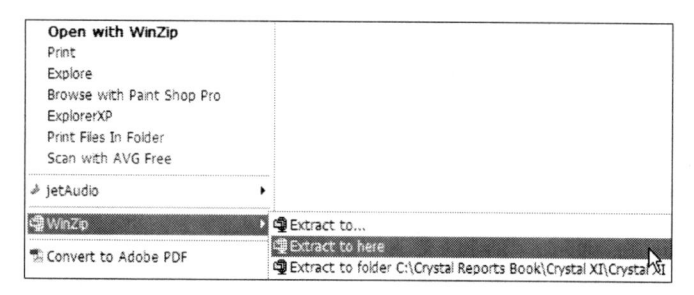

```
Open with WinZip
Print
Explore
Browse with Paint Shop Pro
ExplorerXP
Print Files In Folder
Scan with AVG Free
JetAudio                    ▶
WinZip                      ▶   Extract to...
Convert to Adobe PDF            Extract to here
                                Extract to folder C:\Crystal Reports Book\Crystal XI\Crystal XI
```

Figure 1-3 How to extract the files

7. Repeat the step above for the file new_in_2008.zip and extract it to the Crystal 2008 folder.

Start Page Overview

The Start Page is the most visual difference that you will notice because it has been completely redone as shown in Figure 1-4. The Start Page is like a control panel because you can access every tool from this interface. The Start Page provides a lot of options that you may find helpful. This page should save you some time because you do not have to remember which menu many of the options that you will use most, are on. This section will acquaint you with the features on the Start Page.

> If you close the Start Page either on purpose or by accident, you can still get to all of the options on the Start Page through the menu, toolbar or shortcuts.

> The Start Page is an HTML file that can be modified. Some companies modify this page and use their company logo or company colors. The file name is **START.HTML**. It is in this location: C:\Program Files\Business Objects\Crystal Reports 11\en

> Crystal Reports does not have a **SPELL CHECKER**.

Chapter 1

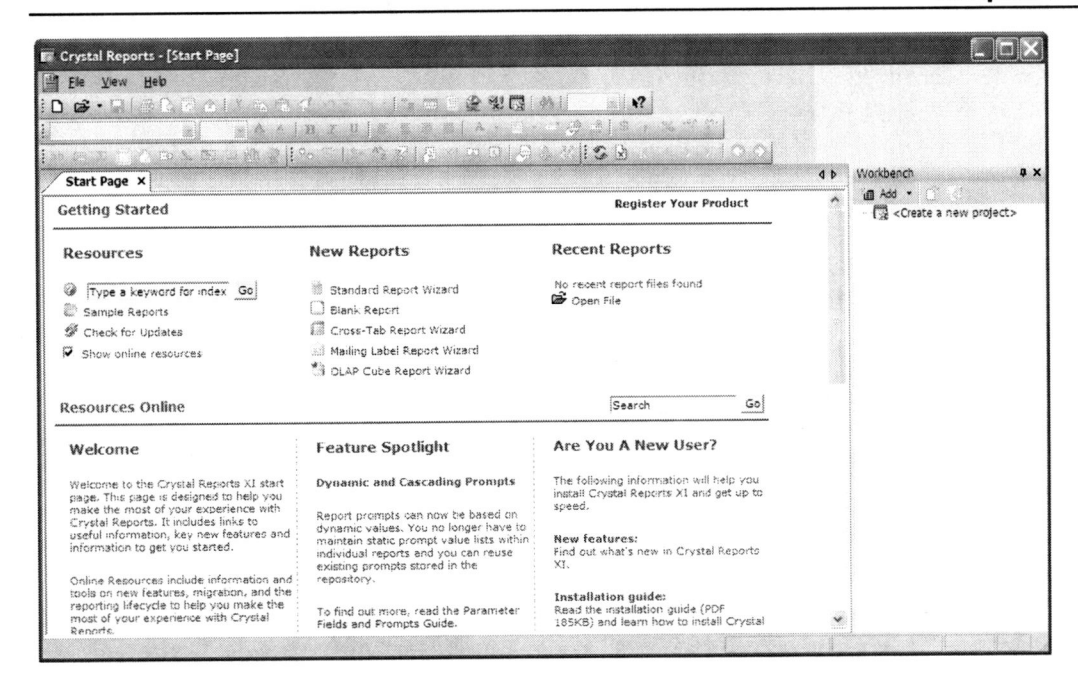

Figure 1-4 Crystal Reports workspace

Open Crystal Reports

1. Double-click on the Crystal Reports icon on your desktop or use the Windows XP Start menu to open Crystal Reports. You will see the Register dialog box if you have not registered the software yet. For now, click the **REGISTER LATER** button. You should see the window shown above in Figure 1-4.

This window replaces the Welcome dialog box in previous versions of Crystal Reports. On the right side of the Start Page, you should see the **WORKBENCH**. You will learn about this new feature later in the chapter.

The options in the **GETTING STARTED** section of the Start Page will let you search the help file, open the sample reports that come with Crystal Reports, check for updates and display or hide the Resources Online section, which is located towards the middle of the Start Page.

New Reports

The options in this section are the report wizards. Having them here makes them easy to get to. They are also on the File ⇒ New menu option shown earlier in Figure 1-1, if you want to access them that way.

> The **BLANK REPORT** option is what you would select when you want to create a report from scratch (not use a wizard).

1-9

What's New In Crystal Reports XI

Recent Reports

This section displays the last five reports that you opened as shown in Figure 1-5. The first report listed is the most recent one that you opened.
I think that it would be great if there was an option to display the last nine reports, like the bottom of the File menu does.

Recent Reports

1. L12.14 Cascading prompts for customer orders.rpt
2. L11.14 Gauge chart.rpt
3. L7 Cross-tab grouped report.rpt
4. L7 Cross-tab basic sort combined.rpt
5. L11.19 OLAP charts.rpt

Open File

Figure 1-5 Recent Reports illustrated

The **OPEN FILE** link will open the last folder that you used in Crystal Reports. Clicking on this link lets you look for the report that you want to open. You can navigate to another folder, if the folder that is displayed is not the one that you need.

Resources Online

If the **SHOW ONLINE RESOURCES** option is checked and your computer is connected to the Internet, you will see the Resources Online section, as shown above in Figure 1-4. This section is how Business Objects will keep you informed about updates for Crystal Reports and much more. What is displayed in this section will change from time to time.

Checking For Software Updates

If you want to keep your Crystal Reports software current, you have to check for updates from time to time. There are several ways that you can check for software updates as explained below.

- ① **Check for Updates on Start Up** If this option is selected, every time that you open Crystal Reports you will be prompted to check for updates. I don't know about you, but this would get on my nerves.
- ② **Check for Updates** This option lets you control when the check for updates will occur. This option is also a link on the Start Page.
- ③ Manually check the BusinessObjects.com web site.

> Depending on the security that you have set in your firewall software, you may be prompted to grant Crystal Reports access to the Internet. It is probably a good idea to grant the access so that you can check for updates. Your firewall software may prompt you if you have the Check for Updates on Start Up option on the Help menu selected.

Chapter 1

1. Open the Help menu on the Start Page. You will see the first two update options discussed above, as illustrated in Figure 1-6.

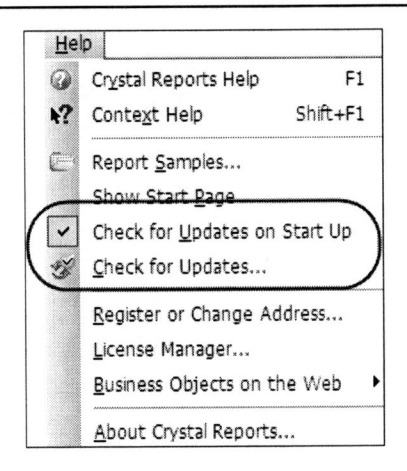

Figure 1-6 Update options illustrated

2. Clear the option **CHECK FOR UPDATES ON START UP**, if you do not want to check for updates every time that you open Crystal Reports.

How To Check For Updates

This exercise will show you how to check for and install updates.

1. Click on the link **CHECK FOR UPDATES**, on the Start Page.

    If updates are available, you will see a dialog box similar to the one shown in Figure 1-7.

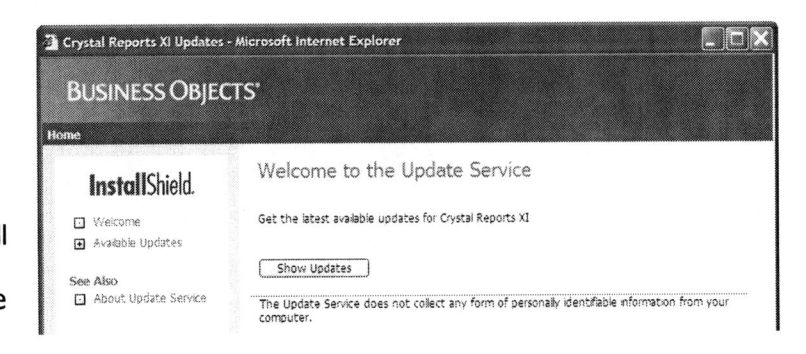

Figure 1-7 Crystal Reports Update window

1-11

What's New In Crystal Reports XI

2. Click the **SHOW UPDATES** button or click the **AVAILABLE UPDATES** link on the left. You will see the window shown in Figure 1-8.

   You may have different updates that need to be installed, then the ones shown in the figure.

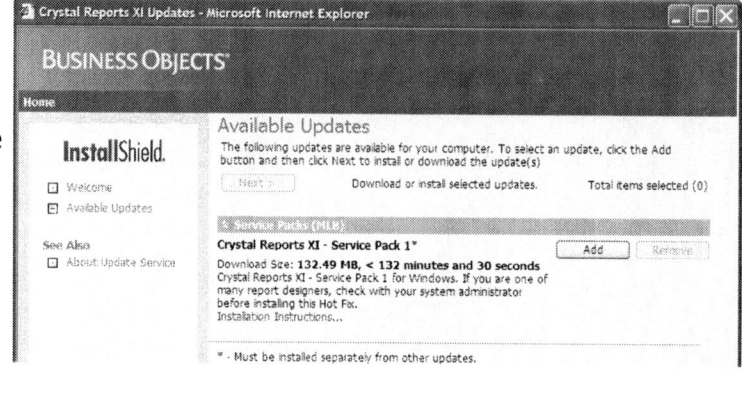

Figure 1-8 List of available updates

3. Click the **ADD** button next to each update that you want to install, then click the Next button.

   You will see the window shown in Figure 1-9.

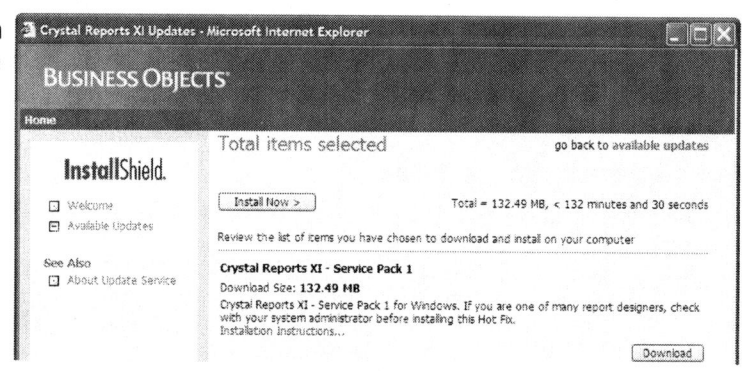

Figure 1-9 Items selected window

The **INSTALL NOW** button will download and install the update(s) that you selected. The **DOWNLOAD** button will download the update files, but will not install them. This option is helpful if you want to download the update files now and install them later.

4. Click on the button for how you want to proceed and follow the directions given. If you do not want to do either now, close the browser window.

How To Manually Check For Updates

If the Show Online Resources option is checked on the Start Page and you scroll to the bottom of the page, you will see the Crystal Product Support, Product Updates and Training sections. You may have different options then the ones shown. These sections provide a lot of help and information about Crystal Reports. The Critical Updates, Monthly Hot Fixes and Service Packs links at the bottom of the window, as shown in Figure 1-10, are another way to manually check for updates.

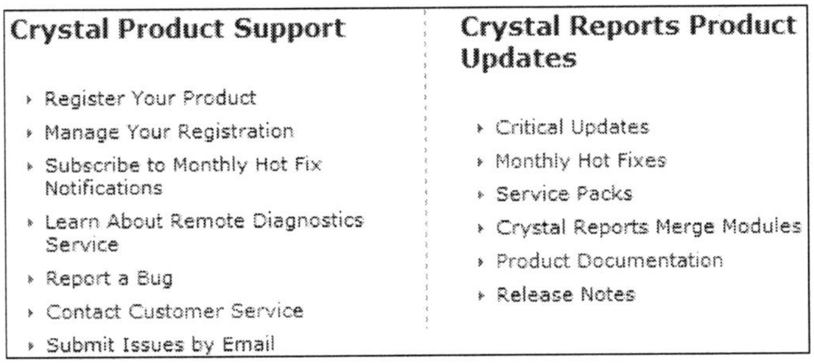

Crystal Product Support	Crystal Reports Product Updates
▸ Register Your Product ▸ Manage Your Registration ▸ Subscribe to Monthly Hot Fix Notifications ▸ Learn About Remote Diagnostics Service ▸ Report a Bug ▸ Contact Customer Service ▸ Submit Issues by Email	▸ Critical Updates ▸ Monthly Hot Fixes ▸ Service Packs ▸ Crystal Reports Merge Modules ▸ Product Documentation ▸ Release Notes

Figure 1-10 Crystal Product Support and Product Update options

As I am writing this book, there are two major updates that are available, as discussed below.

① **SERVICE PACK 1** Provides a lot of fixes. If you do not have this service pack installed, you may want to install it. The link below is for the Business Objects XI Service Packs. The **READ ME** link will open a pdf file that will let you view all of the updates in this service pack.

http://support.businessobjects.com/downloads/updates/service_packs/boenterprise.asp

This service pack is for the entire Business Objects XI suite of products, not just Crystal Reports, but it will only update the components that you have installed.

② **CR XI RELEASE 2** The primary reason to install this release is if you will be using Visual Studio 2005 with Crystal Reports, Crystal Reports Server or the Business Objects Enterprise and are upgrading from the bundled version of Crystal Reports that comes with Visual Studio 2005. This release includes an updated .NET engine for Visual Studio 2005.

Updates in this release that you may find useful if you are not using Crystal Reports XI with Visual Studio 2005 are covered in Chapter 3.

Table Linking Change

In previous versions of Crystal Reports, all of the tables that were used to create a report had to be linked. Now, tables that are not linked can be used to create a report.

Toolbar Changes

This section covers the changes to the toolbars. To help learn about the new toolbar options, you can open a sample report by following the steps below.

1. Click the **SAMPLE REPORTS** link in the Resources section of the Start Page.

What's New In Crystal Reports XI

2. On the **OPEN** dialog box you should see two folders, **FEATURE EXAMPLES** and **GENERAL BUSINESS**.

   Double-click on the Feature Examples folder. You will see the list of reports shown in Figure 1-11.

   These reports were automatically installed when Crystal Reports was installed.

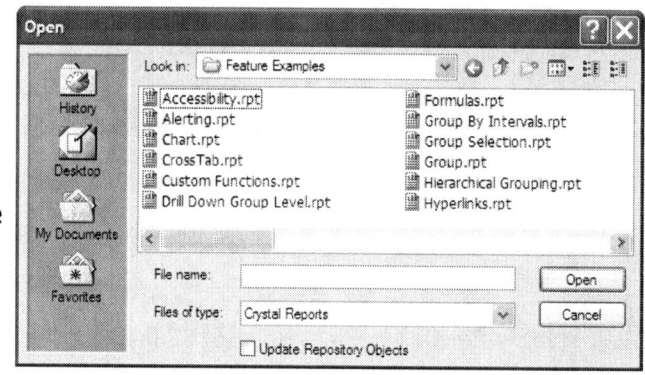

Figure 1-11 Reports in the Feature Examples folder

3. Double-click on the Accessibility report.

   Click OK if prompted that any changes must be saved to a new file.

   The report should look like the one shown in Figure 1-12.

   The only difference should be the date and time.

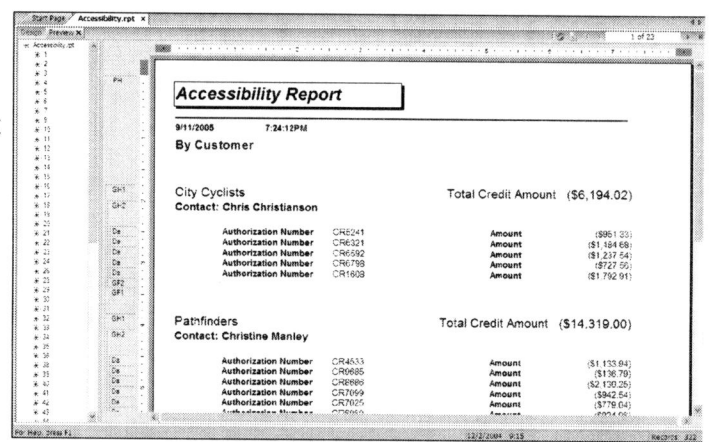

Figure 1-12 Accessibility Report

> The two arrows in the upper right corner on the preview window shown above in Figure 1-12 are used when there are a lot of reports open. Clicking on the right arrow will display the tab for the first hidden report.

> You can make some changes like formatting and moving objects on the preview tab.

Navigation Tools Toolbar

The buttons on the Navigation Tools toolbar shown in Figure 1-13 contain options to move around in a report and refresh data. This toolbar is activated once you preview a report. Table 1-3 explains the purpose of each button on the toolbar.

Chapter 1

> When you have a report open in the preview window, you will see another navigation toolbar that has the first six buttons shown in Table 1-3. The second navigation toolbar is the Report Navigation toolbar and is right above the report as shown in Figure 1-14.

Figure 1-13 Navigation Tools toolbar

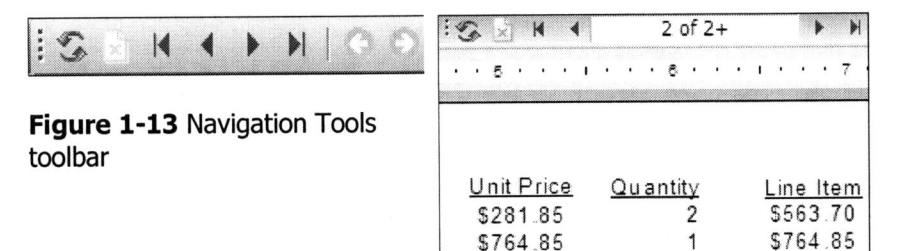

Figure 1-14 Report Navigation toolbar illustrated

Button	Purpose
	Refreshes the report data.
	Stops the processing of data and only displays the report with the data that has been processed prior to clicking this button.
	Displays the first page of the report.
	Displays the previous page of the report.
	Displays the next page of the report.
	Displays the last page of the report.
	Displays the previous page of the report. (3)
	Displays the next page of the report. (3)

Table 1-3 Navigation Tools toolbar buttons explained

(3) This button is only available if you are using the HTML Preview option.

Report Navigation Toolbar

In the previous section you learned about the Navigation Tools toolbar. The preview tab has it's own navigation toolbar. It is located in the upper right corner of the preview tab as shown above in Figure 1-14. One difference between these toolbars is that the one on the preview tab has a **PAGE INDICATOR** section that lets you know what page of the report is currently being displayed. As shown earlier in Figure 1-12 in the upper right corner, the page indicator also lets you know the total number of pages that are in the report.

1-15

What's New In Crystal Reports XI

The plus sign in **2 OF 2+** shown above in Figure 1-14 lets you know that Crystal Reports has not formatted all of the pages for the report. This means that the total number of pages is currently unknown.

> 💡 If you see **1 OF 1+** or something similar and want to know how many pages the report has, click the **SHOW LAST PAGE** button on the Report Navigation toolbar.

View Menu Options

The options on the View menu are explained in Table 1-4. They let you select many of the tools in Crystal Reports.

Menu Option	Description
Design	Opens the design window.
Preview	Opens the preview window.
Print Preview	This option is only available on the design window. It lets you view the report. This is the same as clicking on the preview tab.
Preview Sample	Displays the report with limited data.
HTML Preview	**NEW** Displays the report in HTML format. You may have to set some of the options on the Smart Tag & HTML Preview tab on the Options dialog box shown in Figure 1-15 before you can use this option.
Close Current View	Closes the active tab.
Field Explorer	Opens the Field Explorer.
Report Explorer	Displays all of the fields and objects on the report.
Repository Explorer	Opens the Repository Explorer so that an item from the repository can be added to the report.
Dependency Checker	**NEW** Opens the Dependency Checker so that reports can be checked for errors.
Workbench	**NEW** Displays or hides the Workbench.
Toolbars	**NEW** Customize the toolbars.
Status Bar	Displays or hides the status bar at the bottom of the Crystal Reports window. The status bar provides additional information about the object that you are holding the mouse over, as well as, other information about the active report.
Group Tree	Toggles the group tree on and off on the preview window.
Zoom	Sets the zoom level for viewing a report. You can change the zoom percent on the dialog box shown in Figure 1-16, or you can type the zoom percent in the Zoom field on the Standard toolbar.

Table 1-4 View menu options explained

Menu Option	Description
Rulers	Displays or hides the rulers. (4)
Guidelines	Displays or hides the guidelines. (4)
Grid	Displays or hides the grid. (4)
Tool tips	Displays or hides the tool tips. (4)

Table 1-4 View menu options explained (Continued)

(4) This option works on the design and preview windows.

The Smart Tag & HTML Preview options let you select how Crystal Reports Smart Tags will be used in Microsoft Office Applications.

The HTML Preview Options let you select and configure how reports will be displayed as web pages.

If your reports are not stored in the Business Objects Enterprise you may want to check the **ENABLE HTML PREVIEW** option so that you can preview reports as web pages.

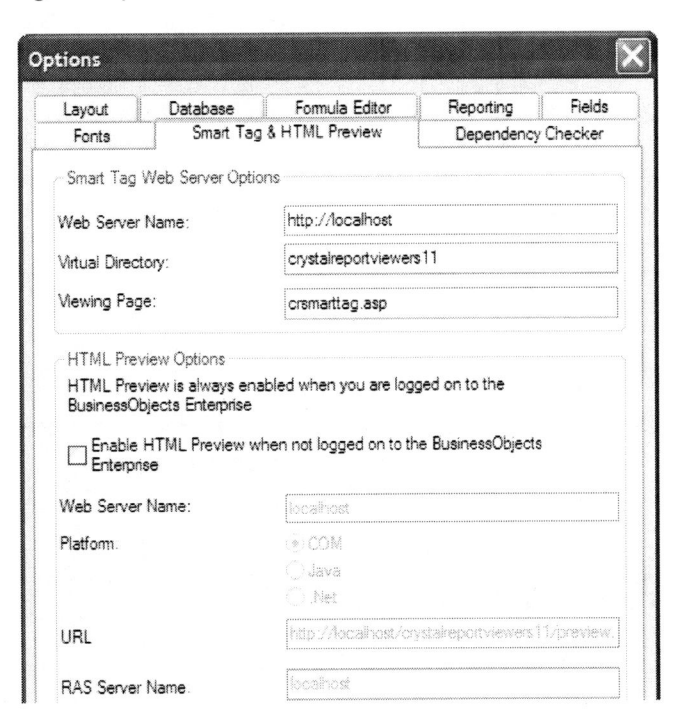

Figure 1-15 Smart Tag & HTML Preview options

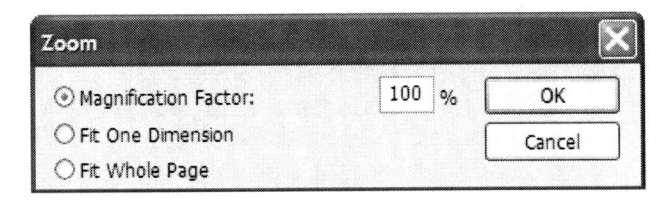

Figure 1-16 Zoom dialog box

The Workbench

This tool will let you organize the reports that you create or are responsible for maintaining. By default, the Workbench is on the right side of the Crystal Reports window. The way that you organize the reports in the Workbench is by placing them in folders which Crystal Reports calls **PROJECTS**. You can also add **REPORT PACKAGES** to the Workbench if you are using the Crystal Reports Server or the Business Objects Enterprise.

Project folders can only contain reports. Unlike other file management tools, you cannot create a folder under an existing folder in the Workbench. A benefit of using the Workbench is that you will be able to access reports without having to know where they are located on your hard drive or which server they are on. The downside is that you have to add the reports one by one to the Workbench.

Once you have added reports to the Workbench, you can move them from one folder to another by dragging the report name link. You can also rearrange the order of the project folders by dragging them to where you want them to be. Using the Workbench is optional. You can create a folder in the Workbench for this book. That way, when you need to go back to a report you will be able to find it easily.

Workbench Toolbar

Table 1-5 explains the purpose of each button on the Workbench toolbar.
If you right-click on a folder in the Workbench you will see the shortcut menu shown in Figure 1-17. If you right-click on a report in the Workbench you will see the shortcut menu shown in Figure 1-18.

Button	Purpose
	The **Add Report** button lets you add three types of objects to the Workbench as discussed below. ① **Add Existing Report** Select this option if you want to add an existing report to the Workbench. ② **Add New Project** Select this option if you want to create a new project folder. ③ **Add Object Package** Selecting this option will prompt you to log into your Business Objects Enterprise System. After you log in, you can select an object or report package to add to the Workbench. It is possible that you will not see this option when you click the Add Report button.
	The **Open** button lets you open a report that is in the Workbench. I find it easier to double-click on the report in the Workbench, then to click this button.

Table 1-5 Workbench toolbar buttons explained

Chapter 1

Button	Purpose
(icon)	The **Check Dependencies** button will start the Dependency Checker. This tool is used to check one report or all reports in a folder in the Workbench for errors.

Table 1-5 Workbench toolbar buttons explained (Continued)

```
Add              ▶   Add Existing Report...
Rename          F2    Add New Project
Remove         Del    Add Object Package...
Check Dependencies ...
Publish to BusinessObjects Enterprise...
```

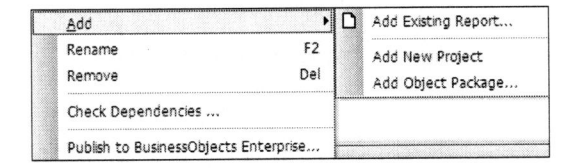

Figure 1-17 Shortcut menu when a folder is selected

```
Add              ▶   Add Existing Report...
Open                  Add New Project
Remove         Del    Add Object Package...
Check Dependencies ...
```

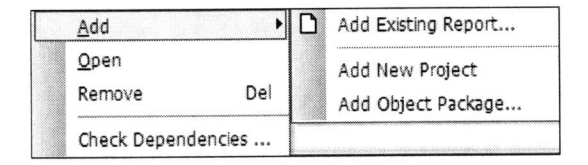

Figure 1-18 Shortcut menu when a report is selected

Report Packages

A report package is a group of related reports that are stored on a Crystal Reports Server or in the Business Objects Enterprise. Report packages allow several reports to be viewed or scheduled as a single entity. After you log in, there are two ways to add a report package, as discussed below.

   ① From the Workbench toolbar, Add ⇒ Add Object Package.
   ② Right-click in the Workbench and select Add ⇒ Add Object Package.

How To Create A Folder In The Workbench

The Workbench has been discussed as a way for you to organize the reports that you create. You can create a folder in the Workbench by following the steps below.

> 💡 View ⇒ Workbench, will display the Workbench if you do not see it in the report design window or on the Start Page. It is probably a good idea to leave the Workbench open all the time because you can use it to quickly open reports that you have already created.

What's New In Crystal Reports XI

1. Add ⇒ Add New Project, as shown in Figure 1-19.
2. Type `My Reports` as shown in Figure 1-20, then press Enter.

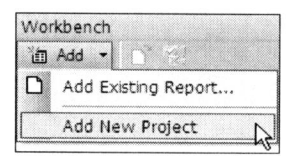

Figure 1-19 Menu option to create a new project folder

Figure 1-20 New project folder created and named

> 💡 If you need to add a report to the Workbench it's easier to do it while the report is open.

Adding Reports To The Workbench

There are three ways to add reports to the Workbench as discussed below.

① From the Workbench toolbar, Add ⇒ Add Existing Report.
② Right-click in the Workbench and select Add ⇒ Add Existing Report.
③ Drag a report from Windows Explorer to the Workbench.

> 💣 The Workbench does not sort the reports in a folder. This means that they appear in the folder in the order that they are added, opposed to be sorted alphabetically for example. You can rearrange the order of the reports in the Workbench. You can also move reports from one folder to another.

Deleting Projects And Reports From The Workbench

Deleting projects and reports from the Workbench works similar to how you delete folders and files in other applications. Reports deleted from the Workbench are not deleted from the hard drive or server that they are stored on. You are only deleting the reference (link) to the report in the Workbench. There are two ways to delete items in the Workbench, as discussed below.

① Click on the project folder or report that you want to delete, then press the **DEL** key on your keyboard.
② Right-click on the project folder or report that you want to delete and select **REMOVE** on the shortcut menu.

> 💣 If you rename, delete or move a report, when you click on the link for it in the Workbench you will get an error message when you try to open the report. If this happens, you have to add the report to the Workbench again.

Maintaining The Workbench

The information for the Workbench is stored in the file **PROJECTEXPLORER.XML**.
This file is automatically saved on your hard drive, in your personal folder under the Documents and Settings folder, which Windows XP creates. The path for the file is listed below.

C:\Documents and Settings\Your account name\Local Settings\Application Data\Crystal Reports

If you have to reinstall Crystal Reports and want to retain your Workbench project folder and report links, you should copy the XML file to another location before reinstalling Crystal Reports and then copy the file back. If you get a new computer, you can copy this file to the new computer and you will have the same projects and folders displayed in the Workbench.

Repository Explorer

The Repository Explorer shown in Figure 1-21, is where you can save objects like images, queries and functions that you want to use in more than one report.
When you use this explorer, you will be prompted to log on to the Business Objects Enterprise, as shown in Figure 1-22.

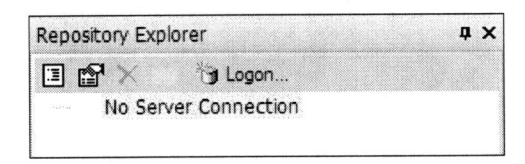

Figure 1-21 Repository Explorer

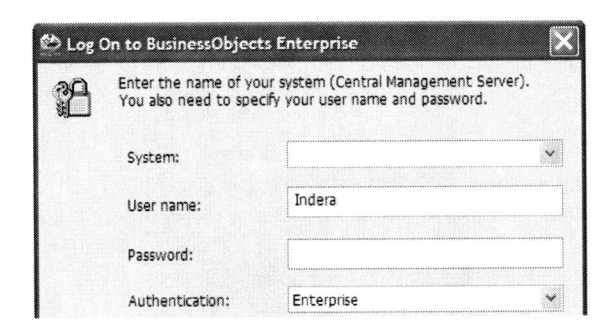

Figure 1-22 Business Objects Enterprise Log on dialog box

The Repository Explorer can only be accessed through the Repository, which is stored in the Business Objects Enterprise. Prior versions of Crystal Reports came with all of the components required to use the Repository Explorer and did not require access to another system. Table 1-6 explains the buttons on the Repository Explorer toolbar.

Button	Purpose
📄	The **CHANGE VIEW SETTINGS** button lets you select options that will change how the Repository Explorer window looks. It lets you limit the items that are displayed in the Repository Explorer.
📄	The **ADVANCED FILTERING** button allows you to only display items based on the author or by specific words.
✕	The **DELETE THE ITEM/FOLDER** button allows you to permanently delete a file or folder from the repository. If you delete a folder, all of the files in the folder are also deleted.
	The **INSERT A NEW FOLDER** button lets you add a new folder to the repository.
Logon...	The **LOGON SERVER** button lets you logon or logoff of the Business Objects Enterprise server.

Table 1-6 Repository Explorer toolbar buttons explained

The Repository

The repository is a database that report designers can use to store objects that will be used by more than one report or share with other people. Actually, anyone that has a valid login account to the Crystal Reports Server or Business Objects Enterprise can connect to the repository. In versions of Crystal Reports prior to XI, there was a stand alone repository database.

Examples of items that are commonly stored in the repository are SQL commands, logos, reports or functions. Interestingly enough, you can store images, parameter fields, SQL commands, lists of values, text objects, reports and even functions in the repository, but you cannot store formulas in the repository. Once connected to the repository you can create, change and delete folders using the Repository Explorer. A benefit of storing objects in the repository is that if the object is updated, all reports that use the object will be updated automatically.

How To Open The Formula Workshop

Like many other tools in Crystal Reports, there is more than one way to open the Formula Workshop. This tool has more ways that it can be opened then most tools.

① Click the **FORMULA WORKSHOP** button on the Expert Tools toolbar.
② Report ⇒ Formula Workshop.
③ Right-click on a formula or SQL Expression field in the design (or preview) window and select Edit.
④ Right-click on a formula or SQL Expression field in the Field Explorer and select New or Edit.
⑤ Click on a formula or SQL Expression field, then click the **NEW** button on the Field Explorer toolbar.
⑥ Click the **FORMULA** button on any tab of the Format Editor dialog box.

Chapter 1

⑦ Open the Select Expert, click the Show Formula button, then click the **FORMULA EDITOR** button.

Formula Editor

The Formula Editor is now part of the Formula Workshop, as shown in Figure 1-23. The contents of each of the trees in the Formula Editor change to display the options that are available for the type of database that the report is based on. The Formula Editor allows you to create formulas by double-clicking on the functions, operators and fields that you need to include in the formula. The Formula Editor will allow you to create the majority of the formulas that you need. The Formula Editor contains the three trees discussed below. You may want to open some of the categories (nodes) in each tree to become familiar with the options.

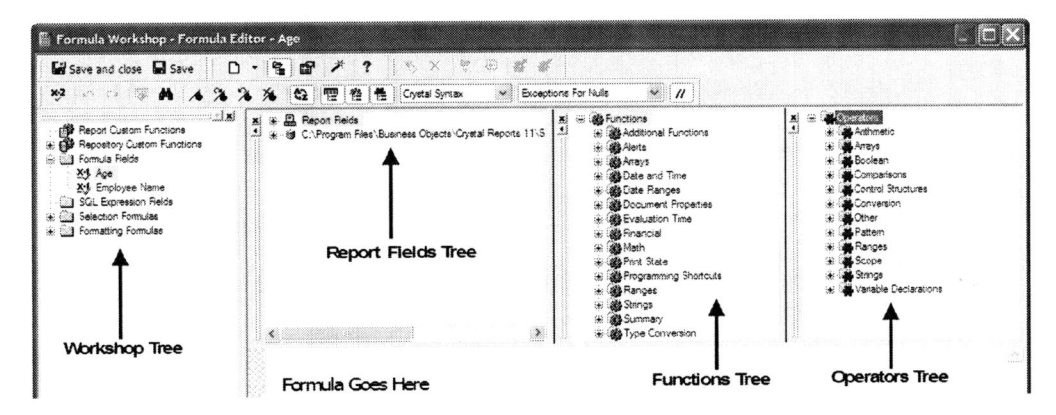

Figure 1-23 Formula Workshop

① The **Report Fields Tree** displays all of the fields that are on the report, including groups, summary fields, running totals, parameters, formulas and the tables that the report uses. This tree is similar to the Field Explorer.
② The **Functions Tree** contains built-in functions. The functions are divided into categories, which makes it easier to find the function that you need.
③ The **Operators Tree** contains the operators (logical and mathematical) that you can use to create formulas. The operators are grouped by type to make them easier to find. Operators use symbols instead of words.

> If you open the Formula Workshop and do not see the Formula Editor. You can do either of the following to open the Formula Editor.

① Select an option in a folder under the Formula Fields, SQL Expression Fields or Selection Formulas in the Workshop Tree.
② Select one of the formula or function options on the New button drop-down list shown in Figure 1-24.

What's New In Crystal Reports XI

The **RECORD SELECTION FORMULA** option lets you create a formula to select which records will appear on the report.

The **GROUP SELECTION FORMULA** option lets you create a formula to select which groups will appear on the report.

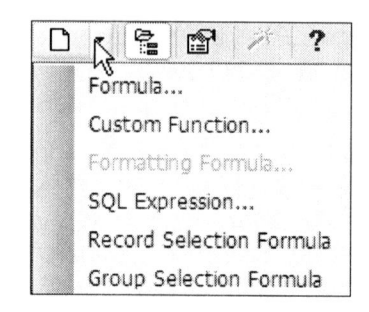

Figure 1-24 New button drop-down list

Customizing The Formula Editor

You can customize the Formula Editor by doing any or all of the following:

① You can resize any of the tree sections by dragging the bar illustrated in Figure 1-25.
② Close a tree by clicking on the ⊠ button to the left of the section that you want to close.
③ Expand a tree by clicking on the ◧ button to the left of the section that you want to expand.
④ Make the Formula section longer or shorter by dragging the section bar above it, up or down.

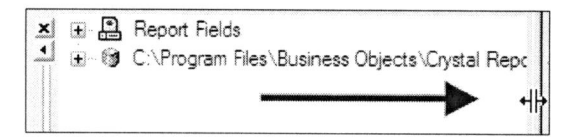

Figure 1-25 Mouse pointer in position to resize a tree

The Workshop Tree

As you saw earlier in Figure 1-23, the Workshop Tree contains several sections called **NODES** or **CATEGORY** folders that formulas can be saved in. This section of the Formula Workshop contains all of the formulas that are in the report and includes formulas that are in the repository that can be used in the report. Items under the Selection Formulas folder are the ones that you created with the Select Expert.

In addition to being able to create formulas, you can also rename and delete formulas, just like you can in the Field Explorer. Each of the categories in the Workshop Tree is explained below.

① **Report Custom Functions** If you create a function or copy a function from the repository into the report, this is where it would be stored. The functions in this category can be used by any formula in your report. Custom functions are used just like the built-in functions that come with Crystal Reports.

② **Repository Custom Functions** The functions stored in this category are stored in the repository. To use a repository custom function, it has to be added to the report so that it will become a report custom function.

③ **Formula Fields** The formulas in this category are server based and are the same ones that are in the Field Explorer in the Formula Fields, Parameter Fields, Running Total Fields and Group Name Fields sections. This is probably the type of formula that you will create and use the most because they are used for calculations and conditional formatting.

④ **SQL Expression Fields** The formulas in this category are the same expression fields that are in the SQL Expression Fields section of the Field Explorer. If you create a new expression or modify an existing expression, the SQL Expression Editor will open in the Formula Workshop instead of the Formula Editor. It has been reported that the SQL Expression Editor may not reflect all of the operators and functions that are really available for certain database types.

⑤ **Selection Formulas** The formulas in this category are created when you use the Select Expert or the selection formula options on the Report menu. You can also create selection formulas in the Formula Workshop. If you click on the Group Selection option, the **GROUP SELECTION FORMULA EDITOR** will open. If you click on the Record Selection option, the **RECORD SELECTION FORMULA EDITOR** will open. The major difference that you will notice with these editors is that the title bar of the Formula Workshop will change as shown in Figure 1-26. Compare this title bar to the one shown earlier in Figure 1-23.

Figure 1-26 Record Selection Formula Editor title bar

⑥ **Formatting Formulas** This category has a folder for each section of the report. All of the objects from each section of the report are listed here. Formatting formulas like changing the color, font or font size for objects in the report are stored in this category. Conditional formatting formulas are also stored in this section.

Formula Expert

The Formula Expert shown in Figure 1-27 allows you to create custom functions. The functions that you create in the Formula Expert can be used in other reports if they are saved in the repository. By design, the Formula Expert will help you create a formula without having to use the Crystal Reports syntax programming language.

While this may sound appealing to those that are new to Crystal Reports or do not want to write code, the Formula Expert only creates formulas that use one custom function. You cannot use the math operators or the Crystal Reports syntax programming language in the Formula Expert.

What's New In Crystal Reports XI

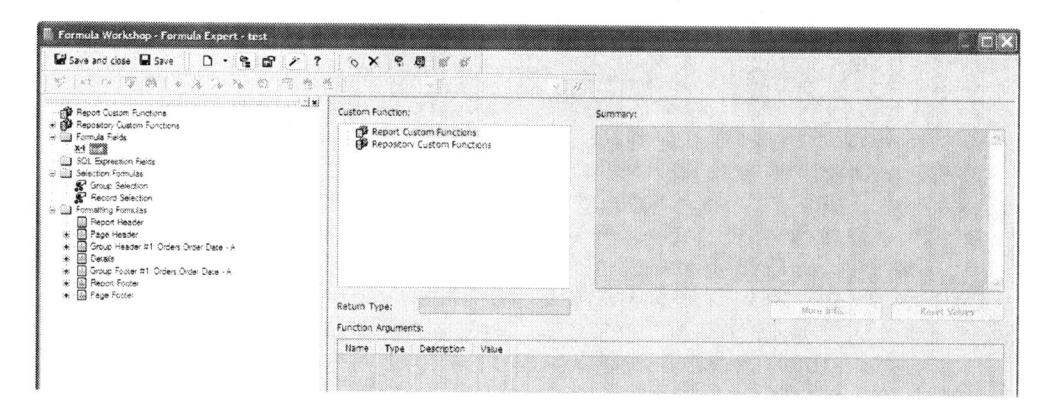

Figure 1-27 Formula Expert

Formula Editor Versus Formula Expert

The main difference between the two is that formulas created in the Formula Editor are saved with the report that they are created in and can only be used in that report. Formulas created in the Formula Expert can be saved as a **CUSTOM FUNCTION** in the repository and can be used in any report. Creating custom functions and using the repository are beyond the scope of this book.

If you find yourself creating the same formula in several reports, copy it to the Formula Expert and save it as a custom function. I often also save the custom functions that I create in a Microsoft Word document because I find it easier to get to them that way, instead of logging into the repository. If you work from home, you will understand what I mean. Many will say that this is not a good technique. There are valid reasons not to save custom functions in a word processing document. I will leave it up to you to decide what works best for you in the environment that you will create reports in.

Exercise 1.1: Create A Formula Field

This exercise demonstrates how to use the modified Formula Workshop. Figure 1-28 displays an order total per customer report. The order total is not correct because the field is adding values from the Order Amount field. In this exercise you will modify the report and create a formula that will calculate the amount for each item. This is known as the line item or extended amount. The formula is Unit Price * Quantity. This will allow the report to have the correct total amount.

Chapter 1

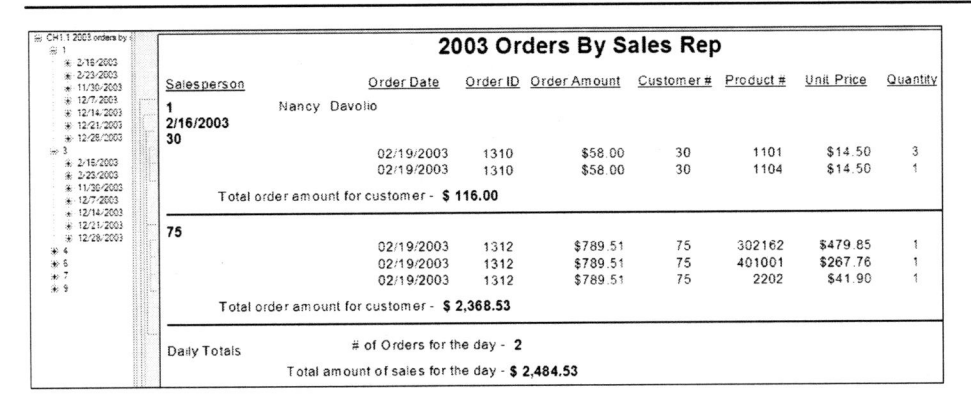

Figure 1-28 Order total per customer report

1. Save the CH1.1 report as `E1.1 Formula field for line item totals`.

2. Right-click on the **FORMULA FIELDS** option in the Field Explorer, then select **NEW**.

3. Type `Line Item Total` in the dialog box shown in Figure 1-29, then click OK.

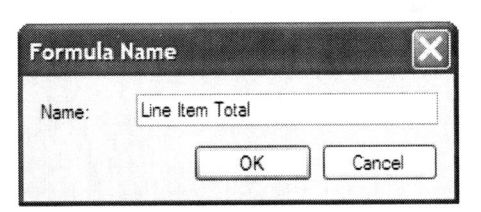

Figure 1-29 Formula Name dialog box

4. In the Report Fields tree, double-click on the Unit Price field in the Orders Detail table.

   > In addition to double-clicking on a field you can also drag the field to the Formula section.

   You should see the field in the Formula section of the Formula Editor, as shown at the bottom of Figure 1-30.

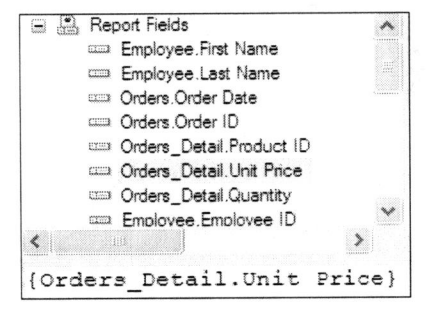

Figure 1-30 Field added to the Formula section

1-27

What's New In Crystal Reports XI

5. Type a * after the Unit Price field, then double-click on the Quantity field.

   > You can use the **MULTIPLY** Arithmetic operator illustrated in Figure 1-31 instead of typing the operator.

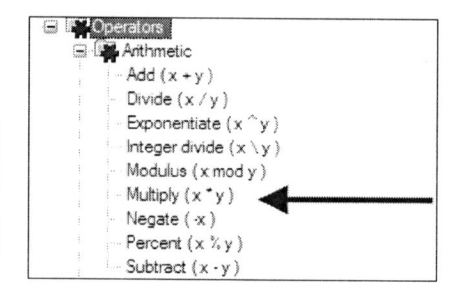

   Figure 1-31 Multiply arithmetic operator illustrated

6. Add a blank line above the formula and type the following comment.
   `// This formula calculates the Line Item Total.`

   Your formula should look like the one shown in Figure 1-32.

   ```
   // This formula calculates the Line Item Total
   {Orders_Detail.Unit Price} *{Orders_Detail.Quantity}
   ```

   Figure 1-32 Line Item Total formula

   > Notice that the comment line is a different color then the formula line. This is one way to know that you have entered the comment correctly. Comments do not have to go above a formula.

7. Click the **CHECK (x+2)** button on the Expression Editor toolbar. You should see the message shown in Figure 1-33.

   > The message shown in Figure 1-33 means that Crystal Reports did not find a syntax error. This does not mean that the formula will produce the results that you are expecting.

   Figure 1-33 No errors found message

If you do not see the message shown above in Figure 1-33, there is an error in your formula. Check to make sure that your formula looks like the one shown earlier in Figure 1-32.

Figure 1-34 shows one error message that you could see. If there is an error, the flashing insertion bar will be in the location in the formula where Crystal Reports thinks that the error is.

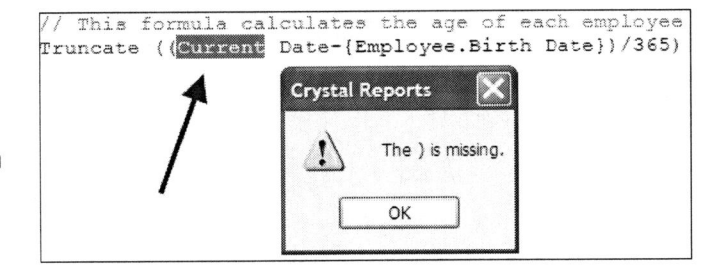

Figure 1-34 Formula error message

The part of the formula where the syntax checker stopped understanding the formula will also be highlighted, as illustrated above in Figure 1-34. You are not required to fix the error immediately. You can save the formula as is and work on something else. Just don't forget to come back and fix it.

8. Click OK, then click the **SAVE AND CLOSE** button.

> If you need to work on another formula, click the **SAVE** button instead of the Save and close button. Doing this will leave the Formula Workshop open.
> When you save a formula it becomes a field, which you can then add to the report or use in another formula.

Using Formula Fields In Reports
You can use formula fields in reports, just like you use fields from a table. Formula fields can be placed in any section of the report. You can create counts and summary fields that are based on formula fields. You can also use formula fields as selection criteria.

Add The Line Item Formula Total Field To The Report
In this part of the exercise you will add the formula field that you just created to the report.

1. Delete the Order Amount field from the report, then move the four fields after the Order Amount field over to the left.

2. Add the Line Item Total field to the report. (**Hint:** The field is in the Field Explorer in the Formula Fields section.)

3. Change the Total Order Amount field to use the Line Item Total formula field instead of the Order Amount field in the three group footer and report footer sections.
The report should look like the one shown in Figure 1-35. Save the changes.
Notice that the customer total amount is now correct.

What's New In Crystal Reports XI

2003 Orders By Sales Rep

Salesperson	Order Date	Order ID	Customer #	Product #	Unit Price	Quantity	Line Item Total
1 Nancy Davolio							
2/16/2003							
30							
	02/19/2003	1310	30	1101	$14.50	3	$43.50
	02/19/2003	1310	30	1104	$14.50	1	$14.50
Total order amount for customer - $ 58.00							
75							
	02/19/2003	1312	75	302162	$479.85	1	$479.85
	02/19/2003	1312	75	401001	$267.76	1	$267.76
	02/19/2003	1312	75	2202	$41.90	1	$41.90
Total order amount for customer - $ 789.51							
Daily Totals	# of Orders for the day - 2						
	Total amount of sales for the day - $ 847.51						

Figure 1-35 E1.1 Line item total field added to the report

Dynamic Graphic Location

In previous versions of Crystal Reports, graphic files had to be stored in the database in order to be used in a report. Now, you can store a link to the location of the graphic file in the database instead. This will greatly reduce the file size of the database, which is a good thing.

This also means that if you need to replace an existing image that is dynamically linked to reports, you can give the new file the same name as the old image file and put the new file in the same path with the file that you want to replace.

The steps below demonstrate how to create an external link to a graphic file after the graphic has been added to the report.

1. Right-click on the graphic in the report and select **FORMAT GRAPHIC**.

2. On the Picture tab, click the Formula button in the **GRAPHIC LOCATION** section, as illustrated in Figure 1-36.

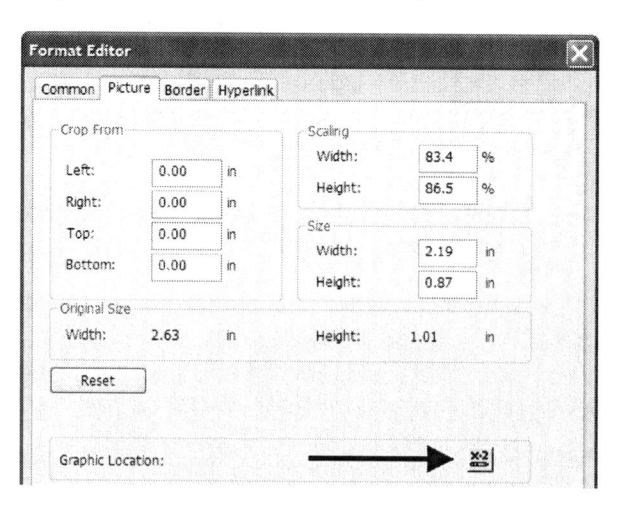

Figure 1-36 Picture tab options

1-30

Chapter 1

3. The Formula Workshop will open. Type in the path for the graphic file. The path can also be a web site address. If the image is on a hard drive, you would enter something similar to "F:\images\filename.jpg". If the image is on a web site, you would enter something similar to "http://tolana.com/photos/filename/jpg". You have to put quotes around the path to the file.

4. Click the Save and Close button, then click OK to close the Format Editor.

The Dependency Checker

As you read earlier in this chapter, the Dependency Checker checks reports for errors. As good as our intentions are, from time to time, the reports that we create will have errors. The Dependency Checker is a debugging tool that will help you find errors in reports. You can check one report at a time or all of the reports that are in a folder in the Workbench at the same time. The areas that the Dependency Checker searches are discussed below.

① **FORMULAS** and **FUNCTIONS** are compiled and checked for syntax errors. This is helpful because you can save a formula even though it has a syntax error.
② The **DATABASE CONNECTION** is checked to make sure that it is valid. The **DATABASE FIELDS** are checked to make sure that the fields are in the tables.
③ **HYPERLINKS** are checked to make sure that they are valid.
④ The location of **SUBREPORTS** are checked to make sure that they have not been moved.
⑤ Objects in the **REPOSITORY** are checked to make sure that they have not been moved.

The options on the Dependency Checker tab on the Options dialog box shown in Figure 1-37 let you select what conditions you want to verify when you check reports. You do not have to select all of these options.

The second set of options shown are for reports that are stored on the Business Objects Enterprise or Crystal Reports Server.

File ⇒ Options, opens this dialog box.

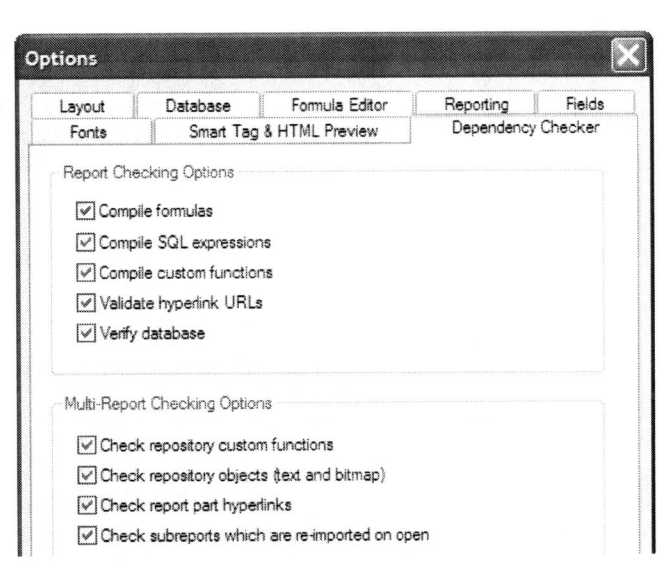

Figure 1-37 Dependency Checker options

1-31

What's New In Crystal Reports XI

The steps below will show you how to use this tool.

1. Open the CH1.2 report. Report ⇒ Check Dependencies.

You should see the window shown in Figure 1-38.

The shortcut menu shown provides additional options and functionality for the Dependency Checker.

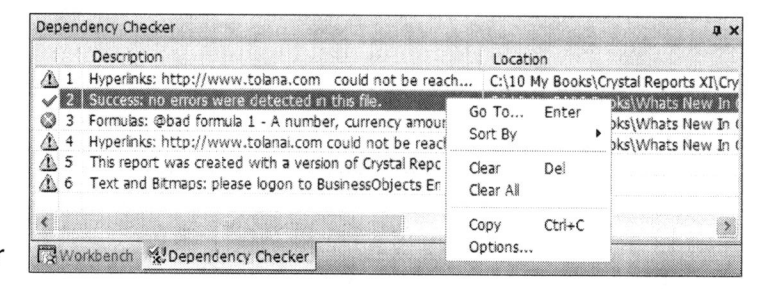

Figure 1-38 Dependency Checker results

2. To fix an error, double-click on it.

In the first column of the Dependency Checker results window you should see icons that are similar to the ones shown earlier in Table 1-1. Like the symbols in Table 1-1, the errors with the red symbol are critical and need to be fixed so that the report can run properly. The errors with the yellow caution sign will not prevent the report from running properly, but you should fix as many of these errors as possible. If you are not able to fix the errors, the information in the tip box below may help.

> **ERROR MESSAGE HELP**
>
> Hopefully you will not create a lot of errors, but if you do, the following files could help you decipher the error messages that you may encounter. On the Search tab of the Help window, type `error message`, then click the List Topics button. You should see the results shown in Figure 1-39. The **CRYSTAL REPORTS ERROR MESSAGES** topic lists each error message. To view the error messages after selecting this topic, click on the right arrow in the topic window on the right, as illustrated. The **ERROR MESSAGES AND FORMULA COMPILER WARNINGS** topic lists the error messages and what may have caused them.

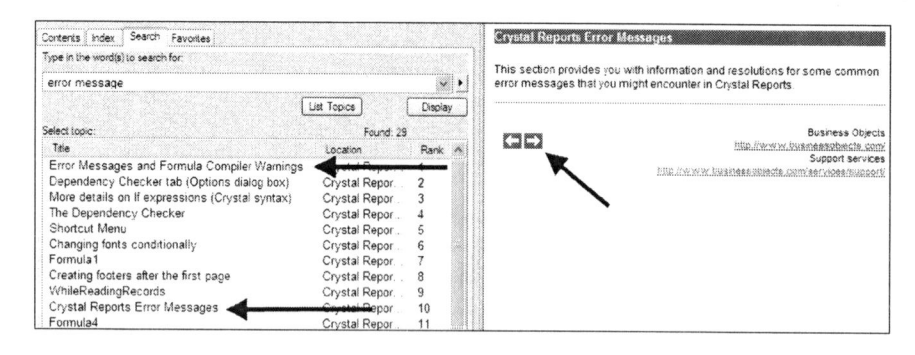

Figure 1-39 Error message topics

1-32

Chapter 1

If you plan to use the Dependency Checker on a regular basis, you may want to dock it with other explorer windows as shown in Figure 1-40.

When you close the Dependency Checker, the entries are not removed, meaning that the next time that you open it, the same entries will still be displayed. To remove an entry you can click on it and then press the Delete key or you can clear it by right-clicking on it and selecting Clear or Clear all as shown earlier in Figure 1-38.

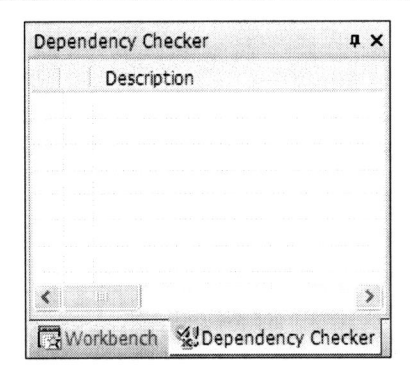

Figure 1-40 Dependency Checker and Workbench windows docked together

If you want to check one report, click on it's name in the Workbench, then start the Dependency Checker. If you want to check all of the reports in a Workbench folder, click on the folder, then start the Dependency Checker.

If you are checking more than one report and want to know which report an error is for, the report name is at the end of the Location column.

Report Options

The settings on the Options dialog box are global report options that are set. They are automatically applied to every report that you create.

There are also options that you can set on a report by report basis, as shown in Figure 1-41. (File ⇒ Report Options, opens this dialog box) The options that are checked, are the default report options.

Figure 1-41 Report Options dialog box

Many of the default options on this dialog box come from options that are checked on the Options dialog box. (File ⇒ Options, opens this dialog box)

1-33

What's New In Crystal Reports XI

Some default (checked) options, like the **DATABASE SERVER IS CASE-INSENSITIVE** is checked here because it is set as a global default on the Options dialog box.

> Changes that you make on the Reporting tab on the Options dialog box will change the default options on the Report Options dialog box. The options selected on the Report Options dialog box override the corresponding option on the Options dialog box (when applicable), for the active report. This means that the options on the Report Options dialog box will always be applied to the report, while the options on the Options dialog box will only be applied if there is no opposing option selected on the Report Options dialog box.

> The **RESPECT KEEP GROUP TOGETHER ON FIRST PAGE** option on the Report Options dialog box should not be selected unless the report is from a previous version of Crystal Reports.

CrystalReports.com

This is a new way to share reports on the Internet. It was introduced after Crystal Reports XI was released. You may have seen information about it on the Start page of Crystal Reports. It is easy to use and it is secure.

You can share up to 10 reports with three users including yourself, for free. If you need to share more than 10 reports or give more than three people access, there is a professional plan that you or your company can purchase.

REPORT DESIGN OPTION CHANGES IN CRYSTAL REPORTS XI

In this chapter you will learn about the following report design option changes in Crystal Reports XI.

- ☑ Cross-Tab
- ☑ Chart Expert
- ☑ Export options
- ☑ Histogram chart
- ☑ Dynamic and cascading parameter fields
- ☑ Hierarchical group reports

CHAPTER 2

Cross-Tab Reports

The Cross-Tab wizard has many of the same screens as the Standard wizard. The major differences between the Standard and Cross-Tab wizards are discussed below.

① There are no detail records in a cross-tab report.
② The functionality of the wizards grouping and summary screens are combined on one Cross-Tab wizard screen.
③ Cross-Tabs are most often placed in the report header or footer section, but they can be placed in other sections.

Cross-Tabs, like the Select Expert, allow you to retrieve records that meet specific criteria. The cross-tab report takes the Select Expert one step further because it allows you to summarize the data that is in the detail section of standard reports. Cross-Tab reports are often used for comparison analysis. Examples of cross-tab reports are:

① Sales by sales rep by year.
② Sales by region.
③ Summarizing how many orders by year and by zip code, each sales rep has.
④ Sales of a specific product by sales rep, by month.
⑤ Summarizing how many customers by region purchased certain products by month or by year.

Cross-Tab reports often give new report designers difficulty. I suspect that this is because this type of report requires one to think in dimensions. Like spreadsheets, cross-tab reports have rows and columns. Each cell in a spreadsheet contains one piece of data. In a cross-tab object, the cell contains one piece of summary data (count, sum, average etc) that is the equivalent of the sub totals that are usually in group footer sections of a report.

Behind the scenes, cross-tab reports take the detail records that you are use to seeing, as well as, the groups and summarizes the detail data and places the result in a cell. Hopefully the following scenario will make the concept of cross-tab reports easier to understand.

Going From Standard Reports To Cross-Tab Reports

This scenario will use the first cross-tab example mentioned above; Sales by sales rep by year. The goal of this cross-tab report from a standard report perspective is to show sales for a year by sales rep.

The report shown in Figure 2-1 is a basic list report that sorts the sales, by sales rep and by year. [See the CH2 Cross-tab basic sort combined report in the zip file] It contains all of the data one would need to determine sales by sales rep, by year. Because there aren't any totals for the groups, it would take a while to manually do the math, especially if there were hundreds of sales reps. Yes, I know what you are thinking, create a report that groups the data by sales rep, then by year. Figure 2-2 shows that report.

Sales By Rep By Year

Last Name	First Name	Order Date	Order Amount	Customer Name
Davolio	Nancy	02/19/2003	$789.51	Belgium Bike Co.
Davolio	Nancy	02/19/2003	$58.00	Spokes for Folks
Davolio	Nancy	02/26/2003	$68.90	Mountain Madmen Bicycles
Davolio	Nancy	02/27/2003	$2,698.53	Pedals Inc.
Davolio	Nancy	02/27/2003	$1,079.70	Mountain Madmen Bicycles
Davolio	Nancy	02/27/2003	$1,529.70	Cycle City Rome
		⋮		
Last Name	First Name	Order Date	Order Amount	Customer Name
Suyama	Michael	02/14/2005	$5,893.20	Crazy Wheels
Suyama	Michael	02/19/2005	$6,005.40	Off the Mountain Biking
Suyama	Michael	02/19/2005	$7,685.25	To The Limit Biking Co.
Suyama	Michael	02/22/2005	$1,664.70	Bike-A-Holics Anonymous
Suyama	Michael	02/24/2005	$138.70	Tienda de Bicicletas El Pardo
Suyama	Michael	02/25/2005	$893.55	Whistler Rentals
Suyama	Michael	02/28/2005	$1,529.70	Belgium Bike Co.

Figure 2-1 Basic sorted report of sales by sales rep by year

Can you tell me how many saddles Robert King sold in total? Or can you tell me who had the lowest number of sales in 2004? Okay, I'll wait while you open the report shown in Figure 2-2 and get a calculator to add up the totals for the sales reps. [See the CH2 Cross-tab grouped report in the zip file] I can wait. I have patience <smile>.

Like the report shown above in Figure 2-1, the report in Figure 2-2 has all of the information that you need to answer these questions.

The problem is that the data is spread out over several pages in the report which makes it difficult for comparison analysis.

- L7 Cross-tab grouped report.rpt
  - Nancy Davolio
    - 2003
    - 2004
    - 2005
  - Janet Leverling
    - 2003
    - 2004
    - 2005
  - Margaret Peacock
    - 2003
    - 2004
    - 2005
  - Michael Suyama
    - 2003
    - 2004
    - 2005
  - Robert King
    - 2003
    - 2004
    - 2005
  - Anne Dodsworth
    - 2003
    - 2004
    - 2005

Sales By Rep By Year

Last Name	First Name	Order Date	Order Amount	Customer Name
Nancy Davolio				
2003				
Davolio	Nancy	02/19/2003	$789.51	Belgium Bike Co.
Davolio	Nancy	02/19/2003	$58.00	Spokes for Folks
Davolio	Nancy	02/26/2003	$68.90	Mountain Madmen Bicycles
Davolio	Nancy	02/27/2003	$1,079.70	Mountain Madmen Bicycles
Davolio	Nancy	02/27/2003	$2,698.53	Pedals Inc.
Davolio	Nancy	02/27/2003	$1,529.70	Cycle City Rome
Davolio	Nancy	12/02/2003	$41.90	City Cyclists
Davolio	Nancy	12/03/2003	$10,259.10	Piccolo
Davolio	Nancy	12/03/2003	$14,872.30	Cyclopath
Davolio	Nancy	12/04/2003	$29.00	Spokes 'N Wheels Ltd.
Davolio	Nancy	12/07/2003	$890.61	Tienda de Bicicletas El Pardo
		⋮		
Davolio	Nancy	05/02/2005	$1,082.50	Warsaw Sports, Inc.
			$138,028.42	
			$660,756.95	
Janet Leverling				
2003				
Leverling	Janet	02/21/2003	$5,219.55	Tienda de Bicicletas El Pardo
Leverling	Janet	02/21/2003	$8,819.55	Bikes, Bikes, and More Bikes
Leverling	Janet	02/25/2003	$2,246.25	Folk och fä HB
Leverling	Janet	02/26/2003	$267.76	Hooked on Helmets
Leverling	Janet	02/26/2003	$61.35	Bike Shop from Mars

Figure 2-2 Data grouped by sales rep by year

As you will see after completing Exercise 2.1, this same data in a cross-tab report will be in an easy to read format. With a cross-tab report you can quickly answer questions like how many sales Robert King had for three products and which sales rep had the lowest number of sales in 2004.

Report Design Option Changes In Crystal Reports XI

How To Create This Cross-Tab

Yes, I hear you grumbling and saying, "Great, I now see the advantages of creating a cross-tab report, but how do I get the data shown earlier in Figures 2-1 and 2-2 into cross-tab format?" Okay, here goes:

① Usually, the field down the left side of a cross-tab (that creates the rows) is the data element that there are more occurrences of. In this example, there are more sales reps than years. You can put the sales reps across the top and still get the same results.

② The field that goes across the top (that creates the columns) represents the data element that there are less occurrences of.

③ The cells in the middle of the cross-tab are the sum (in this example, a count) of orders that the sales rep had for the year. This is the equivalent to grouping and sorting data.

④ The totals at the bottom of the cross-tab report will tell you how many sales are for each year and a grand total number of sales for the entire report in the lower right corner of the cross-tab. These totals are automatically calculated in a cross-tab report.

⑤ I have saved the best for last - the placement of the fields on the Cross-Tab screen. The fields for the row and column were answered above. That leaves the field for the cells in the middle of the cross-tab report. Recall the original statement - Sales by sales rep, by year. You have already determined that the sales rep field (The Employee Name field in the table.), is what will be used for the rows. You have also determined that the Order Date will be used for the columns. The only field left is the sales (the orders). This is what goes in the Summary Fields section of the Cross-Tab screen. In this example, the cells represent a count of orders. The default calculation is Sum. You would change that to **DISTINCT COUNT** for the Order ID field.

> **Cross-Tab Tips**
>
> ① It is best not to place any other objects in the same report section as the cross-tab because they will probably be overwritten.
> ② When more than one field is added to the rows, columns or summarized fields sections, the values will be stacked in the cell.
> ③ If you want the cross-tab to capture all of the data in the report, place the cross-tab object in the report header section.
> ④ It is better to position fields so that there are more rows than columns. Doing this will help keep the cross-tab from being forced to print horizontally on more than one page.

Chapter 2

Cross-Tab Screen

Now that you have a foundation of cross-tab reports, the options on the Cross-Tab and Grid Style screens will hopefully make sense. Figure 2-3 shows the Cross-Tab screen.

Figure 2-4 shows the Grid Style screen.

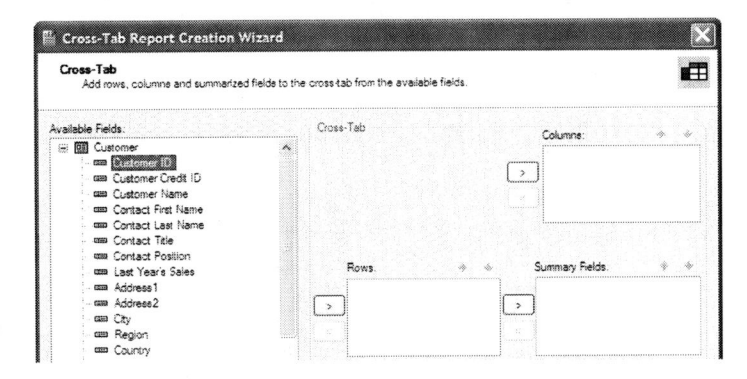

Figure 2-3 Cross-Tab screen

The **AVAILABLE FIELDS** list lets you select the fields that are needed to create the report.

The **ROWS** section contains the field(s) that will be displayed down the left side of the report.

The **COLUMNS** section contains the field(s) that will be displayed across the top of the report.

The **SUMMARY FIELDS** section contains the field(s) that will have the calculation (sum, count, average etc).

At least one field is required in the rows, columns and summary fields sections to create a cross-tab report.

> Text fields cannot be printed in the cells of a cross-tab without selecting a summary type that works with a text field like count, distinct count, minimum or maximum.

The Grid Style screen contains options that add formatting to the cross-tab, similar to templates.

Like other reports, you can format a cross-tab report manually.

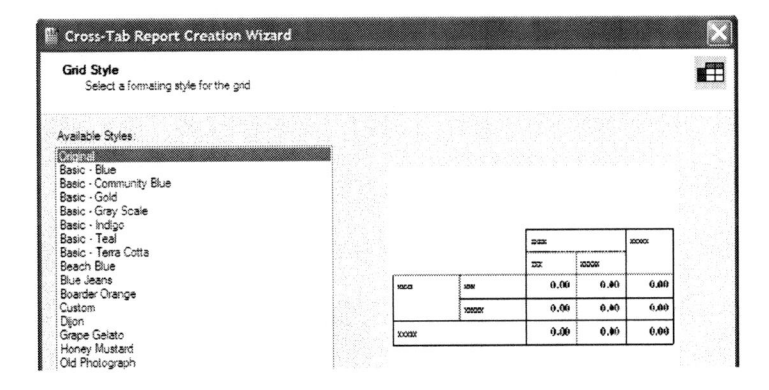

Figure 2-4 Grid Style screen

Report Design Option Changes In Crystal Reports XI

Exercise 2.1: Create A Cross-Tab Product Report

In this exercise you will create a cross-tab report that shows the number of sales for three classes of products: gloves, kids and saddles, by sales rep.

1. Click on the Cross-Tab Report wizard link on the Start Page.

2. Add the Employee, Orders, Orders Detail, Product and Product Type tables, then click Next. Click Next on the Link screen.

3. Click on the Last Name field in the Employee table, then click the right arrow button next to the **ROWS** section.

4. Add the Product Type Name field in the Product Type table to the **COLUMNS** section.

> You can click on the field in the Available Fields list and drag it to the section of the Cross-Tab screen that you need.

5. Add the Quantity field in the Orders Detail table to the **SUMMARIZED FIELDS** section.

6. Select **COUNT** from the drop-down list under the Summary Fields section.
   The Cross-Tab screen should have the options selected that are shown in Figure 2-5.

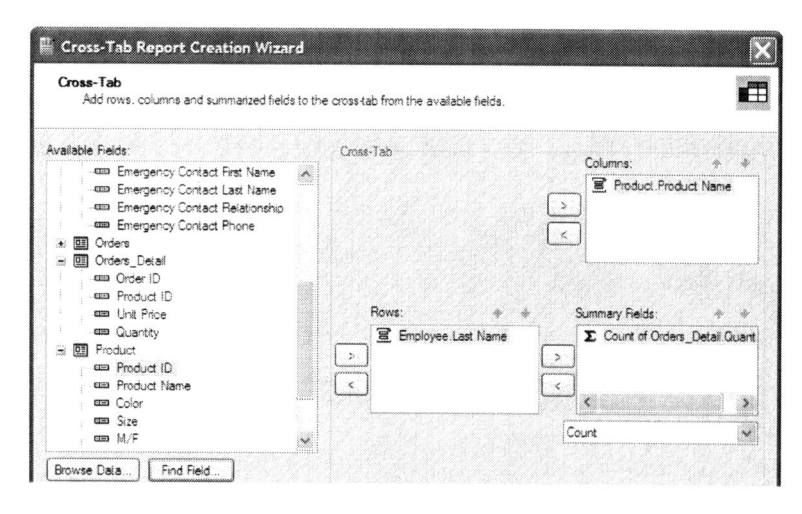

Figure 2-5 Cross-Tab field options

7. Click Next, then select the **NO CHART** option, if it is not already selected and click Next.

> The reason that you added the Orders table and did not use any fields from the table is because it is the "link" between the Orders Detail and Employee tables that is needed to get the Employee Name for each order.

2-6

Chapter 2

8. This report needs to be filtered because you only want totals for three classes of products: gloves, kids and saddles. Add the Product Type Name field from the Product Type table to the Filter Fields list, then open the drop-down list and select **IS ONE OF**.

9. Open the next drop-down list and select gloves, kids and saddles.

   You should have the options selected that are shown in Figure 2-6.

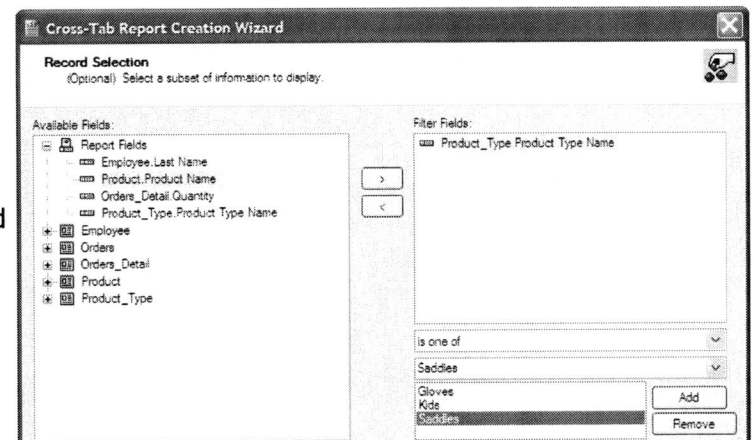

Figure 2-6 Record Selection options

10. Click Next. Click on the **ORIGINAL** grid style if it is not already selected, as shown earlier in Figure 2-4. Click Finish.

    Your report should look like the one shown in Figure 2-7. Now can you tell me how many saddles Robert King sold in total?

    Save the report as `E2.1 Cross-Tab`, then close the report.

	Gloves	Kids	Saddles	Total
Davolio	85	18	49	152
Dodsworth	101	19	58	178
King	97	23	58	178
Leverling	84	25	56	165
Peacock	105	20	59	184
Suyama	84	25	56	165
Total	556	130	336	1,022

Figure 2-7 E2.1 Cross-Tab report

The Chart Expert

This is the tool that allows you to create and modify charts. It has wizard like characteristics because you click on the tabs to accomplish different tasks associated with creating and modifying charts. The biggest benefit of using the Chart Expert instead of the chart options on a wizard is that you have a lot of the chart options available from the beginning and the chart does not have to be based on data that will be printed on the report, like the wizards require. You may gain a better understanding of the options if you have the Chart Expert open.

Report Design Option Changes In Crystal Reports XI

The six tabs on the Chart Expert (Type, Data, Axes, Options, Color Highlighting and Text) contain options for a variety of features that you can use to make the chart as effective as possible. Keep in mind that not all of these tabs are available for all chart types. The tabs and options used most for creating charts from cross-tab data are discussed below.

> You do not have to create a chart from an existing report. You can select the fields that you need on the Chart Expert.

Type Tab

The options on this tab let you select what the chart will look like. There are 16 chart types that you can select from as shown on the left side of Figure 2-8. Many of these chart types have variations that you can select, which gives you more chart options. There are additional chart types, which Crystal Reports refers to as templates that are not on the Chart Expert.

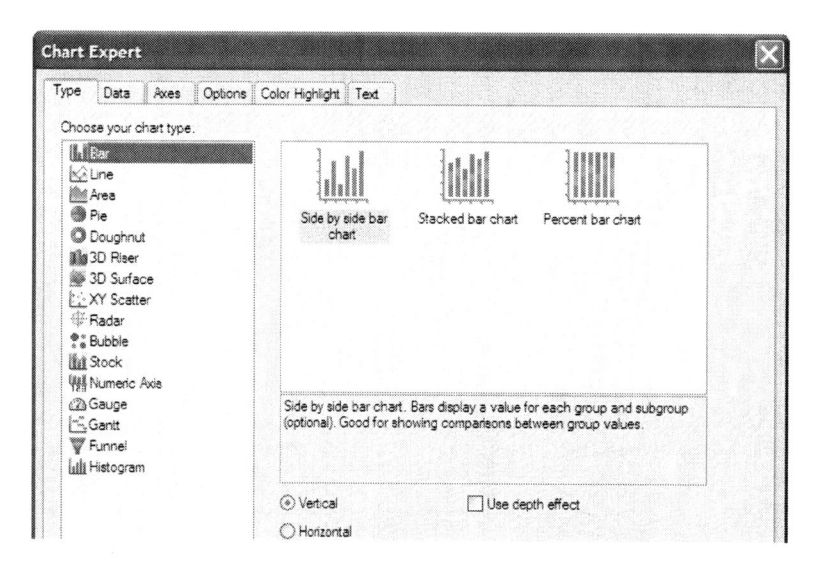

Figure 2-8 Chart Expert Type tab options

If you have created charts in spreadsheet software, you are probably familiar with some of the chart types in Crystal Reports. When selecting the chart type, the most important consideration should be to select the chart type that will best display the data that will be presented in the chart. This is the first thing that you have to do. When you select the chart type on the left you will see variations of the chart on the right. Click on the chart style variation on the right that you want to use. Under the chart variations you will see a description of the chart type.

Chart Layout Options

In addition to chart types, there are four chart layout options as explained in Table 2-1. You have to select one of them.

Chapter 2

Option	Description
Advanced	Creates charts from records in the database, even if the report has groups. The chart must be placed in a report or group header or footer section.
Group	Creates charts from data in summary fields in the group header or footer section. The chart must be placed in a group header or footer section.
Cross-Tab	Creates charts from a Cross-Tab object in the report. The chart must be in the same section type (group, report, etc.) as the Cross-Tab object.
OLAP	Creates charts from an OLAP grid that is already in the report. The chart must be in the same report section type (group, report, etc.) as the OLAP grid.

Table 2-1 Layout options explained

> **Using Formula Fields In Charts**
>
> The Available Fields list on the Advanced layout data screen displays all of the fields that can be used on the chart. You may not see all of the formula fields that you created. You will only see the formula fields whose data is processed during the first pass in the report processing model that Crystal Reports uses.

Cross-Tab Layout Options

This layout option is only available if the report has a cross-tab object in the same or corresponding section of the report that the chart is placed in.

By corresponding section, I mean that if the cross-tab that the chart will be based off of is in the Group 2 footer section, the chart can be placed in the Group 2 header or footer section.

The options shown in Figure 2-9 let you create a chart based on the data in the cross-tab.

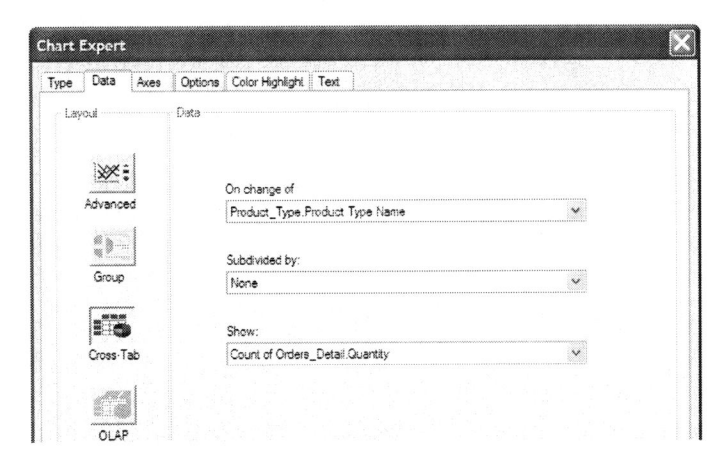

Figure 2-9 Chart Expert Data tab - Cross-Tab options

Cross-Tab charts cannot be placed in the detail section of a report. If you move the cross-tab object to a different section after a cross-tab chart has been created, the report will automatically be moved to the new section also.

Report Design Option Changes In Crystal Reports XI

> 💡 If the report has more than one cross-tab object, you have to select the cross-tab object that you want to create the chart for before you open the Chart Expert.

The options in the **ON CHANGE OF** drop-down list are the first fields in the Rows and Columns sections of the Cross-Tab Expert or Wizard, regardless of how many fields each of these sections have. The field selected in this drop-down list is the first (or only) element that will be used as the primary X axis value.

Selecting a field in the **SUBDIVIDED BY** drop-down list is optional, which is why the default option is **NONE**. The only field that is available in the Subdivided By drop-down list is the one that was not selected in the On Change Of drop-down list.

Selecting a field from the Subdivided by drop-down list will create a second X value, which will add a second series of data to the chart. This will let you create a chart that does a side by side comparison.

Figure 2-10 shows a line chart with the first field in the Row section and the first field in the Column section from the cross-tab selected.

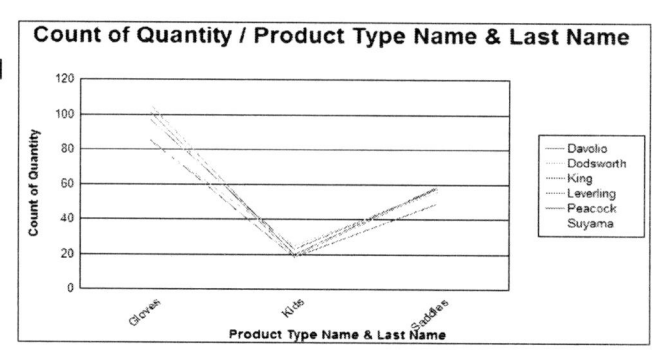

Figure 2-10 Line chart with the row and column fields selected

The options in the **SHOW** drop-down list are the fields that are in the Summary Fields section of the Cross-Tab window. They are the fields that you select from to summarize the report on, like the Show Value list on the Advanced Layout screen.

Exercise 2.2: Create Charts From Cross-Tab Data

Charts that are created from cross-tab data are often easier to create because the data has already been summarized. In this exercise you will create three charts and save them in the same report. Often, cross-tab data is stored in the report header. I find it easier to create additional report header sections and place each chart in it's own section. That keeps the charts from overlapping when the report is viewed or printed.

Add More Report Header Sections

1. Save the CH2.1 report as `E2.2 Cross-Tab data charts`.

2. Open the Section Expert and add three more report header sections.

Create The Quantity Sold By Product Type Chart

1. Add a chart object to the report header b section, then select the Side by side bar chart type, the Horizontal position and the Use depth effect option.

2. Make sure that the On Change Of option on the Cross-Tab layout window has the Product Type Name field selected. The Subdivided By field should be set to None and the Show drop-down list should have the Quantity field selected.

3. Check the Show value option on the Options tab.

4. Change the Title to `Qty Sold By Product Type`.
   Add the Footnote `Report Header B`.
   Change the Group title to `Product Type`.
   Change the Data title to `Qty Sold`.
   Save the changes. The chart should look like the one shown in Figure 2-11.

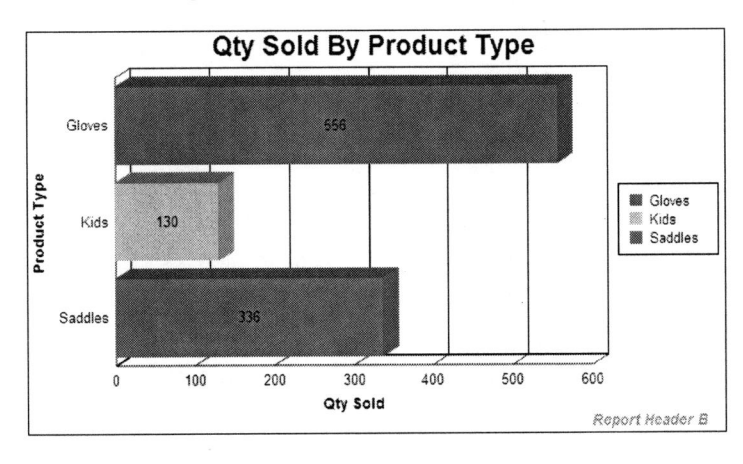

Figure 2-11 E2.2 Quantity sold by product type chart (Report Header B)

Create The Quantity Sold By Product Type By Sales Rep Chart

The chart that you just created provides a high level overview of how many of each product type was sold. The numbers shown across the bottom of the chart represent the totals. The chart that you will create in this part of the exercise will display how many of each product type was sold by each sales rep.

1. Add a chart object to the report header c section, then select the Stacked bar chart type, the Horizontal position and the Use depth effect option.

2. Select the Employee Last Name field from the Subdivided By drop-down list on the Cross-Tab data layout window.

3. Add a major gridline to the Group axis option.

Report Design Option Changes In Crystal Reports XI

4. Check the Show value option on the Options tab.

5. Change the Title to `Product Type & Qty Sold By Sales Rep`.
   Add the Footnote `Report Header C`.
   Change the Group title to `Product Type`.
   Change the Data title to `Qty Sold`. Save the changes. The chart should look like the one shown in Figure 2-12. What you will notice is that each block on the chart is a running total, meaning that the sales rep Dodsworth did not have 186 glove sales. Instead, the sales rep sold the difference between 186 and 85.

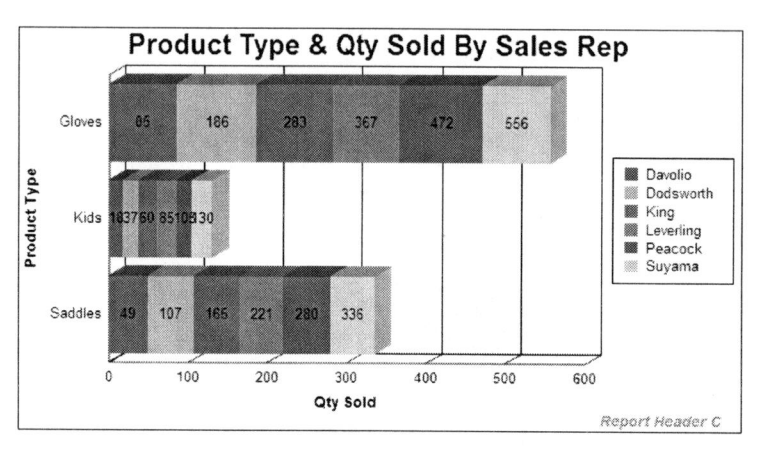

Figure 2-12 E2.2 Product type & quantity sold by sales rep chart (Report Header C)

Create The Percent Of Quantity Sold Chart

The chart that you will create in this part of the exercise will display the total quantity of products each sales rep sold and what percent of the total product quantity their sales represent.

1. Add a chart object to the report header d section, then select the Pie chart type and the Use depth effect option.

2. Add the Employee Last Name field to the first list box on the Advanced tab. Add the Quantity field to the Show value(s) list, then change the summary type to Count.

3. Check the Show label and Show value options, then change the Legend layout option to Percentage. Explode the largest slice of the pie.

4. Change the Title to `Percent Of Qty Sold`.
   Add the Subtitle `The #'s on the chart represent the qty sold`.
   Add the Footnote `Report Header D`.
   Save the changes.

2-12

The chart is on page 2 and should look like the one shown in Figure 2-13.

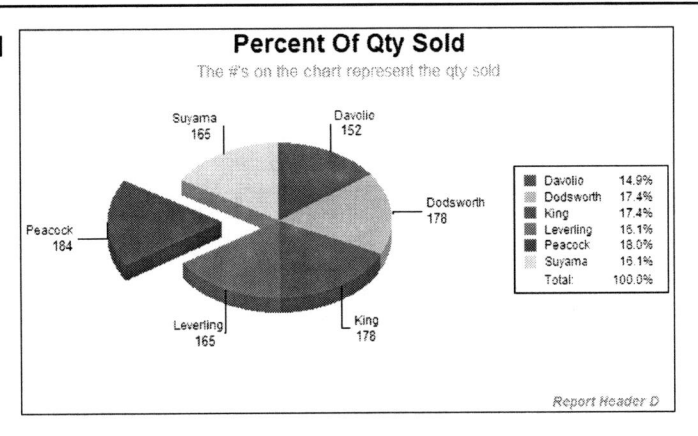

Figure 2-13 E2.2 Percent of quantity sold chart (Report Header D)

Cross-Tab Expert Overview

Earlier you learned how to create a cross-tab report using a wizard. Now you will learn more about cross-tab reports by learning how to use the Cross-Tab Expert. Cross-Tab reports let you summarize large amounts of data in columnar format, in a relatively small amount of space. Cross-Tab reports do not have to be the only object on the report.

You can add a cross-tab object to a report that has field data. In addition to using the Cross-Tab wizard, there are three ways to add a Cross-Tab object to a report as discussed below.

① Right-click on a blank space on the report and select Insert Cross-Tab, then click in the report section where you want to place the cross-tab.
② Click the Insert Cross-Tab button on the Insert Tools toolbar.
③ Insert ⇒ Cross-Tab.

The Cross-Tab Expert has three tabs: Cross-Tab, Style and Customize Style. Many of the options on the first two tabs are on the Cross-Tab wizard.

Figure 2-14 shows the Cross-Tab tab.

Table 2-2 explains the buttons that are not on the Cross-Tab wizard.

Figure 2-15 shows the Style tab. The options on this tab are the same as the ones on the Cross-Tab wizard.

Figure 2-16 shows the Customize Style tab. Tables 2-3 to 2-5 explain the options on this tab.

Report Design Option Changes In Crystal Reports XI

Cross-Tab Tab

The options shown in Figure 2-14 let you select the fields that will be used to create the cross-tab report.

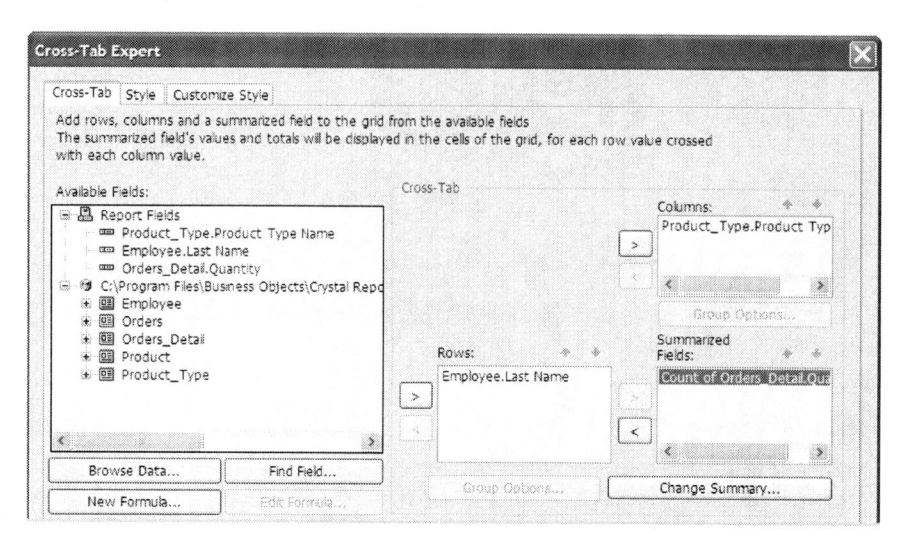

Figure 2-14 Cross-Tab options

Button	Description
New Formula	Opens the Formula Workshop.
Edit Formula	Opens the Formula Workshop so that you can edit an existing formula. You can edit a formula that has been added to the cross-tab or a formula that is listed in the Available Fields list.
Group Options	Opens the Cross-Tab Group Options dialog box shown in Figure 2-15. It is similar to the Insert Group dialog box. After you click on a field in the Rows or Columns section, this button will be enabled, which lets you change the group options for the field.
Change Summary	Opens the Edit Summary dialog box shown in Figure 2-16. It works the same way that the Insert Summary dialog box works and will let you change the summary type for a field in the Summarized Fields section.

Table 2-2 Buttons on the Cross-Tab tab explained

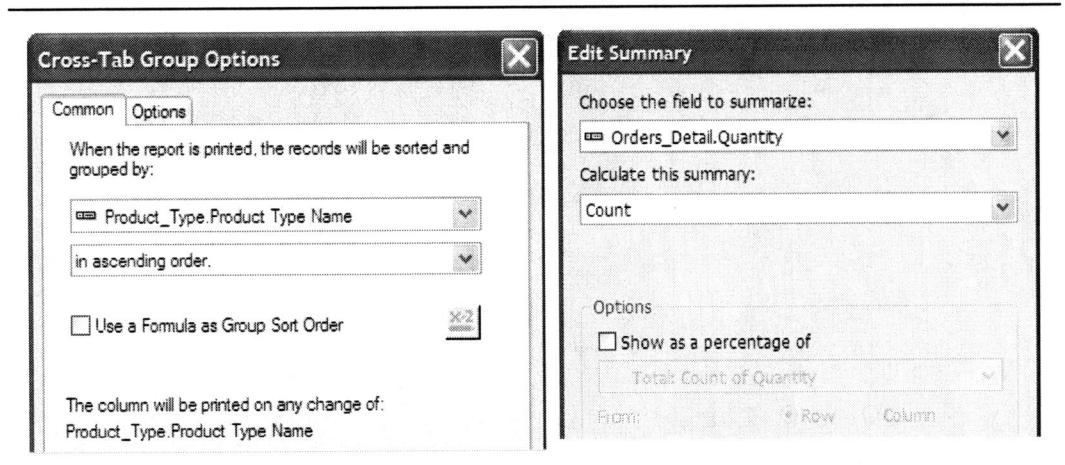

Figure 2-15 Cross-Tab Group Options dialog box

Figure 2-16 Edit Summary dialog box

Style Tab

The options shown in Figure 2-17 are the templates that can be used to format the entire cross-tab object at one time. These are the same styles that are on the Cross-Tab wizard.

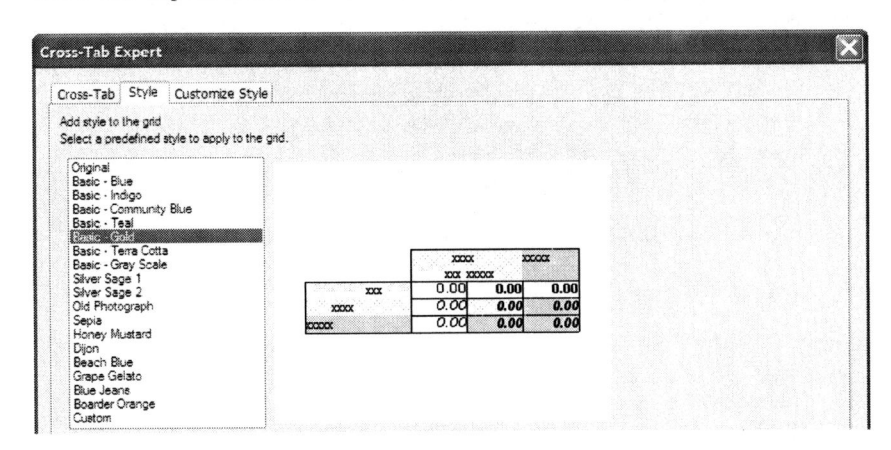

Figure 2-17 Style tab options

Customize Style Tab

The options shown in Figure 2-18 allow formatting to be applied to a specific section of the cross-tab like a row or to the entire cross-tab object. Each field in the Rows and Columns sections represent a group.

The options in the Grid Options section are applied to the entire cross-tab.
The options in the Group Options section can be applied to each field.

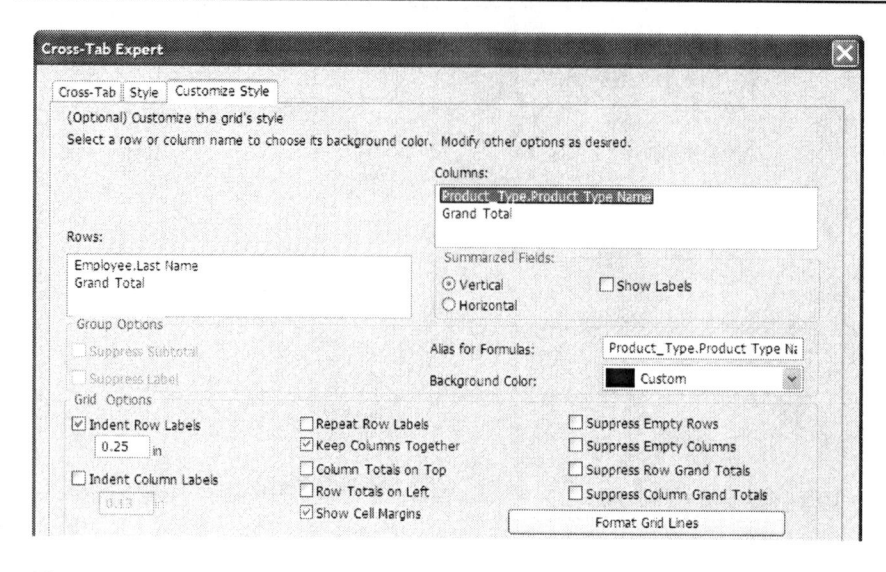

Report Design Option Changes In Crystal Reports XI

Figure 2-18 Customize Style tab options

Option	Description
Vertical/Horizontal	These options determine how the summarized fields will be displayed. There has to be at least two summarized fields to select one of these options. The **VERTICAL** option will stack the summarized fields in the same cell. You will see how this works later in this chapter. The **HORIZONTAL** option will place the summarized fields side by side.
Show Labels	If checked, this option will display the summarized field name in the row or column header.

Table 2-3 Customize style tab Summarized Field options explained

Option	Description
Suppress Subtotal	This option is only available if there are two or more fields in the Rows section or two or more fields in the Columns section. This option cannot be used on grand total fields. If checked, this option will suppress the subtotal for the row or column that is selected.
Alias for Formulas	This option lets you enter a different name for the field that is used on the cross-tab. The name entered in this field can be used in conditional formatting formulas instead of the name in the table.
Background Color	This drop-down list box will let you select a background color for the row or column of data.

Table 2-4 Customize style tab Group Options explained

Chapter 2

Option	Description
Indent Row Labels	Determines how much space the row labels will be indented.
Indent Column Labels	Determines how much space the column labels will be indented.
Repeat Row Labels	This option is only available if the Keep Columns together option is checked. This option will force the row labels to be repeated on other pages when the width of the cross-tab requires more than one page.
Keep Columns Together	Prevents a column from being split across two pages.
Column Totals on Top	Forces column totals to print at the top of the column.
Row Totals on Left	Forces row totals to print on the left of the cross-tab object.
Show Cell Margins	Adds white space on all four sides of the cell.
Suppress Empty Rows	If checked, rows that do not have data will not appear in the cross-tab.
Suppress Empty Columns	If checked, columns that do not have data will not appear in the cross-tab.
Suppress Row Grand Totals	If checked, the grand total row will not appear in the cross-tab.
Suppress Column Grand Totals	If checked, the grand total column will not appear in the cross-tab.
Format Grid Lines button	Clicking this button will open the Format Grid Lines dialog box shown in Figure 2-19. Table 2-6 explains the options on this dialog box.

Table 2-5 Customize style tab Grid Options explained

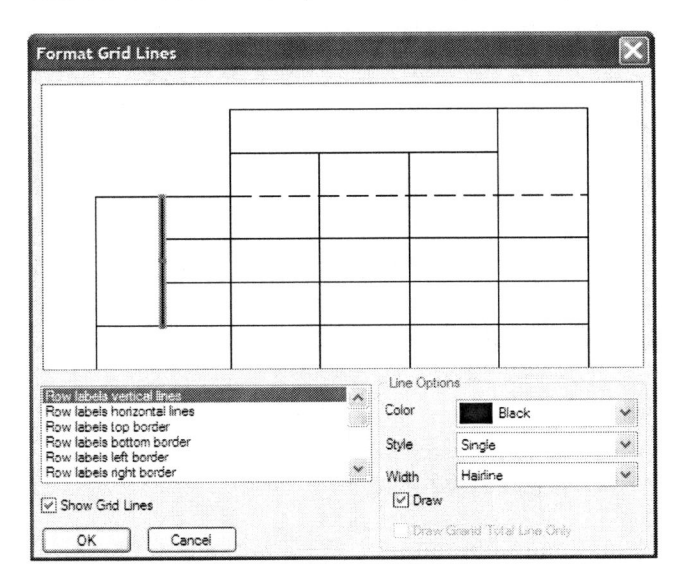

Figure 2-19 Format Grid Lines dialog box

Report Design Option Changes In Crystal Reports XI

Option	Description
Grid Line	Selects the grid line in the list box that you want to modify. The grid line(s) that you select will be highlighted in the grid at the top of the dialog box.
Show Grid Lines	Displays or hides the grid lines.
Color	Select a color for the grid lines.
Style	Select a style for the grid lines.
Width	Select a width for the grid lines.
Draw	Select a specific grid line to hide.
Draw Grand Total Line Only	If checked, this option will only display and print grid lines on grand total rows or columns.

Table 2-6 Format Grid Lines dialog box options explained

Formatting Formulas

You can create conditional formatting formulas in a cross-tab using the Format Editor, similar to how conditional formatting formulas are created for other fields. In addition to being able to use the **CURRENTFIELDVALUE** and **DEFAULTATTRIBUTE** functions, cross-tabs can also use the **GRIDROWCOLUMNVALUE** function. This function lets you create a formula that depends on the value in a row that is related to the current cell. An advantage to using the GridRowColumnValue function is that you can use the Alias field name instead of the real field name. The examples below demonstrate how these functions can be used in a cross-tab object or OLAP grid.

Example #1 The formula below will set the current field (cell) to yellow if it is greater than or equal to 25.

If CurrentFieldValue >= 25 Then crYellow Else DefaultAttribute

Example #2 The formula below will set the current field (cell) to yellow if it is greater than or equal to 100 and the Product Name is "Gloves".

If GridRowColumnValue {Product.Product Name} = "Gloves" and
   CurrentFieldValue >= 100
      Then crYellow Else DefaultAttribute

> You can use the **HIGHLIGHTING EXPERT** to format data fields in a cross-tab object.

Exercise 2.3: Use The Cross-Tab Expert

In this exercise you will recreate the cross-tab report that you created with the wizard in Exercise 2.1. You will enhance the report by adding the following:

① Indenting the row labels.
② Modifying the grid lines.

Chapter 2

③ Applying conditional formatting to change the background of cells that meet a specific condition.
④ Create a formula to calculate the total dollar amount of sales per product, per sales rep.

Create The Product Type Selection Criteria

The Cross-Tab wizard has a Record Selection screen that lets you create selection criteria. If you use the Cross-Tab Expert, you have different options. You can create a formula or create the selection criteria using the Select Expert.

1. Open a new report, then add the following tables to the report: Employee, Orders, Orders Detail, Product and Product Type.

2. Open the Select Expert. Select the Product Type Name field in the Product Type table and click OK. Select the "Is one of" operator, then add the gloves, kids and saddles options and click OK.

Create The Cross-Tab

1. Add a cross-tab object to the report header, then right-click on the cross-tab object and select Cross-Tab Expert.

2. Add the Last Name field in the Employee table to the **ROWS** section.

3. Add the Product Type Name field in the Product Type table to the **COLUMNS** section.

4. Add the Quantity field in the Orders Detail table to the **SUMMARY FIELDS** section. Click the **CHANGE SUMMARY** button and change the summary type to Count, then click OK.

Customize The Cross-Tab

The Customize Style tab has several options that you can use to change the appearance of the cross-tab object.

1. On the Customize Style tab clear the **COLUMN TOTALS ON TOP** and **ROW TOTALS ON LEFT** options.

2. Select the Indent Row Labels option and type .25 in the box below it.

3. Click the Format Grid Lines button. Select the **COLUMN LABEL BOTTOM BORDER** option, then select **DASHED** from the Style drop-down list. Click OK to close the Format Gridlines dialog box, then click OK to close the Cross-Tab Expert.

2-19

Report Design Option Changes In Crystal Reports XI

4. Save the report as E2.3 Cross-Tab.

   The report should look like the one shown in Figure 2-20. Leave the report open to complete the next part of the exercise.

	Gloves	Kids	Saddles	Total
Davolio	85	18	49	152
Dodsworth	101	19	58	178
King	97	23	58	178
Leverling	84	25	56	165
Peacock	105	20	59	184
Suyama	84	25	56	165
Total	556	130	336	1,022

Figure 2-20 E2.3 Cross-Tab report

Add Another Row Of Data To The Cross-Tab

In this part of the exercise you will create a formula that will calculate the total of each product that each sales rep sold.

1. Open the Cross-Tab Expert and click the New Formula button.

2. Type Line Item as the formula name, then type the formula shown below.

   {Orders_Detail.Unit Price} * {Orders_Detail.Quantity}

3. Save the formula, then click on the formula field in the Available Fields list on the Cross-Tab Expert and add it to the Summarized Fields section. Click OK and save the changes. The cross-tab should look like the one shown in Figure 2-21.

If you are wondering why sales reps have the same quantity sold of a product but have different totals for the product, like the sales reps Leverling and Suyama do in the gloves column, it is because the products listed are categories of products, meaning that there are different types of gloves and each type of glove has a different price.

	Gloves	Kids	Saddles	Total
Davolio	85 $2,735.59	18 $11,498.14	49 $1,929.29	152 $16,163.02
Dodsworth	101 $3,404.30	19 $11,625.66	58 $2,492.96	178 $17,522.92
King	97 $2,933.57	23 $15,069.70	58 $2,348.04	178 $20,351.31
Leverling	84 $2,668.06	25 $13,833.10	56 $2,235.63	165 $18,736.79
Peacock	105 $3,174.88	20 $10,830.79	59 $2,647.96	184 $16,653.63
Suyama	84 $2,486.31	25 $13,532.76	56 $2,026.98	165 $18,046.05
Total	556 $17,402.71	130 $76,390.15	336 $13,680.86	1,022 $107,473.72

Figure 2-21 Second row of data added to the cross-tab

I thought the same thing at first, that there was something wrong with the Line Item formula, so I created a detail report and looked at the raw data for the gloves and saw that there are different priced gloves.

Chapter 2

When you see data that does not look right or somehow catches your attention, you should take the time to look at the raw data to see if you can find out why the data looks the way that it does. [See the CH2 Cross-Tab check data report in the zip file] This is the report that I created to figure out if there was really a problem with the formula.

Exercise 2.4: Create Conditional Formatting In Cross-Tabs

Creating conditional formatting in cross-tabs is not that much different then creating conditional formatting in other types of reports. In this exercise you will create conditional formatting on the quantity cells in the gloves column to change the background color to yellow if the quantity is greater than or equal to 100. It would be helpful to quickly be able to see which sales reps sold the most of this particular product.

1. Save the E2.3 report as `E2.4 Conditional formatting Cross-Tab`.

2. In the first column of the cross-tab, right-click on the detail Quantity field and select Format Field.

3. On the Border tab click the Formula button across from the Background option.

4. Type the formula shown below, then click the Save and close button.

   ```
   If GridRowColumnValue("Product_Type.Product Type Name") =
   "Gloves" and CurrentFieldValue >= 100 Then crYellow Else
   DefaultAttribute
   ```

5. Click OK and save the changes. The gloves quantity for two sales reps should have a yellow background.

Cross-Tab Printing Issues

Cross-Tab objects can have printing issues, in particular cross-tab objects that require more than one page to print horizontally. The Cross-Tab Expert has the Repeat Row Labels and Keep Columns Together options that you learned about earlier in Table 2-5, that you can use to resolve some printing issues. If there are horizontal printing issues, there are some options that you can use to resolve them.

- ① **Horizontal Page Number** This special field counts the number of horizontal pages in a report. This field will not work if the cross-tab object is in a section of the report that will not print page footers.
- ② **Repeat Horizontal Pages** This option is on the Common tab on the Format Editor dialog box. If checked, this option will force objects in the page header or page footer section to print on every horizontal page.
- ③ **Relative Positions** This option is on the Common tab on the Section Expert. Use it to control an object that is to the right of a cross-tab object. If checked, this option will cause the object next to the cross-tab to stay in the same relative position, regardless of how much the cross-tab grows.

Cross-Tab Shortcut Menu

Like many features in Crystal Reports, the cross-tab object has it's own shortcut menu. The **PIVOT CROSS-TAB** option lets you move the rows to where the columns are and the columns to where the rows are on the cross-tab object.

Report Viewers

If you do not have Microsoft Word or Excel installed, you can download the free viewers and use them to view some of the exported reports that you will create in this chapter. If the web pages listed below have changed and you can't find the files, search for the file name in parenthesis on Microsoft's web site.

Word 2003 Viewer - (wdviewer.exe)
office.microsoft.com/search/redir.aspx?AssetID=DC011320141033&Origin=HH100152641033&CTT=5

Excel 2003 Viewer - (xlviewer.exe) office.microsoft.com/downloads/2000/xlviewer.aspx

New Report Export Options

The two new export options; editable (RTF) and default export. They are demonstrated in the exercises below.

Exercise 2.5: Create A Word Editable (RTF) Export File

This export option creates a file that allows the report to be edited in Microsoft Word. In this exercise you will only select the first 10 pages of the report to be exported.

1. Open the CH2.2 report, then File ⇒ Export ⇒ Export Report.

2. Select the Word - Editable (RTF) format, then open the Destination drop-down list and select **APPLICATION** as shown in Figure 2-22. Click OK.

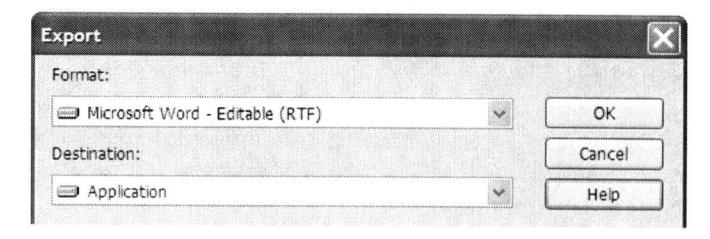

Figure 2-22 Word - Editable (RTF) export options

3. Select the page options shown in Figure 2-23.

   Click OK and the report will be created.

   Your report should look like the one shown in Figure 2-24.

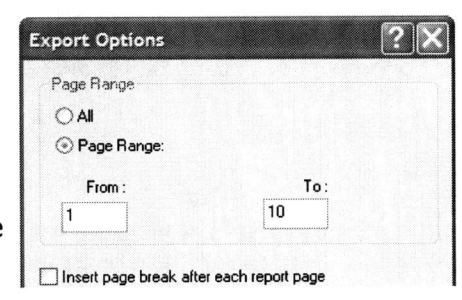

Figure 2-23 Page range export options

Figure 2-24 E2.5 2004 orders by month exported file in Word - Editable (RTF) format

Notice that even though you selected the first 10 pages, there are more pages in the Word document. That is because the page length is different in Crystal Reports then it is in Word. If you scroll down the pages, you will see a blank line between some of the records.

That blank line is where the data would start to print on a new page in Crystal Reports. If the **INSERT PAGE BREAK AFTER EACH REPORT PAGE** option was checked on the Export Options dialog box shown above in Figure 2-23, you may see page breaks in places other then at the bottom of the page. This report is an example of what happens when the page break option is selected.

4. Save the exported file as `E2.5 2004 orders in Word Editable format`, then close the Word document.

Exercise 2.6: Creating Default Export Options

If you know that you always want a report to use the same default export options, you can save the export options by following the steps below. The export options that you select are what will appear in the Format drop-down list on the Export dialog box. Each report can have its own default export options.

1. Open the report that you want to set the default options for. In this exercise, open the CH2.3 2004 Orders by month report, if it is not already open.

2. File ⇒ Export ⇒ Report Export Options, then open the Format drop-down list and select the option, **MICROSOFT EXCEL 97-2000 - DATA ONLY (XLS)**. Click OK.

Report Design Option Changes In Crystal Reports XI

3. Select the **EXPORT IMAGES** and **USE WORKSHEET FUNCTIONS FOR SUMMARIES** options on the Excel Format Options dialog box shown in Figure 2-25 and click OK.

4. Save the exported file as `E2.6 Saved export options`. Close the report. Close Excel.

Now when this report is exported, it will automatically use the export options that are saved with the report. Even though the report now has default export options, you can select other export options.

Histogram Chart

This new chart type places the data into buckets, based on the range that the data falls into and displays a count of the records in each bucket, as shown in Figure 2-25.

Usually, you will not see more than eight bars on a histogram chart, regardless of how many ranges (buckets) there really are.

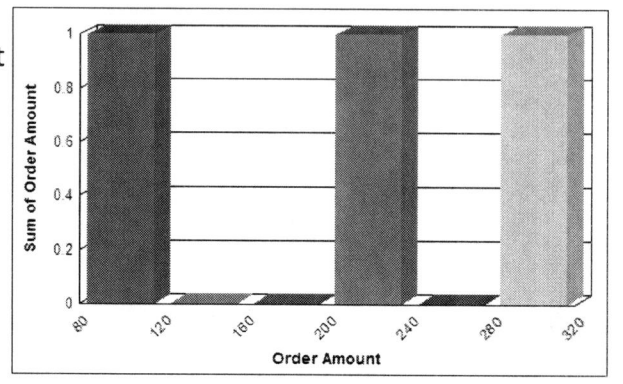

Figure 2-25 Histogram chart

Exercise 2.7: Create A Histogram Chart

In this exercise you will create a histogram chart that shows how many orders per day were placed in 2004.

1. Save the CH2.4 report as `E2.7 Histogram chart`.

2. Select the Histogram chart type, then select the Advanced layout option.

3. Add the Order Date field to the first list box. Add the Order ID field to the Show value(s) list and change the summary type to Distinct Count.

4. Check the Show value option and change the Number format to 1.

5. Change the Title to `Histogram Chart`.
   Change the Subtitle to `Count of orders per day`.
   Change the Data title to `Number of orders`.
   Save the changes. The chart should look like the one shown in Figure 2-26.

Keep in mind that a histogram chart does not display all of the data. A problem that I have noticed is that it is often difficult to know what data is actually being displayed.

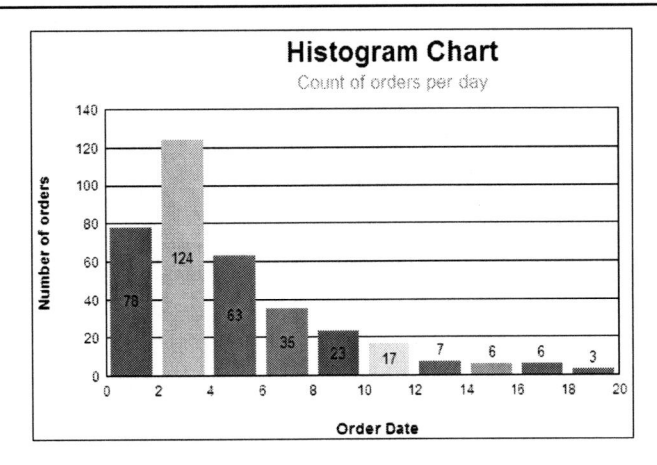

Figure 2-26 E2.7 Histogram chart

Parameter Fields

In previous versions of Crystal Reports, the only type of parameter fields that could be created were static. Now you can create parameter fields that get data directly from a field in a database. Before I cover the new parameter field data options, a brief discussion on importing values and the fields on the Create Parameter Field dialog box will be covered.

Importing Values

If you do not need all of the values in a data field, you have the three options discussed below for selecting which values in the data field will be used in the parameter field.

① You can import all of the values from a field in a table and then delete the values that you do not need.
② Export the values from the table to a text file. This export is done from the database, not from Crystal Reports. Open the text file and delete the values that you do not need, then import the values left in the text file into the parameter field.
③ You can manually import only the values that you need from a field, one by one.

All of these options can be time consuming. The way that I decide which option to select is if I need more than 50% of the values in a data field. If I need more than 50% of the values from a field, I import all of the values from the field, then delete the values that I do not need. If I need less than 50% of the values from a field, I import the ones I need manually, by following the steps below.

1. Create a new parameter field.

2. Enter a name and type for the field.

Report Design Option Changes In Crystal Reports XI

3. Open the **VALUE FIELD** drop-down list and select the field that has the values that will be used in the parameter field.

4. Click in the first row in the **VALUE** column to display the drop-down list arrow.

   Open the drop-down list and select the value(s) that you want, as shown in Figure 2-27, one at a time.

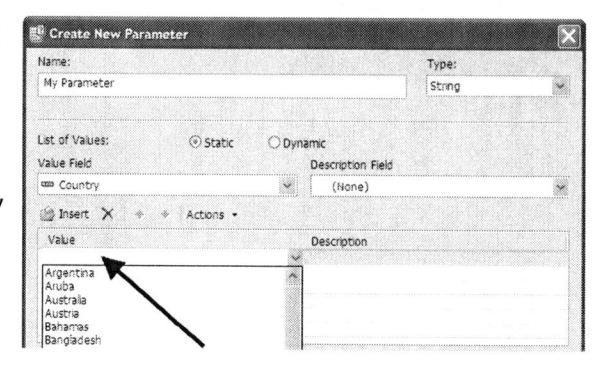

Figure 2-27 Value drop-down list illustrated

The Create New Parameter Dialog Box

The dialog box shown in Figure 2-28 is used to create parameter fields. Reports can and often do have more than one parameter field.

The bottom portion of the dialog box contains a lot of options that can be used to customize the parameter field.

Table 2-7 explains the options on the Create New Parameter dialog box.

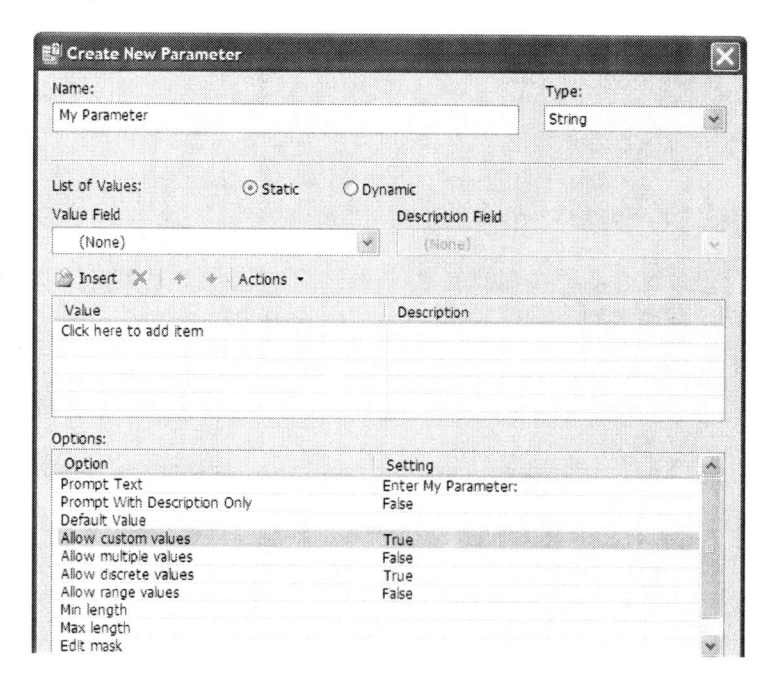

Figure 2-28 Create New Parameter dialog box

2-26

Option	Description
Name	This field stores the name of the parameter field. The name is how you would reference the parameter field. Try to use as descriptive a name as possible, while keeping the name as short as possible. You can use the name of the field in the table that the parameter field will query. You can also use the name of an existing formula. (1)
Type	Select the data type for the parameter field. Select the same data type as the field or data that the parameter field will be compared to. (1)
List of values	If you want to provide values for the parameter field, there are two types of values: Static values that do not change and dynamic values, which can change each time the report is run.
Value Field	The options in this field are the fields from the tables that are connected to the report. This field has two purposes: To select the field for the comparison for the parameter field or to select the field that will be used to import values for a static or dynamic list of values.
Description Field	Allows you to enter text or select another field that will be used to display text next to the Value Field in the list. This is helpful when the value field option is an ID field. Often, the person running the report will not understand the values in an ID field. For example, you may need to use the Customer ID field, but display either the Customer ID field and the Customer Name field or only display the Customer Name field. The Customer Name field contains data that the person running the report understands.
Insert	Clicking this button will retrieve the data that is in the field selected in the Value Field discussed above.
Actions	The options for this drop-down list are shown in Figure 2-29. They are used to create a list of values or export values.
Value/Description	These two columns function like a table. They let you select specific data from the field that is selected in the Value Field. Filling in the Description column is optional. If the field name that is in the Value column is not descriptive enough, you can enter text in the Description column to better explain the data in the Value column.
Option/Setting	The options in this section let you customize the parameter field. The options will change depending on the data type that is selected.

Table 2-7 Create New Parameter dialog box options explained

(1) This option is required to create a parameter field.

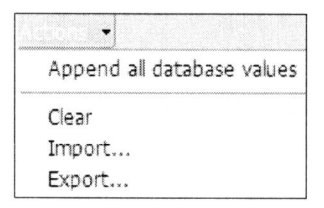

Report Design Option Changes In Crystal Reports XI

Figure 2-29 Actions drop-down list options

There are four ways to open the Create New Parameter dialog box as discussed below.

① Click on the Parameter Fields category in the Field Explorer, then click the **NEW** button on the Field Explorer toolbar.
② Right-click on the Parameter Fields category in the Field Explorer, then select **NEW**.
③ Click the Field Explorer button on the Standard toolbar to open the Field Explorer, then follow one of the options above.
④ View ⇒ Field Explorer, then follow option one or two above.

Adding Values Manually

There are two ways to add values manually on the Create (or Edit) Parameter dialog box as discussed below.

① Click on the **CLICK HERE TO ADD ITEM** option in the Value column.
② Click the **INSERT** button.

Exercise 2.8: Create A Static List Of Values Manually

The report that you will modify is currently limited to two regions: OH and FL. In this exercise you will create a static list of values manually and limit the regions to five, but you will be able to select which of the five regions that you want to appear on the report from a drop-down list.

1. Save the CH2.5 report as `E2.8 Manual static list of values`.

2. Type `Region` in the Name field.

3. Select one of the ways discussed above to add a value and type `OH` in the first row in the Value/Description section of the dialog box, then type `Ohio` in the Description column.

If the data in the Value column contains an ID number, abbreviation or other data that the person running the report may not be familiar with, you should enter a brief explanation in the Description column. The information that you enter in the Description column will appear in the drop-down list next to the content in the Value column. The description is only used for display purposes.

Chapter 2

> You do not have to enter a value in the Description column for every option in the list, only those that you think the person running the report may not understand.

If you have entered a description for every value in the list, you can change the **PROMPT WITH DESCRIPTION ONLY** option at the bottom of the dialog box to True. If you do this, the only values that will appear in the list will be the values in the Description column.

If there is data in a report that you do not want everyone to see, you can create a list of values that will prevent everyone from seeing all of the data. For example, you may not want all sales reps to see sales outside of their region. In this example, you would create a parameter field that lists the regions that you want the sales reps to be able to view. You can create this type of list of values with static or dynamic lists.

4. Add the following regions to the Value column: CA, PA, WI and FL.

5. Change the **ALLOW CUSTOM VALUES** option at the bottom of the dialog box to False.

   In this report, you are only going to allow the report to be run for one of the regions that you added to the static list of values.

   You should have the options shown in Figure 2-30.

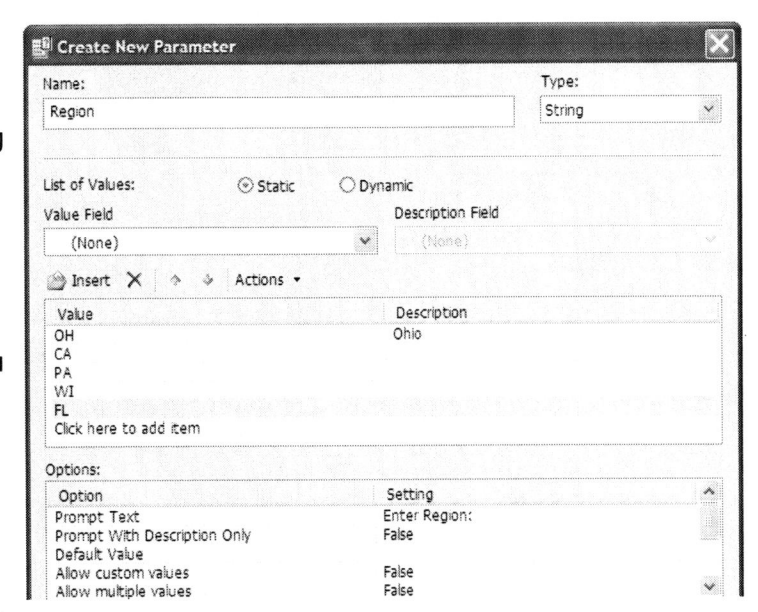

Figure 2-30 Parameter field options for a static list of values

6. Click OK. Open the Select Expert and select the Region parameter field, then remove the other values from the list and click OK.

2-29

Report Design Option Changes In Crystal Reports XI

You will see the Enter Values dialog box. If you open the drop-down list, you will see the values that you added to the static list of values as shown in Figure 2-31. As you can see, the first option also displays the description that you entered. If you try to type in a value you will see that you can't. That is because the **ALLOW CUSTOM VALUES** option is set to False as shown above in Figure 2-30.

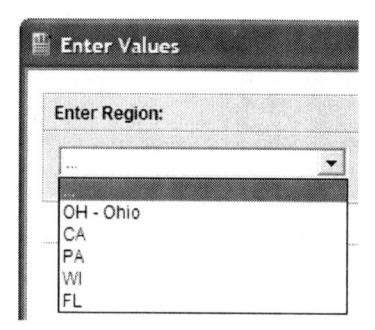

Figure 2-31 Static list of values

Also notice that the values are not in alphabetical order. They are in the order that they were added to the Value/Description table. In the next part of this exercise you will learn how to change the order of values in a static list.

If the Allow custom values option was set to True on the parameter field dialog box shown above in Figure 2-30, you would see a field at the bottom of the Enter Values dialog box that would let you type in the values that you want, as illustrated in Figure 2-32.

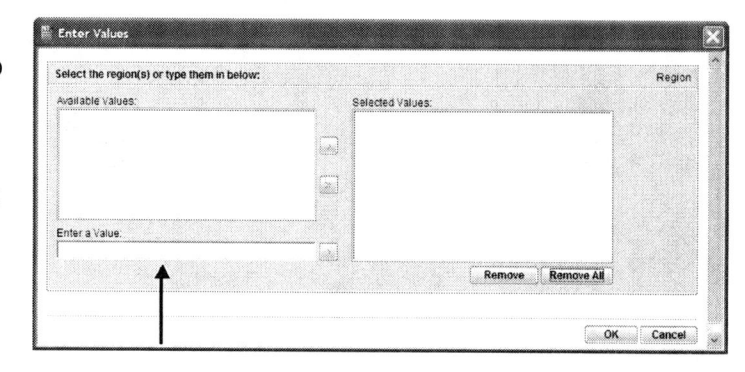

Figure 2-32 Result of the Allow custom values option set to true

The person running the report could select an option from the drop-down list or type in the value that they want. This would be useful for example if the static list contained the 10 most used options, which would keep the list small, while providing additional flexibility by allowing data to be entered manually.

7. Select PA from the list and run the report. You should have five records on the report. Save the changes and leave the report open to complete the next part of the exercise.

Change The Sort Order Of The Static List Of Values

As you saw in the previous part of this exercise, the states are not in alphabetical order. Most text lists are in alphabetical order because it is easier for the person running the report to find the value that they are looking for. In this part of the exercise you will learn how to change the order of the items in the list.

Chapter 2

> 💡 There are two ways to change the sort order of a list of values. The instructions in this exercise are best suited for a list that does not need a lot of changes or for a list that you do not necessarily want in alphabetical order, but just in a different order then the list is currently in.
>
> An example of this would be if you wanted to put a specific value at the top of the list because it is the most used option and then put the rest of the list in alphabetical order. You may have seen this on a web-based form for a country field. You would see "USA" at the top of the drop-down list because the company knows that most of their subscribers or customers are in the USA. Below that option, the rest of the countries are in alphabetical order.

1. Open the Edit Parameter dialog box for the Region field.

2. Click on the CA value, then click the Up button illustrated in Figure 2-33.

   Rearrange the other values in the column so that the entire list is in alphabetical order.

   Click OK, then press F5.

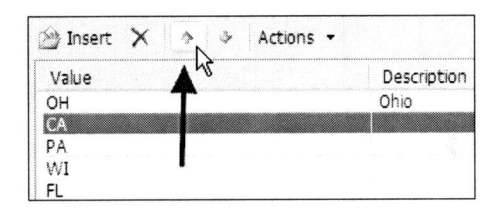

   Figure 2-33 Reorder buttons illustrated

3. Select the second option, then click OK. When you open the drop-down list, the values will now be in alphabetical order. Save the changes and close the report.

How To Sort The Entire Value List At One Time

To sort the entire value list at one time, click on the column heading (Value or Description) that you want to sort the list by. You will see an arrow as illustrated in Figure 2-34. If the arrow is pointing up, the values will be sorted in ascending order.

If the arrow is pointing up and you click on the arrow, it will point down and the values will be sorted in descending order.

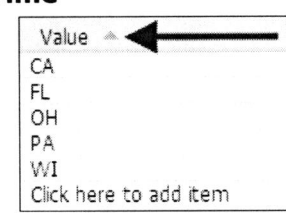

Figure 2-34 Column sorting options illustrated

Dynamic List Of Values

Dynamic and cascading prompts are probably one of the most talked about features in Crystal Reports XI. This type of parameter field allows for greater flexibility when creating reports. Often, you may find that different groups of people may need similar reports. One of the ways that you can create one report that works for slightly different needs is by incorporating dynamic and cascading prompts.

Report Design Option Changes In Crystal Reports XI

Unlike a static list of values that are not refreshed each time the report is run, dynamic and cascading list of values are refreshed each time the report is run. This means that if new values are added to the field in the table that the parameter field is getting the data from, the new values are also available in the parameter field. For example, if the dynamic parameter field is based on the product name field and 12 new products are added, those 12 products would also be available in the parameter field drop-down list. The opposite is also true. If values are deleted from the field in the underlying table, they would no longer be available in the parameter field drop-down list. Dynamic list of values are best suited for data that changes in a table, like new customers or a very large list of products.

> While you will not notice this completing the parameter exercises in this book because the database is stored on your hard drive, dynamic and cascading lists take longer to be retrieved then static lists. Depending on the number of records in the table that the dynamic or cascading list is being retrieved from, you may notice a delay between the time that you open the drop-down list and the time that you actually see the values appear in the list.

Exercise 2.9: Create A Dynamic Region List Of Values

When a customer is added that is in a region that does not currently exist in the values for the parameter field, a report that uses a static list of values would not include the new region on the report. This means that the report will not contain up to date information because static lists are not automatically updated. In this exercise you will create a dynamic list of values for the region field.

1. Save the CH2.6 report as `E2.9 Dynamic region list of values`.

2. Open a new parameter field.

3. Type `Region` in the Name field, then open the List of Values drop-down list and select **DYNAMIC**.

4. Click the Insert button. You will see a list of fields that are available for the dynamic list. Select the Region field.

The **EXISTING** option in the Data Source section is only available when the report already has an existing dynamic list.

The **DESCRIPTION** column works the same for dynamic lists as it does for static lists.

The **PARAMETERS** column is used when creating a dynamic cascading prompt. This is how you create the hierarchy between the fields that will be part of the cascading prompt.

5. Click OK. Open the Select Expert and select the parameter field, then remove the other values from the Region field.

Chapter 2

6. Click OK, then press F5. You will see that you can only select one value from the Region drop-down list. Save the changes and close the report.

> If this report was going to be put into production, it would probably be a good idea to change the operator to "Is equal to" so that when you read the formula, it will match the objectives of the report. Otherwise, it may be confusing later if you have to edit the report. If you leave it as it is, when the report is run, only one region can be selected from the drop-down list because the Allow multiple values parameter option is set to False.

Cascading Prompts And List Of Values

Cascading prompts are created like dynamic prompts. Unlike the dynamic list of values, the cascading prompts contain related data and you must have at least two parameter fields to create cascading prompts. A cascading list of values will reduce the number of items to select from in at least one of the fields on the Enter Values dialog box.

The difference between dynamic and cascading prompts is that the option selected in the first prompt on the Enter Values dialog box is used to filter the values that will be displayed in the second prompt. An example of cascading prompts would be a list of suppliers and a list of products. The first prompt would be for the suppliers. Once a supplier is selected, the values in the second drop-down list would only contain products for the supplier that was selected in the first prompt.

> When you create cascading prompts, Crystal Reports will automatically change the name of the parameter field. It will be renamed to a combination of the name that you entered for the field and the name of the field that it is connected to in the prompt group. You can rename the parameter field in the Field Explorer back to what you had originally named it.

Cascading prompts are also known as a **PROMPT GROUP**. All of the options on the Create New Parameter dialog box are not available for each parameter field in the group. There are some design limitations to creating cascading prompts as discussed below.

① The last parameter field in the group always has access to all of the options.
② Only the last parameter field in the group can select range values. The other parameter fields can only use discrete values.

Exercise 2.10: Create Cascading Prompts For Countries And Regions

In this exercise you will create two prompts. The first one is for the country, the second one is for the region. The region drop-down list will only show states (regions) that are in the country that is selected in the first prompt. The CH2.7 Parameter Fields report (in the zip file) currently displays all countries and regions. The cascading prompts that you will create for this report will allow a specific country and specific region to be selected when the report is run.

Report Design Option Changes In Crystal Reports XI

1. Save the CH2.7 report as
   `E2.10 Cascading prompts for countries and regions.`

2. Type `Countries and Regions` in the Name field, then select the Dynamic List of values option.

3. Type `Select a country, then select a region:` in the **PROMPT GROUP TEXT** field.

4. Click the Insert button, then select the Country field. Click in the second row and select the Region field. Click OK.

5. Open the Select Expert, click on the Region field on the Choose Field dialog box, then click OK. In this step, you have to select the last field that was added on the Create New Parameter dialog box.

6. Select the "Is equal to" operator, then select the Countries and Regions - Region parameter field and click OK.

Your dialog box should look like the one shown in Figure 2-35.

Notice that the Region field is not available. When you select a country, the region field will be available.

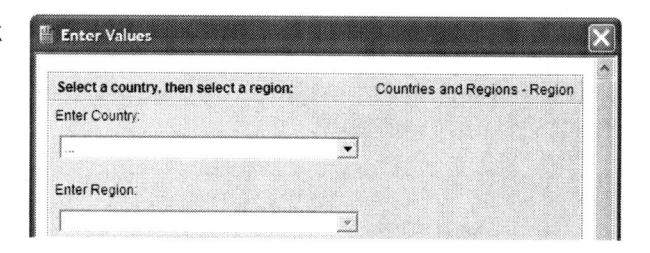

Figure 2-35 Dynamic cascading parameter options

7. Select USA, then select CA and click OK. There should be six records on the report. Save the changes.

Did you notice that the only states (regions) that you saw in the second drop-down list are for the USA? If you select a different country, you will only see regions that are in that country. This is the dynamic cascading (filtering) effect.

Exercise 2.11: Create Cascading Prompts For Customers And Their Orders

Many people in a company may have the need to view a particular customers orders. This is the type of report that dynamic cascading parameters were designed to handle.

1. Save the CH2.8 report as `E2.11 Cascading prompts for customer orders.`

2. Type `Customer Orders` in the Name field, then select the Dynamic List of values option.

Chapter 2

3. Type `Select a customer, then select the Order # that you want to view:` in the Prompt Group Text field.

4. Select the Customer Name field in the Value column.

5. Change the **PROMPT TEXT** option to `Select A Customer:` as illustrated in Figure 2-36.

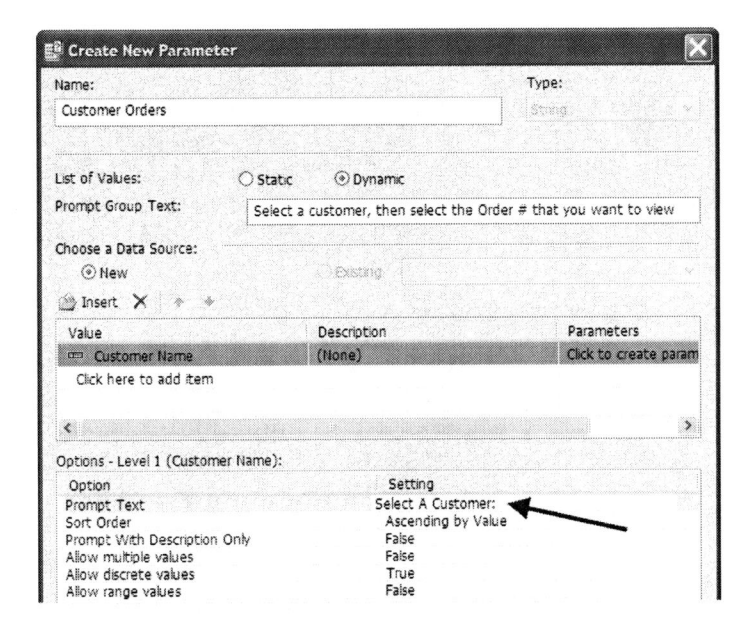

Figure 2-36 Options for the first parameter field

6. Click in the second Value row and select the Order ID field, then change the Prompt Text option to `Select the Order Number that you want to view:`, then click OK.

7. Open the Select Expert, select the Order ID field, then click OK.

8. Select the "Is equal to" operator, then select the Customer Orders - Order ID parameter field in the next drop-down list and click OK.

9. Select the customer, Alley Cat Cycles, then select the order number 2300.
The order numbers in the drop-down list are for the customer that is selected in the first drop-down list.

Report Design Option Changes In Crystal Reports XI

Your dialog box should look like the one shown in Figure 2-37. Click OK.

You should see the data for order number 2300. Save the changes and close the report.

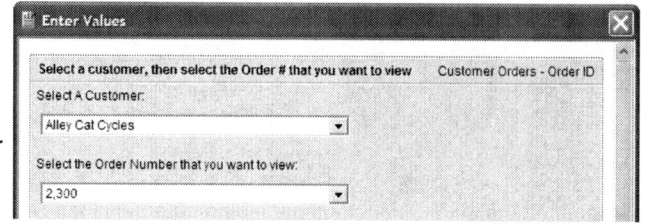

Figure 2-37 Cascading customer parameter options

> What may not be obvious is that once you click OK on the Create New Parameter dialog box, you can't go back and edit cascading parameter field options. You would have to recreate each of the parameter fields. For that reason, I create each of the fields for the group separately and then put them in a group parameter field. Doing this allows you to edit each of the fields in the parameter group if necessary.

Allow Range Values And Allow Multiple Values Options

The reports that you have created parameter fields for so far in this chapter have added a lot of interactivity between the user and the report. This allows the person running the report to have more control over the records that will appear on the report. What you have probably noticed is that each parameter field that you have created only allows one option to be selected. In some instances this can limit the data that displays on reports in a way that is not best suited for the person running the report.

The Create New Parameter dialog box has two options that will allow more flexibility. The **ALLOW RANGE VALUES** option allows the parameter field to accept high and low values. A good use of this option would be for a date range. The **ALLOW MULTIPLE VALUES** option allows more than one value to be selected from the parameter field. A good use of this option would be if you need to select more than one value from the same field.
An example is if you needed to select several products to see which ones are not selling.

Allow Range Values Option

When you set this option to **TRUE**, you will be able to use one parameter field to accept two values, a start of range value and an end of range value. When a parameter field has this option set to true, you have to select the "Is equal to" operator on the Select Expert because the parameter field contains the start and end values in one field. A parameter field with the range value option set to true is the equivalent of the "Is between" operator.

By default, the start and end of range fields have the **INCLUDE THIS VALUE** option checked. This means that the values entered in both fields will be included in the record selection process. If you clear this option for either field, the value will not be included in the record selection process. This is the equivalent of the "Is greater than" and "Is less than" Select Expert operators.

When the Allow range values option is set to True, the **NO LOWER VALUE** and **NO UPPER VALUE** options are not checked. This means that only records that have a value between the start and end range values will be included in the record selection process.
These options can and often are used with date fields. These options also work with non date field ranges. If either of these options are checked, the input field is disabled and you can't enter anything in the field. These options can also be used like the "Is greater than" and "Is less than" Select Expert operators.

Only entering a value in the Start of range input field and checking the No lower value option will retrieve all records that have a value greater than (or equal to, if the Include this value option is also checked for the field) the value in the Start of range field.
Only entering a value in the End of range input field and checking the No lower value option will retrieve all records that have a value less than (or equal to, if the Include this value option is also checked for the field) the value in the End of range field.

Allow Multiple Values Option
When you set this option to **TRUE**, you will be able to select more than one value in the parameter field. This is the equivalent of the "Is one of" Select Expert operator.
In Exercise 2.9 you created a dynamic list of values for the region field. When the report was run, only one region could be selected. You may often have a report request that requires that more than one value be included in the selection process. When the Allow multiple values option is set to True, you are creating what is called an **ARRAY**.
This means that the field can contain more than one value.

> If the **ALLOW CUSTOM VALUES** and **ALLOW MULTIPLE VALUES** options are set to True, values can be added from the **AVAILABLE VALUES** list box and typed in manually if the values in the Available Values list box is from a static list. This cannot be done with dynamic and cascading list of values.

Top N Reports With Parameter Fields
Like other reports that have formulas, the options that you select on the dialog box to create a Top N report are hard coded. You can create a conditional formula and use it with the parameter field to be able to run the Top N report with different **N** values.

Exercise 2.12: Create A Parameter Field For A Top N Report
In this exercise you will create a formula that will be used as the basis for a parameter field that will let the person running the report select the **N** value. You will also remove the hard coded date range and add a parameter field to allow a date range to be selected each time the report is run.

Create The Parameter Field
1. Save the CH2.9 report as `E2.12 Top N parameter field`.

2. Type `Top N` in the Name field, then change the Type to Number.

Report Design Option Changes In Crystal Reports XI

3. Change the following options:
   Prompt Text - `Enter a number between 1 & 100 for the Top N value:`
   Change the Default Value option to 5.
   Change the Min Value option to 1.
   Change the Max Value option to 100.
   You should have the options selected that are shown in Figure 2-38. Click OK and save the changes.

Option	Setting
Prompt Text	Enter a number between 1 & 100 for the Top...
Prompt With Description Only	False
Default Value	5.00
Allow custom values	True
Allow multiple values	False
Allow discrete values	True
Allow range values	False
Min Value	1.00
Max Value	100.00

Figure 2-38 Top N parameter field options

> When you have to create a Top, Bottom or Percent N parameter field you can select the Default, Min and Max Values that you want. If you know that the majority of times that the report will be run that a specific N number will be selected, set that number as the default. It is not a requirement to have Min and Max Values.

Create The Top N Formula

1. Open the Group Sort Expert, then click the Formula button.

2. Type {?Top N} as shown on the right side of Figure 2-39.

   Click the Save and close button.

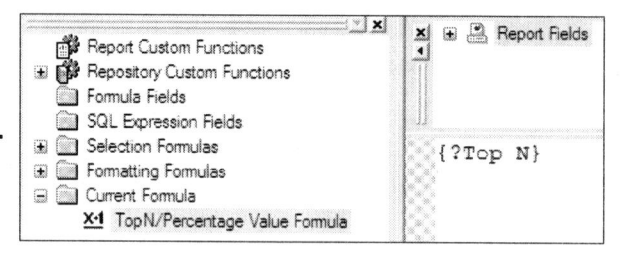

Figure 2-39 Top N Formula

3. Check the **INCLUDE TIES** option, then click OK to close the Group Sort Expert.

> If the **INCLUDE TIES** option is not checked and there are ties, only one of the tied groups will be displayed on the report. I could not find a way to specify which of the tied groups will appear on the report or no way to indicate that there is another group with the same number. Therefore, I think that the best solution may be to always select this option.

Chapter 2

The report needs more changes. The current report title will not be accurate because the person running the report has the option of selecting the Top N value and the order date range.

Create The Order Date Range Parameter Field

In this part of the exercise you will remove the hard coded date range and replace it with a parameter field.

1. Open a new parameter field dialog box and type `Order Date` in the Name field, then change the Type to Date Time and select the Dynamic List of Values option.

2. Add the Order Date field to the Value column, then click in the Parameters column.

3. Change the following options, then click OK.
   Prompt Text - `Select the date range that you want to see orders for:`
   Change the Allow range values option to True.

Modify The Select Expert Options And Parameter Field Order

1. Open the Select Expert. Select the "Is equal to" operator, then select the Order Date parameter field and click OK.

2. Open the Parameter Order dialog box and put the parameter fields in the order shown in Figure 2-40, then click OK and save the changes.

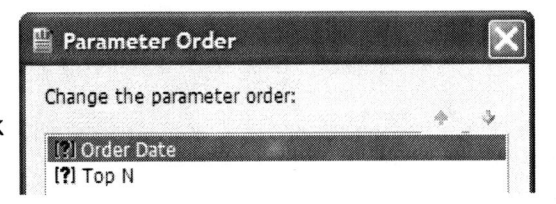

Figure 2-40 Parameter Order dialog box options

Test The Parameter Fields

1. Press F5. Your dialog box should look similar to the one shown in Figure 2-41.

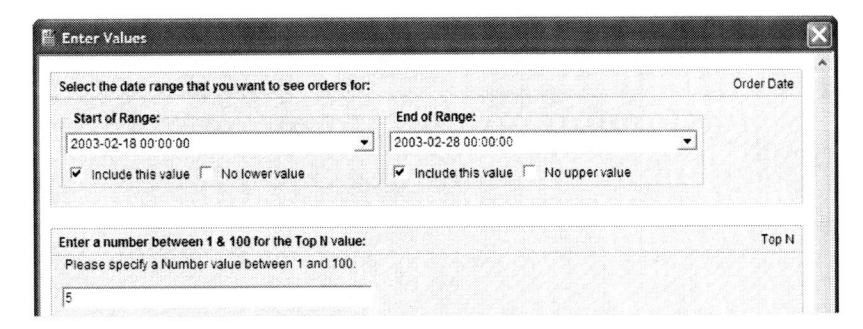

Figure 2-41 Top N parameter options

Report Design Option Changes In Crystal Reports XI

2. Run the report to make sure that it works. If you select a high N number, the chart will be difficult to read. More than likely, you would delete the chart from this report.

Exercise 2.13: Show The Bottom 20% Of Orders

The chart shown in Figure 2-42 plots the data for 12 months. If the marketing department wanted to create a campaign to increase sales in the months that had the lowest number of sales, it could be difficult to tell which months fall into that category.

If the chart was modified to only display the months that are in the bottom 20% of sales based on the total order amount by month, the chart would be easier for the marketing department to use. Creating a report for the bottom 20% is very similar to creating reports in the top 20%.

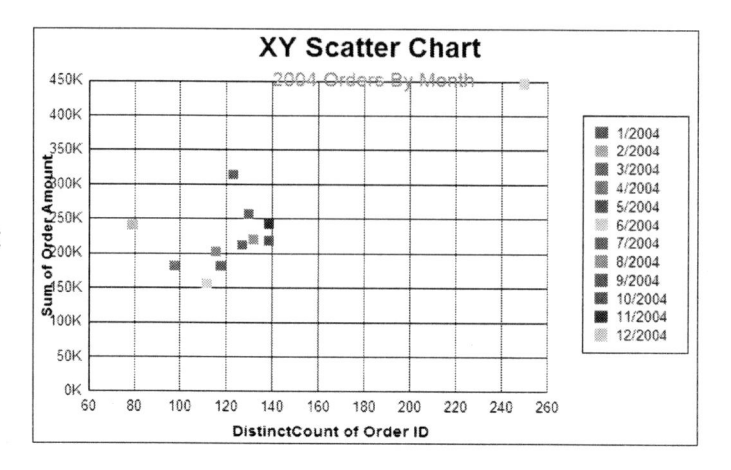

Figure 2-42 XY Scatter chart

1. Save the CH2.10 report as `E2.13 Bottom 20 percent chart`.

2. Open the Chart Expert. On the Data tab click on the Order Date field in the top list on the right, then click the **TOP N** button.

3. Open the Group Sort drop-down list and select **BOTTOM PERCENTAGE**. Change the Percentage field to `20`, then check the **INCLUDE TIES** option. The options that are shown in Figure 2-43 will display the months that are in the bottom 20%, based on the number of orders placed that month. Click OK.

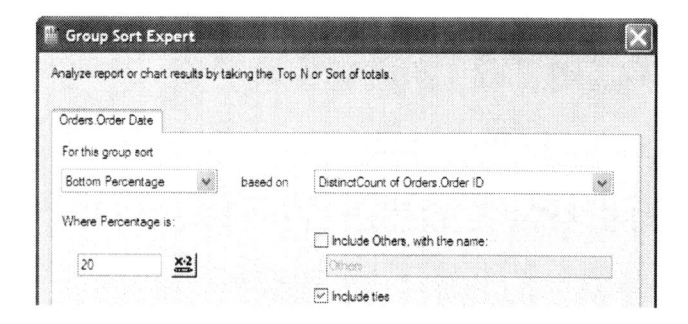

Figure 2-43 Group Sort Expert options

2-40

Chapter 2

4. Change the Title to Bottom 20% Of Orders.
   Delete the Subtitle.
   Change the Group title to Number of orders.
   Change the Data title to Total monthly order amount.

   Click OK and save the changes. The chart should look like the one shown in Figure 2-44.

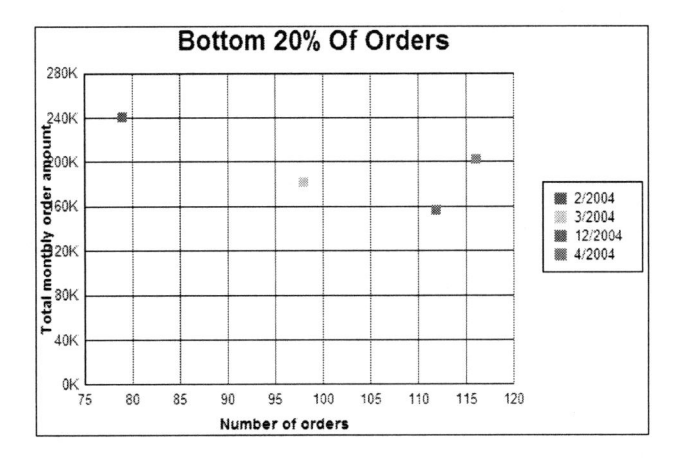

Figure 2-44 Bottom 20 percent chart

> If you create a Top N report and do not add the records that do not meet the Top N criteria to the "Others" group option, any grand total fields that are placed in the report footer will include totals for all records that meet the report criteria, whether or not they appear on the report. This means that the report grand totals will not be accurate. This may not be what you want. If you only want the grand totals to include records that print on the report, in this case the Top N records, you have to create running total fields and place them in the report footer instead of summary fields.

Using Parameter Fields To Select The Sorting And Grouping Options

Parameter fields will let you create formulas to sort or group data because the Insert Group dialog box has a Formula field button. You can sort and group data by selecting options on the Record Sort Expert and Insert Group dialog boxes. There will be times when a report needs to be sorted or grouped in several different ways. Rather then hard code this information and have to create several reports, one for each way that the report needs to be sorted or grouped, you can create a parameter field that will be used to find out what field the person wants the report to be sorted or grouped on. The value collected from the parameter field will be passed to the Record Sort Expert or Insert Group dialog box.

Parameter fields cannot retrieve a formula or table name. Therefore, you have to create a formula that uses the value in the parameter field as the field to sort or group on.

Report Design Option Changes In Crystal Reports XI

Exercise 2.14: Create A Parameter Field To Sort The Records

The customer information report that you will modify is not sorted or grouped. In this exercise you will create a formula and parameter field that will allow the report to be sorted on one of the following three fields: Customer Name, Region or Country.

Create The Sort By Parameter Field

1. Save the CH2.11 report as `E2.14 Sort records parameter field`.

2. Open a new parameter field, then type `Sort By Field` in the Name field.

3. Type the values `Customer Name`, `Region` and `Country` in the Value column. Type `State` in the Description column of the Region value.

4. Change the following options, then click OK.
   Prompt Text - `Select the field that you want to sort by:`
   Change the Allow custom values option to False.

Create The Sort Formula And Add It To The Parameter Field

1. Open the Formula Workshop and create a new formula. Type `SortBy` as the formula name.

2. Type the formula shown below, then click the Save and close button.

   ```
   If {?Sort By Field} = "Customer Name" Then
   {Customer.Customer Name}
   Else
   If {?Sort By Field} = "Region" Then {Customer.Region}
   Else
   {Customer.Country}
   ```

3. Open the Record Sort Expert, then add the SortBy formula field to the Sort Fields list box and click OK.

   Save the changes and preview the report.

   The Enter Values dialog box shown in Figure 2-45 will open.

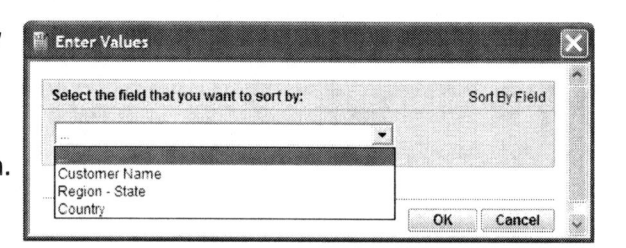

   Figure 2-45 SortBy options

Test The Sort Parameter
1. Select the Customer Name option from the drop-down list and click OK.
   The report should be sorted in Customer Name order.

2. Run the report again and sort the report by Region. Leave the report open to complete the next exercise.

Exercise 2.15: Create A Parameter Field To Group Data
In the previous exercise you learned how to sort the detail records using a parameter field. Selecting the field to group on via a parameter field basically works the same way. The difference is that you attach the formula field to the Insert Group dialog box instead of the Record Sort Expert.

In this exercise you will create a group for the customer information report from the previous exercise. One parameter field that you will create in this exercise will let you select which of the three fields; Customer Name, Region or Country to group on. You will create another parameter field that lets you select the group sort order, ascending or descending.

Create The Group Sort Parameter Field
1. Save the L2.14 report as E2.15 Group data parameter field.

2. Open a new parameter field, then type Group By Field in the Name field.

3. Type the values Customer Name, Region and Country in the Value column.

4. Change the following options, then click OK.
   Prompt Text - Select the field that you want to group by:
   Change the Default Value option to Region. You can select it from the drop-down list.
   Change the Allow custom values option to False.

Create The Group Formula And Add It To The Parameter Field
1. Open the Formula Workshop and create a new formula. Type GroupBy as the formula name.

2. Click on the SortBy formula field under the Formula Fields node on the left of the Formula Workshop. Copy and paste the SortBy formula into the GroupBy formula.

3. Change the word "Sort" to Group in two places in the formula, then click the Save and close button.

Report Design Option Changes In Crystal Reports XI

Create The Group Sort Order Parameter Field

The parameter field that you will create in this part of the exercise will let the person running the report select the sort order of the group, either ascending or descending. Parameter fields are displayed on the Enter Values dialog box in the order that they were created in. The more logical order in this exercise would be to have the Sort By Field last.

1. Open a new parameter field, then type `Group Sort Order` in the Name field.

2. Type the options `Ascending` and `Descending` in the Value column.

3. Change the following options, then click OK.
   Prompt Text - `Select the order that you want to sort the groups in:`
   Change the Default Value option to Ascending.
   Change the Allow custom values option to False.

4. Change the order of the parameter fields so that the Sort By Field is last.

Create The Group And Add The Group Formula To The Insert Group Dialog Box

As you have noticed, the report that you are working on does not have any groups.
In this part of the exercise you will create the group based on a formula field and sort the group based on a different formula field.

1. Click the Insert Group button on the Insert Tools toolbar.

2. Open the first drop-down list and select the GroupBy formula.

3. Check the option, **USE A FORMULA AS GROUP SORT ORDER**, then click the Formula button and type the formula shown below.

   ```
   If {?Group Sort Order} = "Ascending" Then crAscendingOrder
   Else
   crDescendingOrder
   ```

4. Click the Save and close button, then click OK to close the Insert Group dialog box. Save the changes.

Test The Parameter Fields

1. Refresh the report.

   You should see the dialog box shown in Figure 2-46.

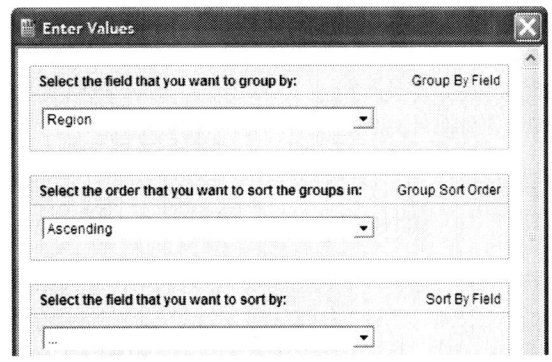

Figure 2-46 Group and field sort parameter options

2. Run the report a few times, selecting different options.

Adding Parameter Field Criteria To A Report

While this is not a new feature, it is a question that I am asked frequently, so I am covering it here in hopes of helping more people.

You have learned how to create parameter fields that add a lot of interaction. The one thing that is missing is adding the parameter field criteria to a report. With all of the parameter field selection combinations that a report can have, including the selection criteria on the report would be helpful. Single value parameter fields can be dragged from the Field Explorer on to the report like other fields.

> Range value and multiple value parameter fields cannot be dragged onto the report and printed like single value parameter fields. If these fields are added to the report, only the first value in the field will print. Printing solutions for these types of parameter fields are discussed below.

Printing Parameter Range Fields

There are two functions, **MINIMUM()** and **MAXIMUM()** in Crystal Reports that will print the range in a parameter field. These functions return the beginning and ending values. The formula below will print the date range on the report as long as the **NO LOWER VALUE** and **NO UPPER VALUE** options are not checked on the Enter Values dialog box. To create your own formula, replace the {?Date_Parameter} field with the name of the parameter field that has multiple values that you want to print.

"Starting Date " & Minimum ({?Date_Parameter}) & " and Ending Date " & Maximum ({?Date_Parameter})

> You can use the Minimum and Maximum functions for any type of range parameter field data. It is not just for date ranges.

Report Design Option Changes In Crystal Reports XI

Exercise 2.16: Print Parameter Range Fields

1. Save the CH2.12 report as `E2.16 Print parameter range fields`.

2. Create a formula field called `Print Date Range`. Type the code shown below. Type the formula on one line.

   `"Starting Date " & Minimum ({?Date Range}) & " and Ending Date " & Maximum ({?Date Range})`

3. Add the Print Date Range formula field to the top of the page header section. Make the field at least four inches long, then save the changes. Preview the report. You should see the date range at the top of the report, similar to the one shown in Figure 2-47. You will have different data on the report.

Starting Date 2/18/2003 12:00:00AM and Ending Date 2/7/2004 12:00:00AM				
Customer Name	Order Date	Ship Date	Order ID	Unit Price
City Cyclists	12/02/2003	12/10/2003	1	$41.90
Deals on Wheels	12/02/2003	12/02/2003	1,002	$33.90

Figure 2-47 Parameter field range printed on the report

Printing Multi Value Parameter Fields Using The Join Function

All of the values that are selected in a multi value parameter field are stored in one field and are separated by a comma in the array. The **JOIN** function will print all of the values in the array. The formula below will print all of the values in a multiple value parameter field. Replace the {?ShipVia} field with the name of the multi value field that you want to print.

`"Shipping Methods Selected: " + Join ({?ShipVia}, ", ")`

Exercise 2.17: Print Multi Value Parameter Fields

1. Save the CH2.13 report as `E2.17 Print multi value parameter fields`.

2. Create a formula field called `Print Regions`. Type the code shown below.

   `"Regions Selected: " + Join ({?Region}, " , ")`

3. Add the Print Regions formula field to the top of the page header section. Make the field longer, then save the changes.

4. Preview the report. Select two regions from the list and type in other regions. Your report should look similar to the one shown in Figure 2-48. You will have different data on the report. The regions should have printed at the top of the page.

Regions Selected: CA, FL, WI, TX			
Customer Name	Address1	Region	Country
Sporting Wheels Inc.	480 Grant Way	CA	USA
Rockshocks for Jocks	1984 Sydney Street	TX	USA
Trail Blazer's Place	6938 Beach Street	WI	USA

Figure 2-48 Multi value parameter field printed on the report

Hierarchical Group Reports

A hierarchical group is a special type of parent-child, one-to-many relationship. It shows the relationship between records that are in the same table. If it helps, think of the parent field as the field that is displayed in the group header section and the child fields will be displayed in the details section of the report. The **RECURSIVE JOIN** is required to create hierarchical reports.

Hierarchical groups are useful when you need to create a report where two fields in the same table relate to each other. This is what Crystal Reports refers to as a hierarchical group. This is how you can create organizational charts. An Employee table lists the employees that work for the company. It also contains who each employee reports to. Remember that the person that has someone reporting to them is also an employee.

In this example, the people that have someone reporting to them are the "parent" portion of the relationship. Employees that do not have anyone reporting to them are the "child" portion of the relationship.

The Hierarchical Group Options dialog box shown in Figure 2-49 is used to create a hierarchical group report.

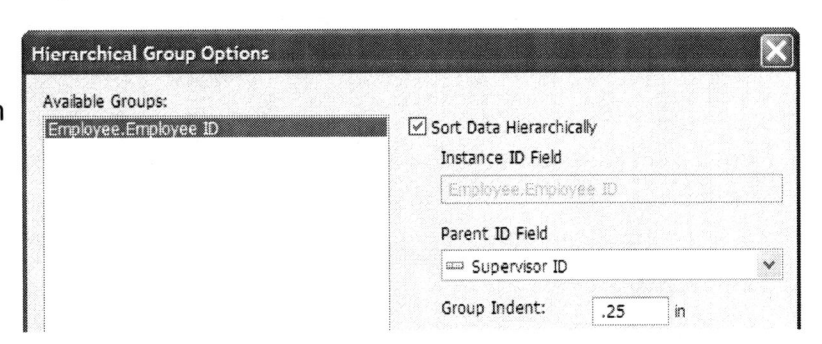

Figure 2-49 Hierarchical Group Options dialog box

The **AVAILABLE GROUPS** list contains all of the groups that the report has. The hierarchical report must be created using one of the groups that are listed in this section.

Once you select a group, check the **SORT DATA HIERARCHICALLY** option to indicate that you want to apply hierarchical sorting to the group that is selected.

The **INSTANCE ID FIELD** contains the field that will be used as the child field.

Report Design Option Changes In Crystal Reports XI

The **PARENT ID FIELD** drop-down list contains the fields that can be used as the parent field. The parent record (in this example, the supervisor) will print first and then the employees that report to the supervisor will print. All of the fields in this drop-down list are the same data type as the group field.

The **GROUP INDENT** option lets you select how much the child records should be indented. Using this feature is optional. If the columns do not contain a lot of data and the Group Indent option is greater than zero, it is possible that some data will not line up properly with the field headings. One way to fix this is to make the Group Indent number smaller. Another option is to resize some of the fields on the report. Leaving this option set to zero means that the child records will not be indented, which will make it difficult to see who reports to who.

Hierarchical Report Requirements

To create a hierarchical report, the following three requirements must be met.

① The table must have two fields that represent the same data. This allows the data in one field to point to another record in the same table.
② The parent and child fields must have the same data type.
③ The report must be grouped on the child field.

Exercise 2.18: Create A Hierarchical Group Report

In this exercise you will create an organizational report that shows who each employee reports to.

1. Create a new report and add the Employee table, but do not add any fields to the report.

2. Create a group on the Employee ID field. Use the Options tab to create a group name formula that combines the Employee first and last name fields.

3. Report ⇒ Hierarchical Grouping Options. You will see the Hierarchical Group Options dialog box.

4. Check the Sort Data Hierarchically option, then select the Supervisor ID field from the Parent ID Field drop-down list.

5. Change the Group Indent option to .25. You should have the options shown above in Figure 2-49. Click OK.

6. Add the Position and Hire Date fields to the group header section, then format the Hire Date field so that the time does not show.

7. Save the report as `E2.18 Hierarchical report`.

   The report should look like the one shown in Figure 2-50.

Andrew Fuller	Vice President, Sales	07/12/1996
Steven Buchanan	Sales Manager	09/13/1997
Nancy Davolio	Sales Representative	03/29/1996
Janet Leverling	Sales Representative	02/27/1996
Margaret Peacock	Sales Representative	03/30/1997
Michael Suyama	Sales Representative	09/13/1997
Robert King	Sales Representative	11/29/1997
Laura Callahan	Inside Sales Coordinator	01/30/1998
Anne Dodsworth	Sales Representative	10/12/1998
Albert Hellstern	Business Manager	03/01/1998
Tim Smith	Mail Clerk	01/15/1998

Figure 2-50 Hierarchical report

CRYSTAL REPORTS XI RELEASE 2 (R2)

Overview

In this chapter you will learn about the following features that were added or modified in the Crystal Reports Release 2.

- ☑ Workbench
- ☑ Field Explorer
- ☑ Object Size and Position dialog box
- ☑ Custom colors
- ☑ Insert Summary dialog box
- ☑ Swapping Fields
- ☑ Formula Workshop
- ☑ Auto Complete
- ☑ Export options

Crystal Reports XI Release 2 (R2)

Crystal Reports XI Release 2 Overview

The main purpose of this free update makes Crystal Reports XI more compatible with Visual Studio 2005 and the Business Objects Enterprise software.

While compatibility appears to be the main purpose of the Release 2 update, which is also known as Crystal Reports 11.5 or R2, other changes were made which you may find helpful, even if you are not using Crystal Reports with Visual Studio 2005 or the Business Objects Enterprise. These changes are what is covered in this chapter.

You can download this update from the link below.
www.businessobjects.com/products/reporting/crystalreports/xi_release_2.asp

Adding Reports To The Workbench

There are now four ways to add reports to the Workbench as discussed below.

① From the Workbench toolbar, Add ⇒ Add Existing Report.
② **NEW** From the Workbench toolbar, Add ⇒ Add Current Report.
③ Right-click in the Workbench and select Add ⇒ Add Existing Report.
④ Drag a report from Windows Explorer to the Workbench.

Workbench Toolbar

The options on the Add Report button on the Workbench toolbar have changed. Table 3-1 explains the purpose of each option on the Add button. The other buttons on the toolbar are the same as the original Crystal Reports XI version. [See Chapter 1, Table 1-5]

Button	Purpose
Add ▼	The **Add Report** button lets you add three types of objects to the Workbench as discussed below. ① **Add Existing Report** Select this option if you want to add an existing report to the Workbench. ② **Add Current Report** **NEW** Select this option if you want to add the active report to the Workbench. The report does not have to be saved before using this option. ③ **Add New Project** Select this option if you want to create a new project folder.

Table 3-1 Add Report button options explained

Field Explorer

The Field Explorer toolbar shown at the top of Figure 3-1 now has a button that will let you duplicate formula fields.

The buttons on the toolbar are explained in Table 3-2.

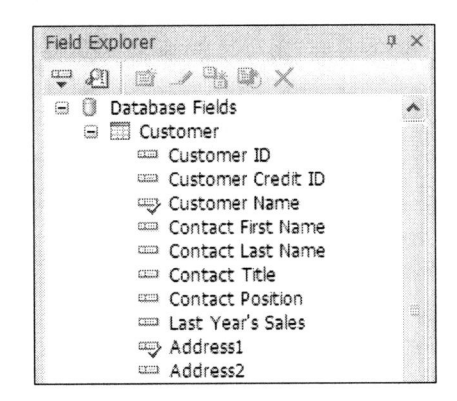

Figure 3-1 Field Explorer

Button	Purpose
	The **INSERT TO REPORT** button lets you add a field to the report.
	The **BROWSE** button lets you view the data in the field that you select.
	The **NEW** button lets you create formula, parameter, SQL Expression or running total fields. (1)
	The **EDIT** button lets you modify formula, parameter, SQL Expression or running total fields. You can double-click on the formula in the Field Explorer to edit it, instead of clicking on the Edit button. (1)
	NEW The **DUPLICATE** button creates a copy of a formula, SQL Expression or running total field. This option does not duplicate parameter fields. (2)
	The **RENAME** button lets you rename formula, parameter, SQL Expression or running total fields. (1)
	The **DELETE** button lets you delete formula, parameter, SQL Expression or running total fields. (1)

Table 3-2 Field Explorer toolbar buttons explained

(1) Before clicking on this button, click on the category below the toolbar of the field type that you want to use.

(2) **Duplicating A Formula**

If you need to create a formula that is similar to one that is already in the report, you can duplicate the formula, instead of creating the second formula from scratch. Right-click on a formula field in the Field Explorer and select **DUPLICATE**. You can accept the default formula name of you can right-click on the duplicated formula and select **RENAME** to change the name.

Crystal Reports XI Release 2 (R2)

> **Copying A Formula From One Report To Another**
>
> You can also copy a formula from one report to another. Open the report that has the formula that you want to copy and the report that you want to copy the formula to. Click on the formula field that you want to copy in the report layout, then Edit ⇒ Copy. Click on the tab of the report that you want to copy the formula to, then Edit ⇒ Paste.

Sort Fields In The Field Explorer

By default, the fields are displayed in the table in the order there were created. If you do not like the default order that the fields are displayed in the Field Explorer, you can sort the fields alphabetically by right-clicking on the table name and selecting **SORT FIELDS ALPHABETICALLY** as illustrated in Figure 3-2. Figure 3-3 shows the fields after they have been sorted.

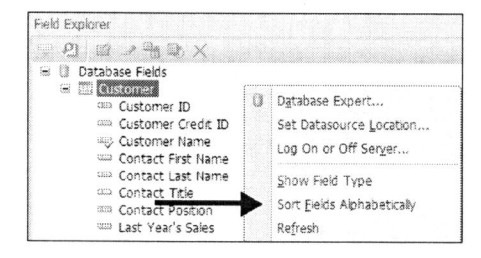

Figure 3-2 Fields in table before sorting

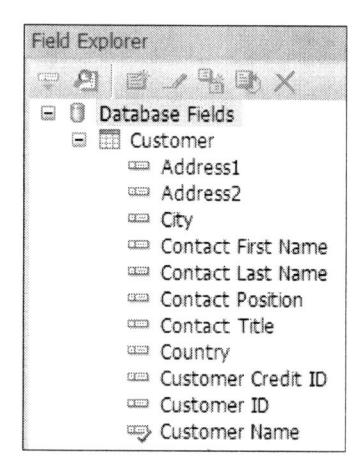

Figure 3-3 Fields in table after sorting

Object Size And Position Dialog Box

In addition to resizing a field manually, you can also use the Size and Position option on the shortcut menu by following the steps below.

> The options that you change on the Object Size and Position dialog box will **NOT** automatically be applied to the fields title.

3-4

Chapter 3

1. Right-click on the field that you want to resize and select **SIZE AND POSITION** as illustrated in Figure 3-4.

    The options on the menu change, depending on how many objects are selected or the type of object that is selected.

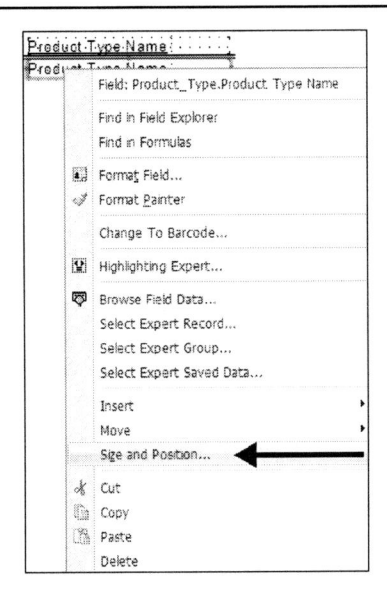

Figure 3-4 Object shortcut menu

2. Change the **UNITS OF MEASUREMENT** as needed, as shown in Figure 3-5, then click OK.

> **NEW** The **WIDTH** option now has a Formula field button as shown in Figure 3-5.

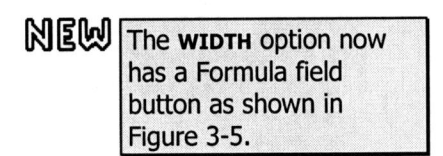

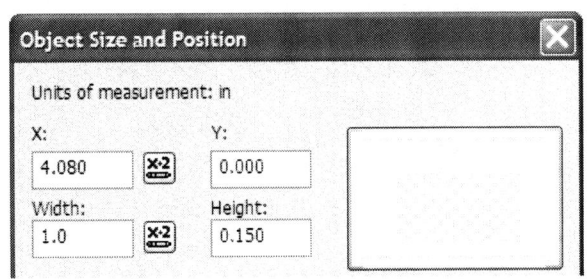

Figure 3-5 Object Size and Position dialog box

If you enter a larger number in the **WIDTH** field, the field will be longer. If you do not have a need for such field size precision, you will probably not have a need to use the options on this dialog box. I have been using Crystal Reports for years and other then writing this book, I have never used this dialog box.

Custom Colors

If you create a custom color, it can be saved. To create a custom color, follow the steps below.

1. Open the Format Editor, then click on the Border tab or any tab that has a **COLOR** drop-down list field.

3-5

Crystal Reports XI Release 2 (R2)

2. Open the Color drop-down list and select **MORE** as illustrated in Figure 3-6.

   You will see the Color dialog box.

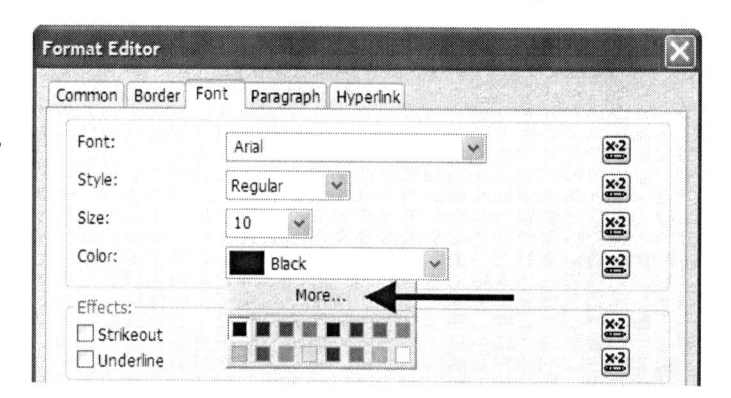

Figure 3-6 Color option illustrated

3. Use the options to create the custom color that you want. When you are finished, click the **ADD TO CUSTOM COLORS** button shown in Figure 3-7.

   The color that you created should be in one of the custom color boxes on the left, as illustrated.

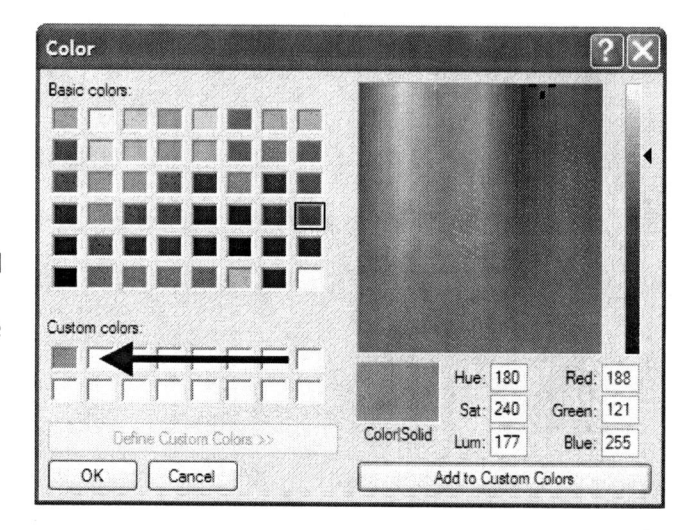

Figure 3-7 Color dialog box

4. Click OK twice to close both dialog boxes. Save the report. When you re-open the Color dialog box shown above in Figure 3-7, you will see the custom color that you created.

Insert Summary Dialog Box

Table 3-3 explains the options on the bottom of the Insert Summary dialog box.

Option	Description
Summary Location	This option allows you to select the section of the report where you want to place the summary field. The good thing is that you are not limited to the options in the drop-down list. You can manually copy or move the summary field to another section of the report.
Add to all group levels	**NEW** If checked, this option as illustrated in Figure 3-8, will add the summary field to all existing group levels on the report. This means that you no longer have to create the same summary field manually for every group section that needs the summary field.
Show as a percentage of	This option will calculate a comparison of the percent of one group that is part of a larger group. If selected, this option lets you select the group or total that you want the comparison to be based on. For example, this option can calculate the percent of sales for June compared to the sales for the entire year. The result would display what percent (out of 100%) the sales in June accounted for, compared to the sales for the entire year. This option is not available for all types of calculations. (3)
Summarize across hierarchy	On reports that have hierarchical groups (groups that have parent/child relationships), an identical summary field will be added to all subgroups under the primary hierarchical group. An example of a report that could have hierarchical groups would be one that displays a list of department managers (the parent group) and the employees (the child group) that are in each department. Figure 3-9 illustrates this option.

Table 3-3 Summary options explained

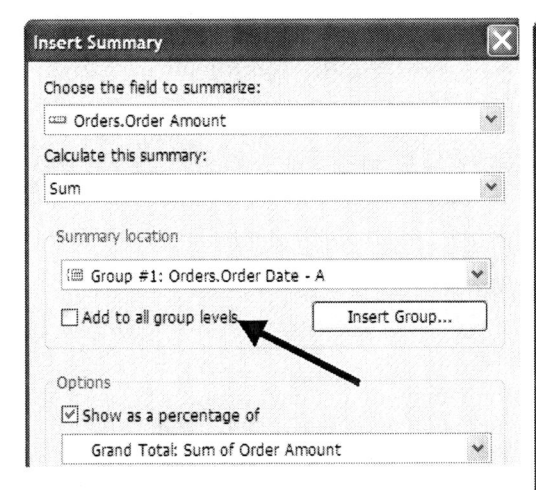

Figure 3-8 Group level option illustrated

Figure 3-9 Hierarchy option illustrated

3-7

Crystal Reports XI Release 2 (R2)

> (3) Percentage summaries cannot be placed in the report footer section.

Find In Formulas Option

The **FIND IN FORMULAS** shortcut menu option can be used if you need to find out if a field is used in a formula or if you need to change the field or variable in a formula. Right-click on the field either in the report or in the Field Explorer and select Find in Formulas as illustrated in Figure 3-10.

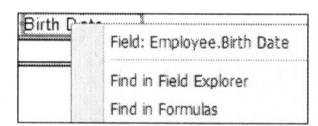

Figure 3-10 Find in formulas option illustrated

If the field is being used in a formula, the Formula Workshop will open and display all of the formulas that use the field at the bottom of the window as shown in Figure 3-11. Double-click on the formula that you need to edit.

Formula	Line	Matches for "{Employee.Birth Date}"
Age	2	Truncate ((CurrentDate - {Employee.Birth Date})/365)
test	1	{Employee.Birth Date} - 10
test age	1	{Employee.Birth Date} * 2

Figure 3-11 Formula search results window

Exercise 3.1: Swapping Fields

You may have the need to swap a field on the report with a field in the database or a formula field. I find being able to swap fields helpful when I want the new field to have the same formatting as the original field on the report. Using this option saves some time because the formatting does not have to be applied to the field that is added to the report.

Prior to Release 2, the two ways that swapping fields was accomplished was by deleting the field from the report and adding the new field. If the field that you wanted to replace had formatting, you would use the Map Fields dialog box.

Release 2 makes it easier to swap fields on the report and keep the formatting of the existing field. The steps below show you how to swap a field.

1. Save the CH3.1 report as `E3.1 Swapping Fields`.
   Notice the formatting of the Order Amount field.

2. Display the Formula fields in the Field Explorer.

3. Press and hold down the Shift key, then drag the Line Item Total formula field on top of the Order Amount field. You should see two arrows, as shown in Figure 3-12. This lets you know that the fields are being swapped.

Figure 3-12 Swap field arrows

Chapter 3

4. You should see the Line Item Total field on the report with the formatting of the original field. Save the changes.

Formula Workshop Changes

The two changes in the Formula Workshop are the ability to create a copy of a formula as explained in Table 3-4 and additional Auto Complete functionality.

Workshop Tree Toolbar

A new button has been added to the toolbar as explained below.

Button	Purpose
NEW	**NEW** Duplicates the formula selected in the Formula Fields section of the Workshop tree.
	Renames the selected formula, custom function, or SQL Expression.
X	Deletes the selected formula, custom function, or SQL Expression.
	Expands the selected node(s) in the Workshop Tree.
	The Show Formatting Formulas button displays or hides all of the report objects in the Formatting Formulas folder or only the objects that have a formatting formula.
	The Add To Repository button opens the Add Custom Function To Repository dialog box so that the custom formula can be added to the repository.
	The Add To Report button adds the selected repository custom function to the report.

Table 3-4 Workshop Tree toolbar buttons explained

Auto Complete Option For Functions

You could already use the **AUTO COMPLETE** feature in the Formula window in the Formula Workshop by typing in the first few letters of the function that you need and then press the **CTRL + SPACEBAR** keys.

You will see a list that has functions that start with the letters that you typed in, as shown in Figure 3-13. If you type in enough letters to only display the function that you want, the drop-down list will not be displayed. Instead, the function will be filled in for you. If you press the CTRL + Space bar keys before typing any letters, you will see all of the functions.

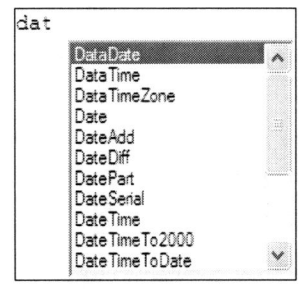

Figure 3-13 Auto complete list

3-9

Auto Complete Option For Tables And Fields

Now, the Auto Complete list will also display all of the tables and fields in the data source when you type the left curly bracket in the Formula window. When you type the bracket, all of the tables connected to the report will be displayed as shown in Figure 3-14.

Use the arrow keys on the keyboard to select the table that the field is in that you need, then press Enter to display the fields for the table as shown in Figure 3-15. Use the arrow keys to select the field that you need, then press Enter.

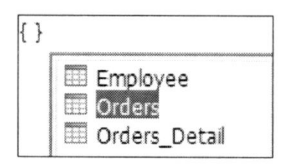

Figure 3-14 Tables displayed in the Auto complete list

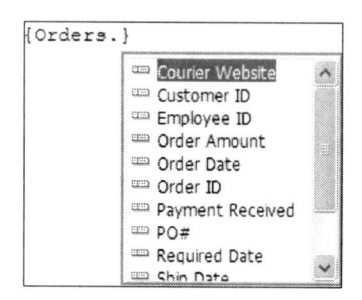

Figure 3-15 Fields displayed in the Auto complete list

Export Options

The next three exercises demonstrate new export features and options. Before you start each of the export exercises, open the CH2.6 report, then File ⇒ Export ⇒ Export Report.

Exercise 3.2: Create An Adobe Acrobat PDF Export File

This export file type will create a PDF (Portable Document Format) file of the report. End-users that need to open reports in this file type will need to have the Adobe Acrobat Reader installed. This software is free and can be downloaded from http://www.adobe.com/products/acrobat/readstep2.html.

This export file type can also be opened and viewed with Adobe Acrobat, which is the full version of the software that lets you create PDF files.

1. Select the PDF format, then open the Destination drop-down list and select **DISK FILE** if it is not already selected. Click OK.

> If you select the **APPLICATION** destination option, you will get the same PDF export file. The difference is that the Application option will not let you select where the export file will be saved initially. Once the report is exported you can save it to a different location. In Windows XP, the exported file will automatically be stored in this location: C:\Documents and Settings\{username}\Local Settings\Temp\.
>
> Usually the files are not automatically deleted from this folder, so you may want to check this folder from time to time and delete the files.

Chapter 3

The dialog box shown in Figure 3-16 lets you select whether to include all or some of the pages from the report in the PDF export file. If you were going to send each sales rep their stats for the month, you would enter the corresponding page numbers in the From and To fields in the dialog box. If the report has **PARAMETER FIELDS**, you would not have to do this to get a specific sales reps stats.

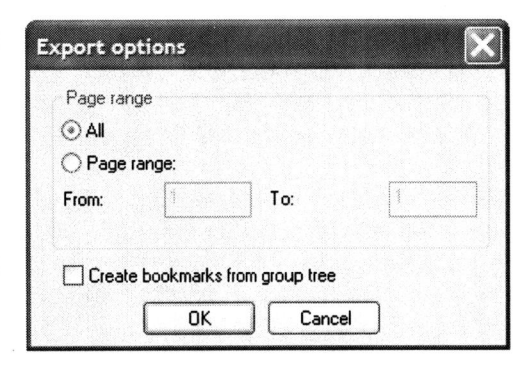

Figure 3-16 Export page range options

NEW The **CREATE BOOKMARKS FROM GROUP TREE** option if checked, will create bookmarks (similar to hyperlinks) in the PDF file for each group in the group tree. This will make it easier for the person reading the PDF version of the report to find specific information.

2. Check the Create bookmarks from group tree option.

    Click OK to include all of the pages. You will see the dialog box shown in Figure 3-17.

    This dialog box lets you select where the export file will be saved.

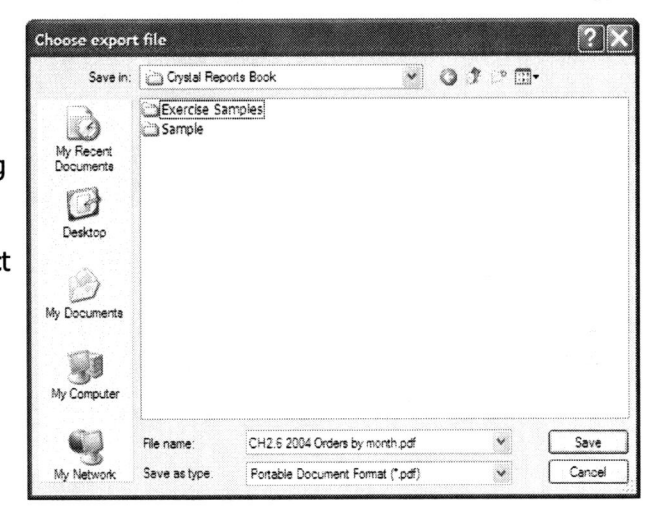

Figure 3-17 Choose export file dialog box

3. Navigate to your folder, as shown above in Figure 3-17 and type `E3.2 2004 Orders by month exported PDF file` as the file name and press Enter or click the Save button.

3-11

Crystal Reports XI Release 2 (R2)

You will see the dialog box shown in Figure 3-18. This dialog box lets you know that the export file is being created and how many records will be exported.

When the export is complete, you can open the PDF file in either the Adobe Acrobat Reader or Adobe Acrobat. The exported PDF file should look similar to the one shown in Figure 3-19.

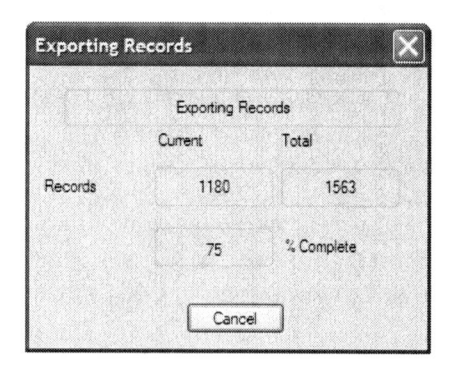

Figure 3-18 Exporting Records dialog box

The bookmarks shown on the left side Figure 3-19 are the groups on the report. Like the report, you can click on the group in the PDF file and the corresponding section of the report will be displayed.

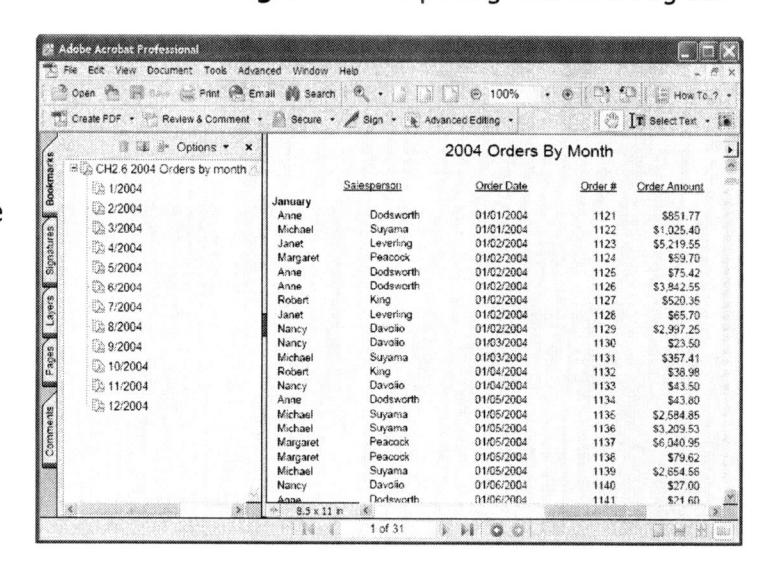

Figure 3-19 Exported PDF file with bookmarks

4. Close the PDF file.

Exercise 3.3: Create A Separated Values (CSV) Export File

In Crystal Reports XI, there was a problem exporting to a CSV file. The problem was that the information in the page header section appeared at the beginning of each detail record. This problem has been fixed in Crystal Reports XI Release 2. In this exercise you will create a CSV export file.

1. Select the **SEPARATED VALUES (CSV)** format, then open the Destination drop-down list and select **APPLICATION**. Click OK.

Chapter 3

The options in the top portion of the dialog box shown in Figure 3-20 let you select the format for how the report data will be exported.

The Mode, Report and Page sections and Group sections are new. They are discussed below.

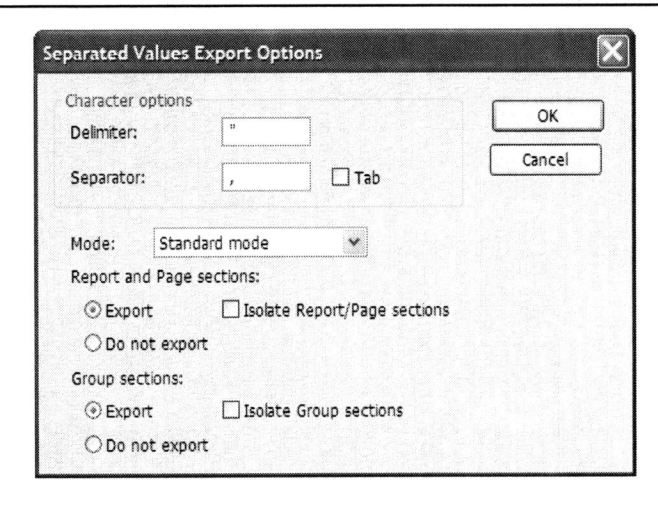

Figure 3-20 Separated Values Export Options

The **MODE** option lets you select one of the following options:

① **STANDARD MODE** stops the data in the report header section from being exported. Exporting data in the report header section is a problem because the report header section is repeated at the beginning of each detail section.
② **LEGACY MODE** allows the data in the report header section to be exported.

If checked, the **ISOLATE REPORT/PAGE SECTIONS** option will export the report and page header and footer sections of the report as separate records.

If checked, the **ISOLATE GROUP SECTIONS** option will export the group header and footer sections of the report as separate records.

2. For this exercise, the default options are fine. Click OK. Because the Application destination option was selected, the CSV file will be opened in Excel, unless you have another software package associated with .CSV files.

3. Any columns with the pound signs means that the column is not wide enough for the data that it contains.

   To make the column wider, double-click on the line after the column that you want to widen, as illustrated in Figure 3-21.

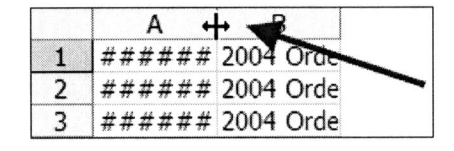

Figure 3-21 Mouse pointer in position to widen the column

After the column is made wider, it should look like the one shown in Figure 3-22. Notice that some of the columns (B, C and D for example) don't have data. They have field titles. That is because everything is exported. You can delete the columns that are not needed.

Crystal Reports XI Release 2 (R2)

	A	B	C	D
1	3/24/2008	2004 Orders By Month	Salesperson	Order Date
2	3/24/2008	2004 Orders By Month	Salesperson	Order Date
3	3/24/2008	2004 Orders By Month	Salesperson	Order Date
4	3/24/2008	2004 Orders By Month	Salesperson	Order Date
5	3/24/2008	2004 Orders By Month	Salesperson	Order Date

Figure 3-22 E3.3 CSV exported file with column A made wider

4. Save the file as E3.3 Exported CSV file. You will see a message similar to the one shown in Figure 3-23. This message is asking if you want to keep the formatting. For this exercise, click Yes.

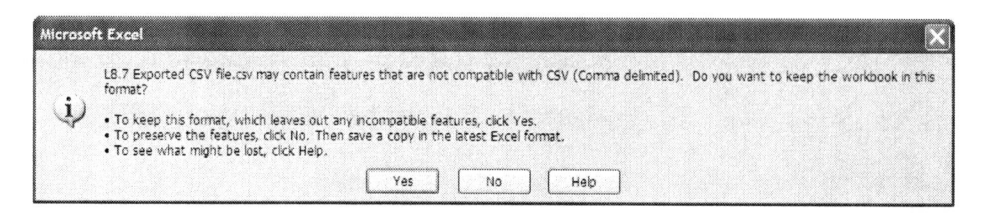

Figure 3-23 Excel formatting message

5. Close Excel. You will be prompted to save the file again. Save it with the same name.

Exercise 3.4: Create An Excel Data Only Export File

If the data in the spreadsheet will be used to create formulas or some type of analysis, it is best to turn off as many formatting options as possible before the data is exported to Excel. Using the Excel Data Only export option instead of the other Excel export option makes this task easier. The steps below will show you hot to only export the data.

1. Select the **EXCEL 97-2003 DATA ONLY** format, then open the Destination drop-down list and select **DISK FILE** and click OK. You will see the dialog box shown in Figure 3-24. The typical and minimal options pre-select some options on the bottom portion of the dialog box for you. Table 3-5 explains the Excel format options.

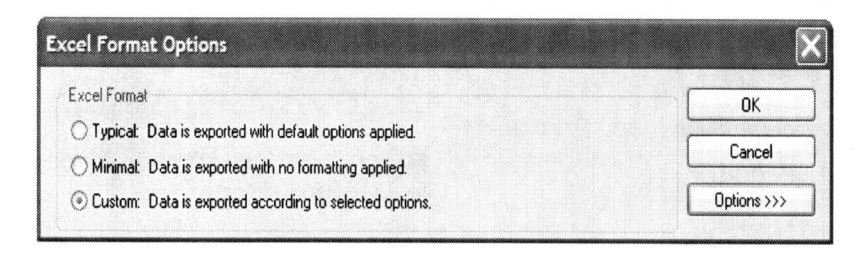

Figure 3-24 Excel 97-2003 Data Only Format Options dialog box

3-14

Chapter 3

Format	Description
Typical	Pre-selects the most common options in the bottom section of the dialog box, which are shown in Figure 3-25.
Minimal	Pre-selects the basic options shown in Figure 3-26, to export the report without any formatting options.
Custom	You select the export options.

Table 3-5 Excel Data Only export format options explained

The pre-selected options shown in Figures 3-25 and 3-26 can be used as a starting point. You can select one of these options and then add or remove options as needed. This may be helpful if one of these export formats has some of the options that you need already selected. Selecting one of these options and then making changes to it may save you some time.

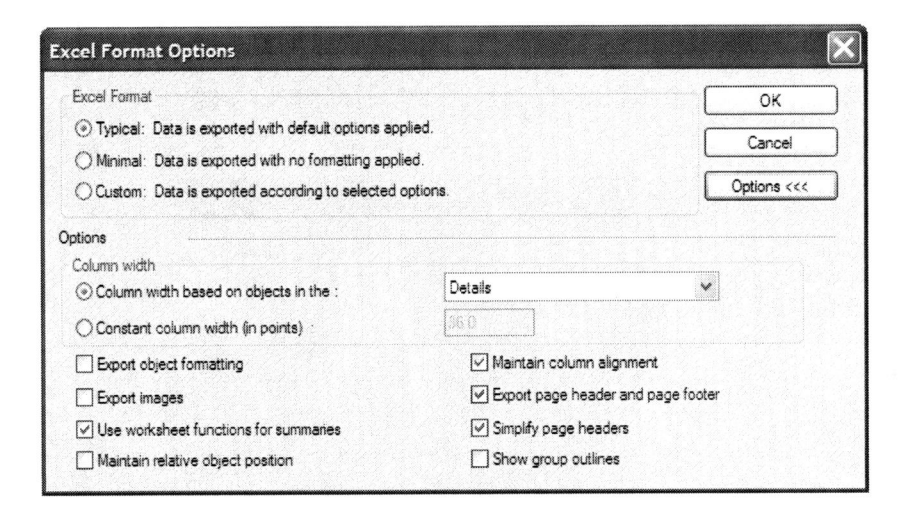

Figure 3-25 Typical pre-selected default options

> Changing an option after selecting the typical or minimal option changes the export format to custom.

Crystal Reports XI Release 2 (R2)

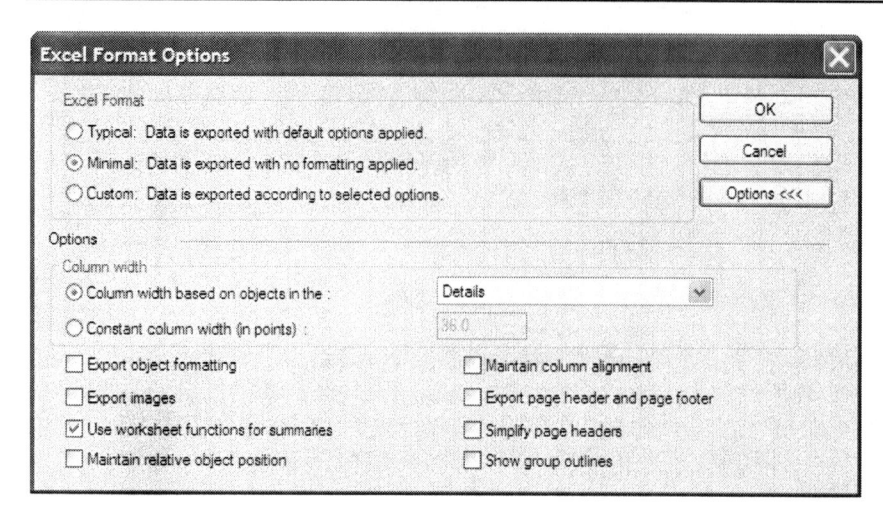

Figure 3-26 Minimal pre-selected default options

2. Click the **OPTIONS** button. You will see the options shown in Figure 3-27. Table 3-6 explains the options.

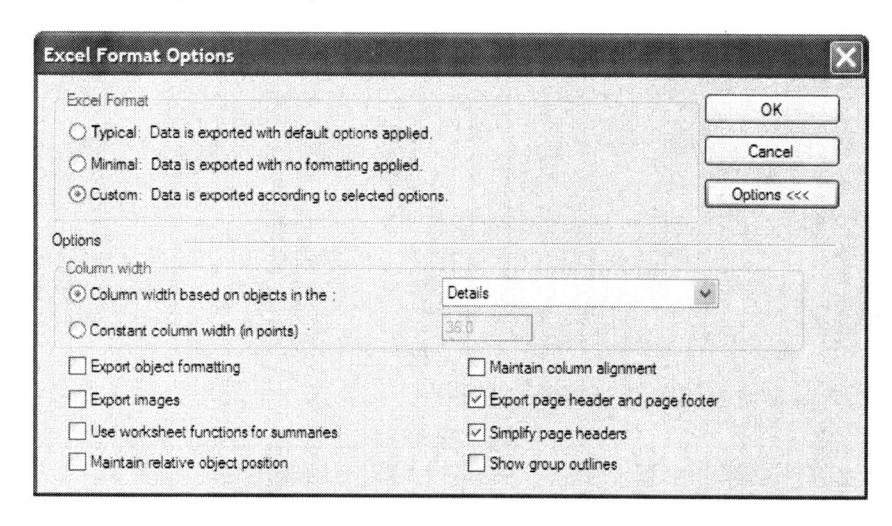

Figure 3-27 Custom pre-selected default options

Option	Description
Column Width	These options let you select the column widths in Excel. ① The **COLUMN WIDTH BASED ON OBJECTS IN THE** option lets you select the Excel column width based on a section in the report. ② The **CONSTANT COLUMN WIDTH (IN POINTS)** option lets you select a free form column width.
Export object formatting	Exports as much formatting as possible.
Export images	Exports images that are in the report.
Use worksheet functions for summaries	If checked, Crystal Reports will try to convert summary fields to Excel functions. If a matching function is not found, the summary field will be exported as a number without the formula.
Maintain relative object position	Adds rows and columns as needed to keep objects in the Excel file in the same location/position that they are, in the report.
Maintain column alignment	Will force summary fields to appear in the correct column in Excel. By default, the export process ignores blank spaces to the left of fields, which causes fields to be shifted.
Export page header and page footer	If checked, the information in the page header and footer sections will be exported.
Simplify page headers	If checked, the last row of the page header section will be exported. Usually the last row of the page header section contains the field headings.
Show group outlines	**NEW** If checked, the group information will be exported. This will allow the Excel outline options to be used, which will make navigating in the spreadsheet easier.

Table 3-6 Excel Data Only export options explained

3. Select the options **USE WORKSHEET FUNCTIONS FOR SUMMARIES** and **MAINTAIN COLUMN ALIGNMENT**, then click OK. Save the exported file as
   `E3.4 2004 orders by month data only exported file`.

4. Open the E3.4 spreadsheet in Excel and make columns A through H wider.

5. Scroll down to row 130 and click in cell F130, then look in the Formula Bar. You will see the equivalent of the summary calculation that was created in the report, as shown in Figure 3-28. Save the changes and close the spreadsheet.

Figure 3-28 Summary calculation in the Formula Bar

WHAT'S NEW IN CRYSTAL REPORTS 2008

Overview

This chapter covers additions and changes to existing features in Crystal Reports 2008.

- ☑ Start Page changes
- ☑ Workbench changes
- ☑ Preview window changes
- ☑ Menu changes
- ☑ Toolbar changes
- ☑ Data Source connections
- ☑ Connecting to an Excel spreadsheet
- ☑ Format Editor
- ☑ Special Fields
- ☑ Select Expert
- ☑ Printing changes
- ☑ Section Expert
- ☑ Formula Workshop

If you skipped the chapters on Crystal Reports XI, please go back and follow the instructions in the "Create A Folder For Your Reports" section in Chapter 1 to download the sample files for Crystal Reports 2008.

CHAPTER 4

What's New In Crystal Reports 2008?

The older the version of Crystal Reports that you are upgrading from, the more new features you will notice. The following list does not include all of the new features, but it should be enough to make you want to learn more.

Single Edition

Prior to Crystal Reports 2008, there were multiple editions of the software. Now there is only one. It is the equivalent of the developer edition from previous versions. That means that you have all of the features of the software.

Reduced Installation File Size

The installation file size has been reduced because the sample database and reports have been removed from the installation. You can download them separately.

New Interface

The interface will remind you of Office 2007. The icons on the toolbar buttons have been redesigned.

Parameter Panel

The Parameter Panel allows the person running the report to select different parameter values from the preview tab.

Sort Control

This option allows the person running the report to sort the data on their own.

Built-In Bar Code Support

Basic bar codes can be added to a report by converting data in a field that is on the report.

Enhanced Cross-Tabs

This feature allows calculations to be added to rows or columns of cross-tab reports and charts. There are also new functions for cross-tabs.

Save Reports Directly To CrystalReports.com

If you have an account on crystalreports.com, you can save reports directly to this web server instead of having to upload them.

Locale Settings

If you purchase language packs, you can select the language that users will see when they run reports and the language that objects in the design interface will use.

Adobe Flash & Flex Integration
These options allow you to link or embed a Flash (SWF) file into a report. They also provide the ability to create mashups (pulling different types of data from multiple sources) in reports, which makes the reports interactive.

Xcelsius Integration
This option allows Crystal Xcelsius created SWF files to be incorporated into a report. Xcelsius files provide enhanced "What If" analysis functionality from Excel spreadsheets. Crystal Xcelsius is a software package owned by Business Objects.

Flexible Pagination
This option allows more control over how reports can be printed and viewed online. Reports can have different page orientations (landscape and portrait) in the same report by selecting options on the Section Expert.

Other New Features
Integrated SalesForce.com drivers
Interactive Report Viewing
Enhanced Report Designer features
Hyperlinking Wizard
Improved XML Exporting
.Net Report Modification SDK

Start Page Changes
The topics discussed below are the changes to the Start Page.

There are now five tabs on the Start Page as shown in Figure 4-1. The content on these tabs come from the Business Objects web site. The tabs provide information, help, updates and add-ons for Crystal Reports. Each tab is discussed below.

① **HIGHLIGHTS** Provides free product add-ons, updates and news stories.
② **DOWNLOAD** Provides free product add-ons, service packs, sample applications and reports.
③ **DEVELOPER** Has links to How To articles, forums and online documentation. (1)
④ **IT PROFESSIONAL** Has links to How To articles, forums and online documentation. (1)
⑤ **REPORT DESIGNER** Has links to How To articles, forums and online documentation. (1)

(1) As of July 24, 2008, the **SUPPORT FORUM** link on this tab did not work. This is probably because they recently shut down the forums on their web site. They were combined with the forums on the SAP (parent company of Business Objects) Community Network web site. (www.sdn.sap.com) Hopefully, this link will be fixed soon.

What's New In Crystal Reports 2008

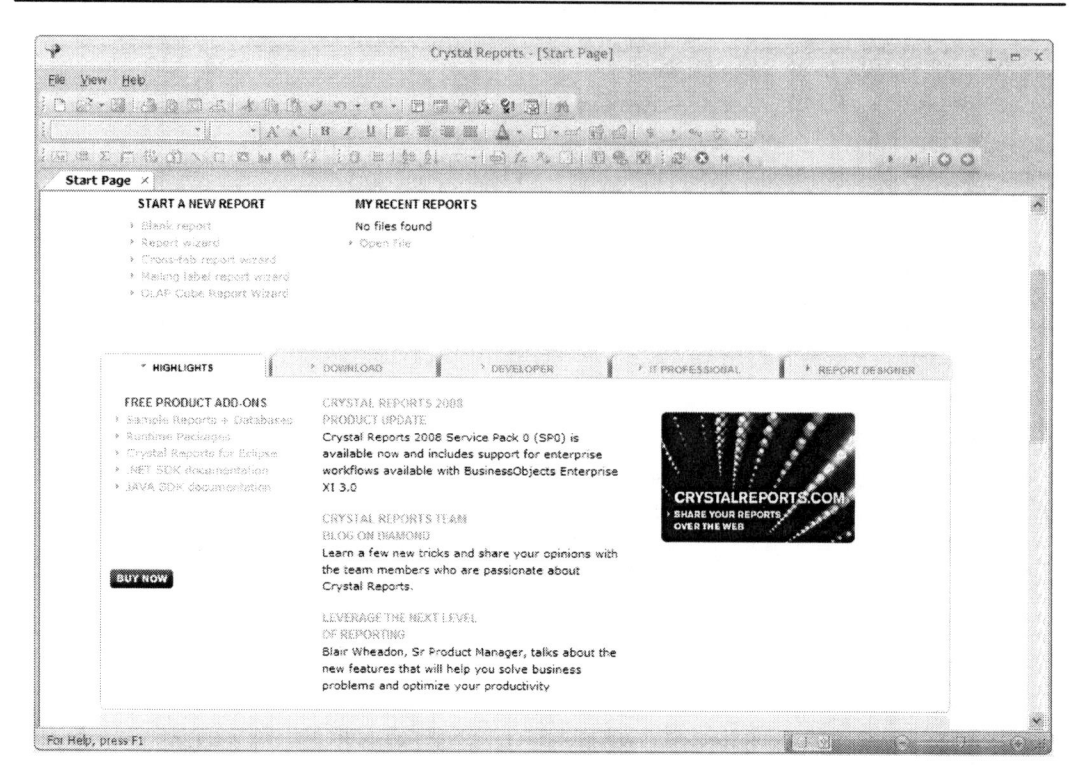

Figure 4-1 Crystal Reports workspace

The **MY RECENT REPORTS** section on the Start Page will display the last five reports that you opened, as shown in Figure 4-2.

The first report listed is the most recent one that you opened. This section was called Recent Reports in Crystal Reports XI.

Figure 4-2 My Recent Reports section

Report Wizard Change
The Standard Wizard has been renamed to Report Wizard as shown above in Figure 4-1.

Download The Sample Reports And Database
In prior versions of Crystal Reports, the sample reports and database were automatically installed when you installed the software. If you have the reports and database from Crystal Reports XI, you can skip this section. In Crystal Reports 2008, you have to install them manually by following the steps below.

1. Create a folder on your hard drive to store the reports in. If you read Chapter 1, you should already have created a folder.

Chapter 4

2. On the Highlights tab on the Start Page click on the **SAMPLE REPORTS + DATABASES** option, then click on the link for Crystal Reports XI samples. Yes, I know what you are thinking, but Crystal Reports 2008 uses the same database as Crystal Reports XI.

3. On the Samples page, click on the Crystal Reports XI Xtreme sample reports and database option, then click on the link for English.

4. On the web page shown in Figure 4-3 click on the link in the Title column, then click Save.

Title	Product Version	File Name	File Type
Crystal Reports XI Xtreme Report Samples and Database - English	**Crystal Reports XI**	cr_xi_xtreme_report_samples_en.zip	**Sample Report**

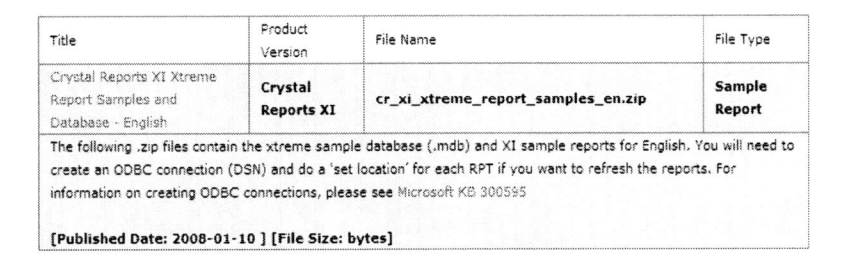

The following .zip files contain the xtreme sample database (.mdb) and XI sample reports for English. You will need to create an ODBC connection (DSN) and do a 'set location' for each RPT if you want to refresh the reports. For information on creating ODBC connections, please see Microsoft KB 300595

[Published Date: 2008-01-10] [File Size: bytes]

Figure 4-3 File to download

5. Navigate to the folder that you created and save the zip file in that folder. Open Windows Explorer and click on your folder. Right-click on the zip file and select the option, Extract to here.

Open A Sample Report

1. Click the **OPEN FILE** link on the Start Page.

2. Open the Look in drop-down list and navigate to the folder where you stored the sample reports.

3. Double-click on the **FEATURE EXAMPLES** folder.

   You will see the list of reports shown in Figure 4-4.

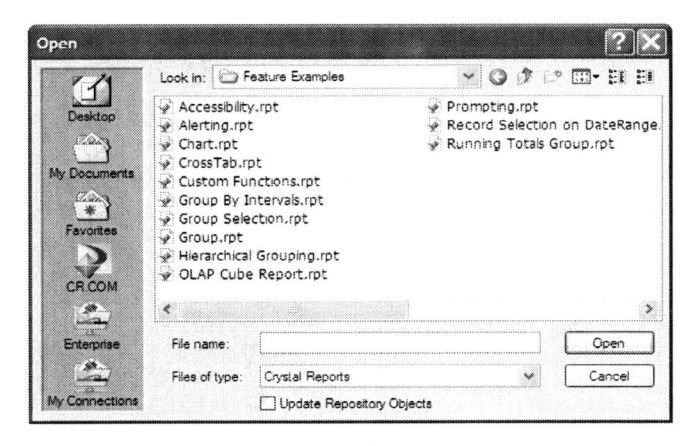

Figure 4-4 Reports in the Feature Examples folder

4-5

4. Double-click on the Accessibility report.
   Click OK when prompted that any changes must be saved to a new file.
   The report should look like the one shown in Figure 4-5.
   The only difference should be the date and time.

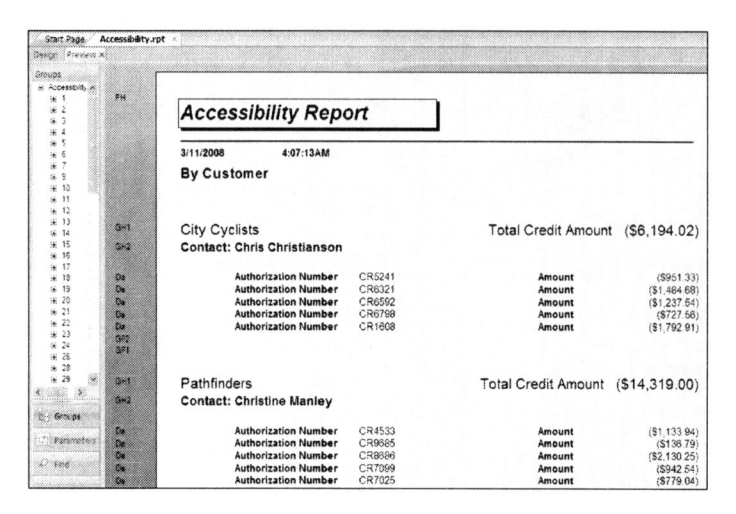

Figure 4-5 Accessibility Report

> The **REPORT NAVIGATION TOOLBAR** that was above the report in Crystal Reports XI has been removed. [See Chapter 1, Report Navigation Toolbar]

Status Bar

You can now see the number of records that are on the report in the Status bar on the design window as shown in Figure 4-6. If you do not see the number of records, resize the window.

Figure 4-6 Status bar with report information

On the right side of the status bar are the **ZOOM** options as shown in Figure 4-7.
The first button displays the entire report in the workspace.
The second button displays the report so that it takes up the entire size of the available workspace. The slider lets you change how large or small the report will be displayed.

Figure 4-7 Zoom options

Chapter 4

Workbench Change

> The Add ⇒ Add Object Package option has been removed from the Add Report button on the Workbench toolbar. To add an Object Package, right-click in the Workbench window, then Add ⇒ Add Object Package. This option allows you to add a Report Package to the Workbench.

Preview Panel

The Preview Panel is a section on the preview tab. It stores the group tree, parameter panel and the Find tab as shown in Figure 4-8. This new feature ads more interactive options. This panel can be displayed or hidden by clicking the **TOGGLE PREVIEW PANEL** button on the Standard toolbar.

If the report has groups, a group section is automatically added to the preview panel. If you click on the groups button you will see the groups as shown in Figure 4-8. Clicking on a group will display that section of the report.

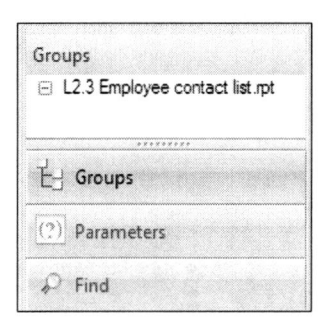

Figure 4-8 Preview Panel

If the report has a parameter field you will see options similar to those shown in Figure 4-9.

The **FIND TAB** is used to search the report for words or phrases. Clicking on this button opens the Search field shown in Figure 4-10. Type in the word or phrase that you are looking for, then click the magnifying glass button or press Enter to start the search. You will see results similar to what is shown in Figure 4-11. Double-clicking on a search result option will display that part of the report.

Figure 4-9 Parameter panel

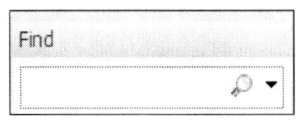

Figure 4-10 Search field

Figure 4-11 Search results

What's New In Crystal Reports 2008

Menu Changes

This section discusses the changes to the menus.

View Menu Options

The options on the View menu let you select many of the tools in Crystal Reports as explained in Table 4-1.

Menu Option	Description
Design	Opens the design window.
Preview	Opens the preview window.
Print Preview	This option is only available on the design window. It lets you view the report. This is the same as clicking on the preview tab.
Preview Sample	Displays the report with limited data.
HTML Preview	Displays the report in HTML format. You may have to set some of the options on the Smart Tag & HTML Preview tab on the Options dialog box before you can use this option.
Close Current View	Closes the active tab.
Field Explorer	Opens the Field Explorer.
Report Explorer	Displays all of the fields and objects on the report.
Repository Explorer	Opens the Repository Explorer so that an item from the repository can be added to the report.
Dependency Checker	Opens the Dependency Checker so that reports can be checked for errors.
Workbench	Displays or hides the Workbench.
Toolbars	Customize the toolbars.
Status Bar	Displays or hides the status bar at the bottom of the Crystal Reports window. The status bar provides additional information about the object that you are holding the mouse over, as well as, other information about the active report.
Preview Panel	NEW The Group Tree, Parameters Panel and Find tab are stored in the Preview Panel. This option replaces the Group Tree menu option in Crystal Reports XI.
Zoom	Sets the zoom level for viewing a report. You can change the zoom percent on the dialog box or you can type the zoom percent in the Zoom field on the Standard toolbar.
Rulers	Displays or hides the rulers. (2)
Guidelines	Displays or hides the guidelines. (2)
Grid	Displays or hides the grid. (2)
Tool tips	Displays or hides the tool tips. (2)

Table 4-1 View menu options explained

Chapter 4

Menu Option	Description
Product Locale	**NEW** Change the language that the menus and commands are displayed in.
Preferred Viewing Locale	**NEW** Selects a language other then the one selected during the installation to display menus and commands.

Table 4-1 View menu options explained (Continued)

(2) This option works on the design and preview windows.

Insert Menu Options

The options on the Insert menu let you add objects to a report as explained in Table 4-2. Many of these objects are available on the shortcut menu for an object.

Menu Option	Description
Text Object	Add a text object to the report.
Summary	Add a summary field to the report.
Field Heading	Creates a field heading for the selected field. If the **INSERT DETAIL FIELD HEADINGS** option is checked on the Layout tab of the Options dialog box, you will probably not have the need to use the field heading option because field headings will be created automatically for fields that are added to the details section.
Sort Control	**NEW** Add a control to a report that lets the person running the report sort it in a different order or on a different field. This option also appears on the object shortcut menu when certain conditions are met.
Group	Add a group to the report.
OLAP Grid	Opens the OLAP Expert, which allows you to create an OLAP grid. (3)
Cross-Tab	Opens the Cross-Tab Expert, which allows you to create a cross-tab object. (3)
Subreport	Opens the Insert Subreport dialog box, which lets you create a subreport or select an existing report to use as a subreport.
Line	Draws lines on the report. You can draw horizontal and vertical lines.
Box	Draws a box on the report. Boxes can also be drawn across sections of the report.
Picture	Add graphic files to a report. The supported file types are .bmp, jpeg, png, tiff and Windows metafile.
Chart	Create a chart using the Chart Expert.
Map	Create a map using the Map Expert.

Table 4-2 Insert menu options explained

What's New In Crystal Reports 2008

Menu Option	Description
Flash	**NEW** Link or embed a Flash (SWF) file to the report.
OLE Object	Add an OLE object to the report.
Template Field Object	This object is used as a placeholder for a field in a template. Template field objects are not connected to fields in a database.

Table 4-2 Insert menu options explained (Continued)

> (3) There can be more than one OLAP grid or cross-tab object in the same report.

Format Menu Options

> The **LINE HEIGHT** option illustrated in Figure 4-12 in Crystal Reports XI has been removed.

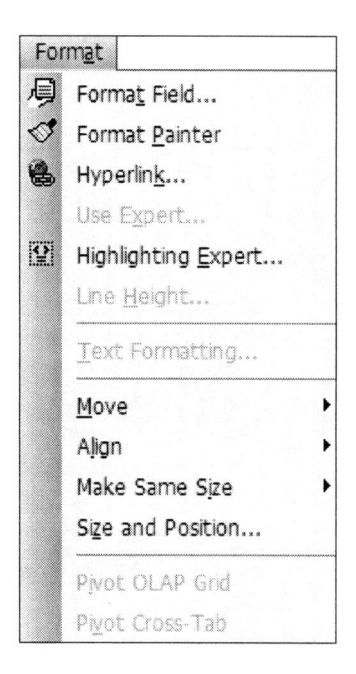

Figure 4-12 Format menu in Crystal Reports XI

4-10

Database Menu Options

The Database menu provides options that make modifying and connecting to databases easier. The options are explained in Table 4-3.

Menu Option	Description
Database Expert	Opens the Database Expert, which is used to add or delete data sources to or from the report.
Set Data Source Location	Select a different database for the report or a different location for the database that the report is currently using. This option is useful when you are using a copy of the database to create and test the report(s) and are now ready to move the report(s) into production (go live).
Log On or Off Server	Used to log on or off of an SQL or ODBC server, set database options and maintain the Favorites folder. Most of the tasks that you can complete on the Data Explorer window can be done another way.
Browse Data	View data in a field. This is the same as the Browse button that you have seen on some dialog boxes.
Set OLAP Cube Location	Change the location of an OLAP Cube that is being used in the report.
Verify Database	Compares the structure of the data source that is used in the report to the structure of the actual database.
Show SQL Query	View SQL queries if the report is using any. Parameter fields are included if they are used in the selection formula.
Perform Grouping on Server	If checked and the report has a group and the details section of the report is hidden, the grouping process will be done on a server.
Select Distinct Records	If checked, duplicate records will not appear on the report. A duplicate record has the same data in every field in both records.
Query Panel	**NEW** Opens the Business Objects Query Panel, which lets you create queries that will be used in the report.

Table 4-3 Database menu options explained

Report Menu Options

> The **XML EXPERT** option illustrated in Figure 4-13 in Crystal Reports XI has been removed in Crystal Reports 2008.

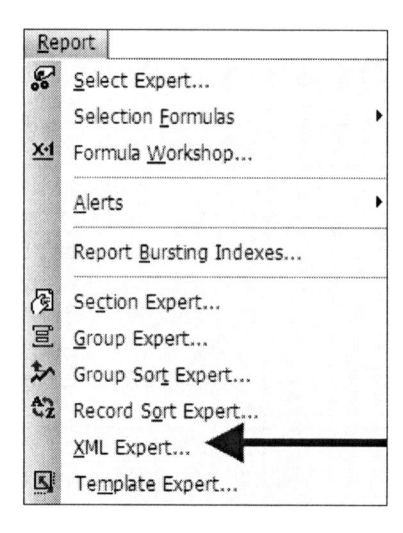

Figure 4-13 Report menu in Crystal Reports XI

Help Menu Options

The options on the Help menu provide several ways to get assistance. Other options let you register and manage the software. Table 4-4 explains the Help menu options.

Menu Option	Description
Crystal Reports Help	Opens the Online Help file.
Context Help	Displays help for windows, buttons and menus that you click on. After selecting this option, click on an item in the Crystal Reports workspace that you want to know more about and a tool tip will appear that explains the item that you clicked on. For example, select this option and then click on a button on a toolbar. The Help file will open. On the right side of the help window, you will see a page for the button that you clicked on.
Show Start Page	Displays the Start Page if it is closed.
Check for Updates on Start Up	If checked, this option will automatically check for software updates each time that you open Crystal Reports.
Check for Updates	If checked, this option will let you check for software updates when you want to.
Register or Change Address	Opens the registration wizard which lets you register your copy of Crystal Reports or change your address.
License Manager	Add and remove Crystal Reports and Integration kit key codes and license information.

Table 4-4 Help menu options explained

Chapter 4

Menu Option	Description
Contact Us	**NEW** Opens the Contact Us page on the Business Objects web site. This page lists several ways for you to get in touch with the company.
Documentation	**NEW** Opens the Product Guides web page on the Business Objects web site. This page has documentation for all of the software Business Objects sells.
About Crystal Reports	Opens the About dialog box which displays information about the version of Crystal Reports that is installed. Clicking the **MORE INFO** button will display the Loaded Modules window. This information could be helpful if you have to troubleshoot some types of report problems.

Table 4-4 Help menu options explained (Continued)

> The Reports Samples and Business Objects on the web options have been removed from the Help menu.

Toolbar Changes

This section discusses the toolbar changes in Crystal Reports 2008. The change that is most noticeable is the graphics on the buttons are slightly different.

Standard Toolbar

The buttons on the Standard toolbar contain the most used options from the File, Edit, Format, View, Report and Help menus. Table 4-5 explains the purpose of each button on the Standard toolbar.

Button	Purpose
	Creates a new report.
	Opens an existing report. If you click on the arrow at the end of the button, you will see the last nine reports that you opened.
	Saves the active report.
	Opens the Print dialog box.
	Displays the active report in the Preview window. This is the same as clicking on the Preview tab. You can click this button if the Preview tab is not visible.

Table 4-5 Standard toolbar buttons explained

What's New In Crystal Reports 2008

Button	Purpose
	Displays the active report as a web page in the HTML Preview window.
	Opens the Export dialog box which will let you export the report to one of several popular formats.
	Removes the selected object(s) from the report and places it on the clipboard.
	Copies the selected object(s) to the clipboard.
	Pastes object(s) from the clipboard into the report.
	Copies (absolute or conditional) formatting properties from one object to one or more other objects. This is a shortcut to the Format Painter command.
	Undoes an action. (4)
	Redoes the last action that was undone. (4)
	NEW Toggles the Preview Panel on the preview window, on and off. In Crystal Reports XI, this was called the Toggle Group Tree button.
	Opens the Field Explorer. (5)
	Opens the Report Explorer. (5)
	Opens the Repository Explorer. (5)
	Opens the Dependency Checker so that you can check reports for errors.
	Displays or hides the Workbench.
	Opens the Find dialog box, which lets you search for information in the report.

Table 4-5 Standard toolbar buttons explained (Continued)

(4) You can select how many changes that you want to undo and redo from the drop-down list. This capability is not available from the Edit menu.
(5) Clicking this button a second time does not close the Explorer window.

4-14

Chapter 4

Insert Tools Toolbar

The buttons on the Insert Tools toolbar contain additional report options.
Table 4-6 explains the object types that you can add to a report. These options are also available on the Insert menu.

Button	Lets You Insert A . . .
	text object
	group
	summary field
	Cross-Tab object
	OLAP grid object
	subreport
	line
	box
	picture
	chart
	map
	NEW Flash object

Table 4-6 Insert Tools toolbar buttons explained

4-15

Expert Tools Toolbar

The buttons on the Expert Tools toolbar provide access to the experts, including the database, group and template experts. The buttons on this toolbar open dialog boxes that provide options to complete a task. Table 4-7 explains the purpose of each button on the Expert Tools toolbar. These options are also available on the Report menu.

Button	Purpose
	Opens the Database Expert which is used to add (or remove) data sources for the report.
	Opens the Group Expert which is used to create, modify and delete groups.
	Opens the Group Sort Expert which lets you select the Top or Bottom N records or lets you sort the report on summary fields.
	Opens the Record Sort Expert which lets you set the order that the detail records will be sorted in.
	Opens the Select Expert which lets you create report selection criteria. (6)
	Opens the Section Expert which lets you format any section of the report.
	Opens the Formula Workshop which lets you create formulas and add functions to the report.
	Opens the OLAP Cube Wizard which lets you create a report that uses an OLAP Cube or a .car file as the data source.
	Opens the Template Expert which lets you apply a template to a report.
	Opens the appropriate Format Editor which lets you modify the formatting properties of the selected object.
	Opens the Hyperlink tab on the Format Editor which lets you add a hyperlink to a report.
	Opens the Highlighting Expert which lets you apply conditional formatting to an object.

Table 4-7 Expert Tools toolbar buttons explained

(6) The Select Expert button now has a submenu as shown in Figure 4-14.

Table 4-8 explains the Select Expert submenu options.

Figure 4-14 Select Expert submenu

4-16

Chapter 4

Option	Description
Record	Creates selection criteria based on a field.
Group	Creates selection criteria based on a group name or summary field. Group processing is done after the record processing.
Saved Data	**NEW** Filters data that has already been saved with the report. This option reduces the number of times a database has to be refreshed. This is helpful for reports that have parameter fields. When selected, this option only uses data that has already been saved with the report instead of retrieving data from the database.

Table 4-8 Select Expert submenu options explained

It may be me, but in prior versions of Crystal Reports, I did not pay that much attention to the group selection option, did you?

External Command Toolbar

By default, this new toolbar is not displayed because it is empty. After you have added an application to the toolbar, it can be displayed. This toolbar provides quick access to third party applications that you add to it. The **ADD-INS** menu can also be used to store custom controls. It is not displayed by default either.

How To Remove Toolbars

Like many features in Crystal Reports, there is more than one way to remove toolbars. There are two ways to remove a toolbar as discussed below.

① View ⇒ Toolbars. You will see the dialog box shown in Figure 4-15. Clear the check mark for the toolbar option that you do not want to be visible on the workspace, then click OK.
② Right-click near the toolbars at the top of the Crystal Reports window. You will see the **TOOLBAR SHORTCUT MENU** shown in Figure 4-16. Click on the toolbar that you want to remove. Notice the **TOOLBARS** option at the bottom of the shortcut menu. Selecting this option will open the Toolbars dialog box shown in Figure 4-15.

What's New In Crystal Reports 2008

Figure 4-15 Toolbars dialog box

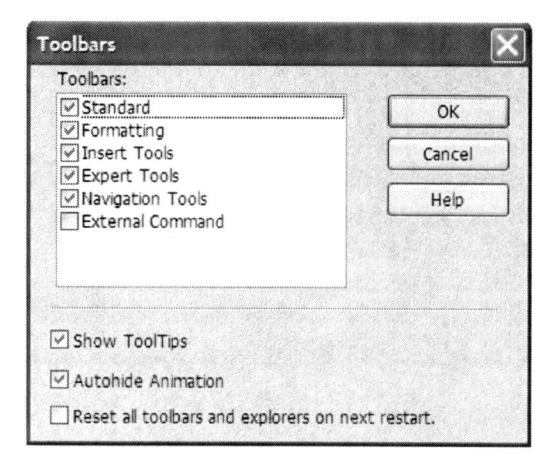

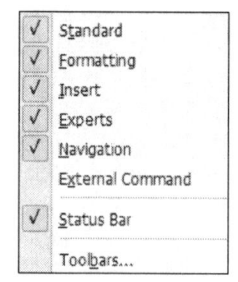

Figure 4-16 Toolbar shortcut menu

> 💣 The **VISUAL THEME** option shown in Figure 4-17 on the Toolbars dialog box in Crystal Reports XI that let you customize the interface has been removed.

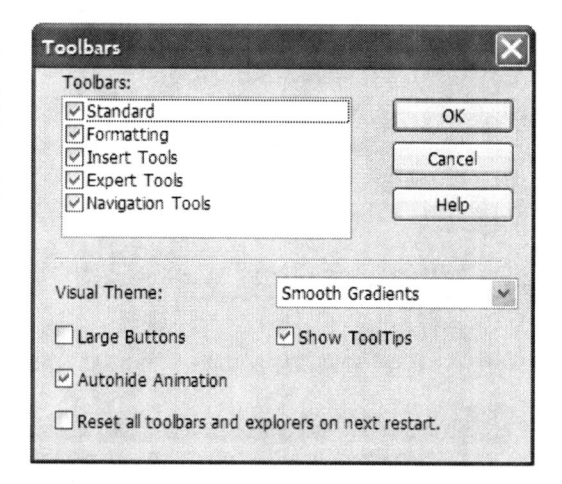

Figure 4-17 Crystal Reports XI Toolbars dialog box

4-18

Chapter 4

Data Source Connections
There are minor changes to the data source connection options.

Create A Connection To The Data Source

There are several types of data sources that you can use in Crystal Reports. Figure 4-18 shows the categories of connection options that are available. Table 4-9 explains some of the more popular connection options.

The list of data sources have been rearranged. The more frequently used data sources now have their own folder. ACT! was moved from the More Data Sources folder to it's own folder. Data sources that are used less, have been moved to the **MORE DATA SOURCES** folder. Some of the connection types have been renamed. For example, XML has been renamed to XML and Web Services.

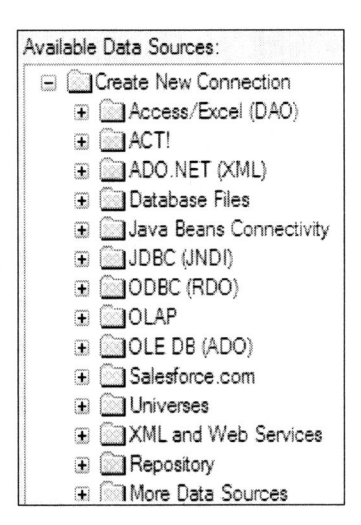

Figure 4-18 Available connection options illustrated

> You may see different data source options depending on the data components that were selected when you installed Crystal Reports. You will also see data source options that you have added.

Connection Option	Lets You Connect To . . .
Access/Excel (DAO)	Access databases and Excel files.
Database Files	Standard PC databases including FoxPro, Paradox, Clipper and dBASE.
ODBC (RDO)	Any ODBC complaint database including Oracle, Sybase, Access and Visual FoxPro.
OLAP	OLAP cubes and .car files. OLAP stands for Online Analytical Processing. CAR stands for Crystal Analysis file.
OLE DB (ADO)	Data link files that contain connection information that is saved in a file.
Universes	Business Objects query and analysis tools like Web Intelligence.
More Data Sources	Databases through ODBC drivers including Btrieve, Informix, Sybase, Outlook/Exchange and Web/IIS log files.

Table 4-9 Connection options explained

What's New In Crystal Reports 2008

If you haven't created a connection, either for the Access/Excel (DAO) or the ODBC (RDO) connection type for the Microsoft Access Xtreme sample database that comes with Crystal Reports, you can follow the steps below. You can go to the section, Step 2: Select The Tables, if you already have a connection to the Xtreme database.

How To Create An Access/Excel (DAO) Connection

1. Click on the **REPORT WIZARD** link on the Start Page.

2. Click on the plus sign in front of the **CREATE NEW CONNECTION** folder, then click on the plus sign in front of the Access/Excel (DAO) option.

3. Click on the button at the end of the **DATABASE NAME** field.

   Navigate to the folder that you saved the Xtreme database in, similar to what is shown in Figure 4-19.

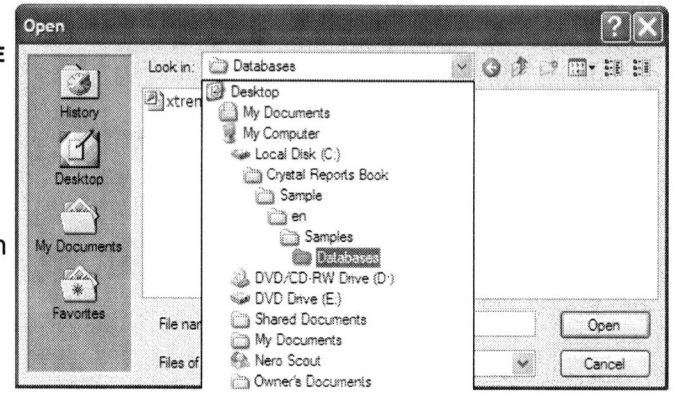

Figure 4-19 Path to the Xtreme database

4. Double-click on the **XTREME.MDB** database file. The database should have been added to the Database Name field on the dialog box, as shown in Figure 4-20.

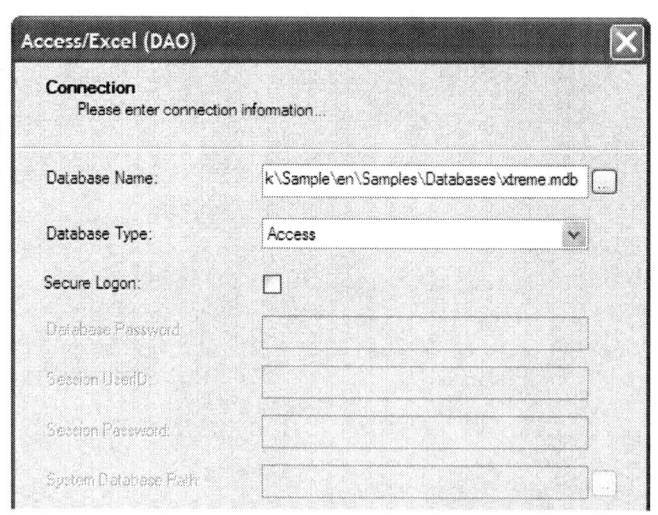

Figure 4-20 Xtreme database added to the Connection dialog box

Chapter 4

> If you want to make sure that you added the correct database, click in the Database Name field, then press the END key. You will be able to see the database name as shown above in Figure 4-20.

> If the database required logon information, you would check the **SECURE LOGON** option shown above in Figure 4-20. The remaining fields on the dialog box would become available for you to enter the password information.

5. Click the **FINISH** button. You have completed creating a connection to a database in Crystal Reports 2008. That wasn't so bad, was it?

Selecting A Data Source

In the previous section you used the options in the Create New Connection folder to create a connection to the Xtreme database.

That connection stays live until you close Crystal Reports. When you reopen Crystal Reports any previous connections are moved to the **MY CONNECTIONS** folder shown in Figure 4-21.

If you right-click on the connection, you will see the shortcut menu shown in the figure. Some of the options are explained below.

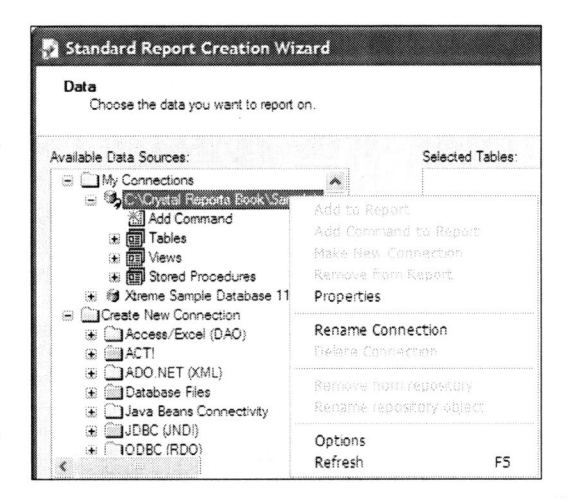

Figure 4-21 My Connection data source folder

The **PROPERTIES** option will let you see information about the data source of the connection as shown in Figure 4-22.

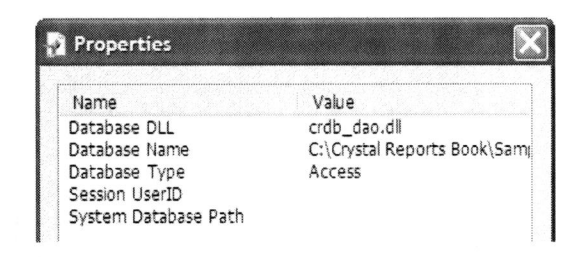

Figure 4-22 Data source connection properties

The **RENAME CONNECTION** option lets you give the connection a more user friendly name.

The **OPTIONS** option opens the Database tab of the Options dialog box.

The Database Expert now only has two folders (called Nodes): My Connections and Create New Connections. When you open a report or create a connection, the connection is automatically saved in the My Connections folder.

What's New In Crystal Reports 2008

> Crystal Reports XI offered four ways to select a data source as discussed below. The last three options discussed below have been removed.

① If you opened the data source after you opened the current session of Crystal Reports, you could select the data source under the **CURRENT CONNECTIONS** folder shown in Figure 4-23. Once you close Crystal Reports, all data source connections in the Current Connections folder were closed. The Current Connections option has been replaced with the **MY CONNECTIONS** option in Crystal Reports 2008.

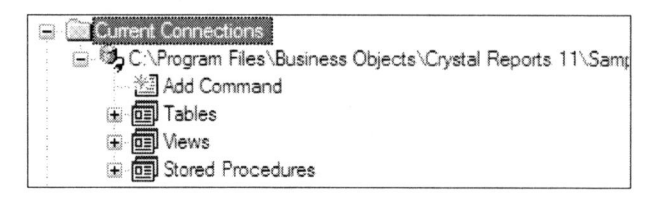

Figure 4-23 Current Connections folder option

② If you knew that you would be using a data source on a regular basis, you could add it to the **FAVORITES** folder by right-clicking on the data source under another folder and selecting **ADD TO FAVORITES**, as illustrated in Figure 4-24.

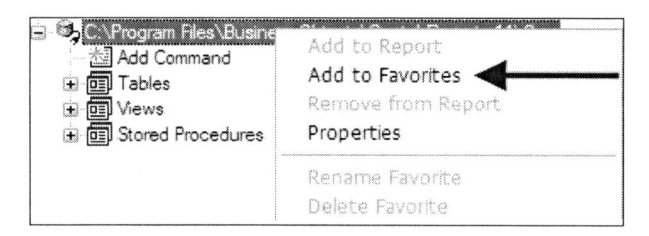

Figure 4-24 Add to Favorites option illustrated

③ The **History** folder contains the last five data sources that were opened.

④ The **Repository** folder would let you select a Business Objects View or an SQL command. The repository lets you connect to data on the Crystal Reports Server or in the Business Objects Enterprise repository.

Connecting To An Excel Spreadsheet

Connecting to an Excel spreadsheet is not new, but spreadsheets are often used as the data source for a report. The process is very similar to connecting to an Access database. If the spreadsheet has data on more than one worksheet (tab) in the spreadsheet, you may find it helpful if each worksheet or at least the worksheets that will be used for the report, have a name instead of Sheet 1, Sheets 2, etc. Crystal Reports treats each worksheet like a table and each column in the spreadsheet is treated like a database field. The steps below demonstrate how to connect to an Excel spreadsheet.

Chapter 4

1. Click on the **REPORT WIZARD** link on the Start Page.

2. Click on the plus sign in front of the **CREATE NEW CONNECTION** folder, then click on the plus sign in front of the Access/Excel (DAO) option.

3. Click on the button at the end of the **DATABASE NAME** field, then navigate to and double-click on the Excel spreadsheet. You may have to change the **FILES OF TYPE** option on the Open dialog box to Microsoft Excel Files.

4. Change the **DATABASE TYPE** field on the Connection dialog box to match the version of the Excel file that you are using, as illustrated in Figure 4-25.

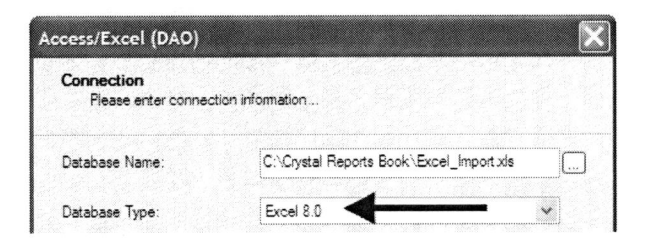

Figure 4-25 Excel selected as the data source

5. Click Finish. You should see the spreadsheet and each worksheet in the My Connections section, as illustrated in Figure 4-26.

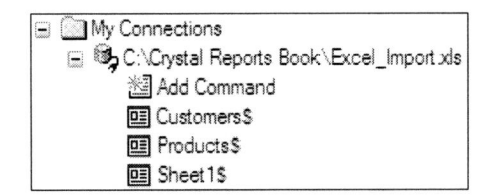

Figure 4-26 Connection to the Excel spreadsheet

Notice that you see three worksheets. Crystal Reports will import all of the worksheets. If you do not want to import all of the worksheets, save the Excel file with a new name and delete the worksheet(s) that you do not need for the report.

6. Select the worksheet(s) that you need to create the report and add them to the Selected Tables list, just like you would tables in a database. The columns in the spreadsheet will be in the Database Fields section of the Field Explorer.

What's New In Crystal Reports 2008

Shortcut Menus

Crystal Reports has several shortcut menus that you can use instead of selecting menu options or clicking on toolbar buttons. As you know, you spend a lot of time formatting and editing reports. A great time saver in my opinion to completing these tasks is using the options on the shortcut menus. The options will change on the shortcut menu depending on the object that is right-clicked on.

In addition to the object shortcut menu, there is a general shortcut menu available when you right-click on an empty space in the design or preview window.

Many of the shortcut menus have new options as illustrated in Figure 4-27. Some of the lesser used options are explained below.

> You can also open this shortcut menu by right-clicking on the design or preview tab.

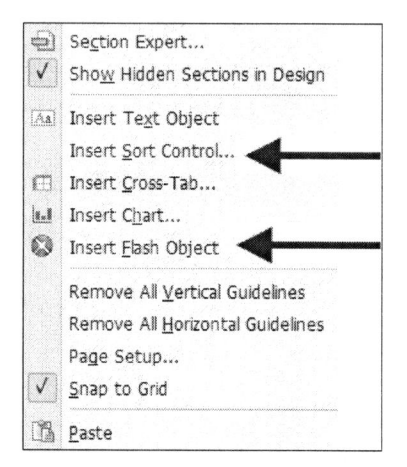

Figure 4-27 General shortcut menu

① **Show Hidden Sections In Design** By default, this option is turned on. It allows you to see hidden sections of the report in the design window. If this option is turned off (not checked), hidden sections have a small space between the sections, as illustrated in Figure 4-28. Suppressed sections have slanted lines as shown in Figure 4-29.

② **NEW Insert Sort Control.** Adds a control that lets the person running the report sort it in a different order or on a different field.

③ **Insert Cross-Tab** Adds a cross-tab object to the report.

④ **Insert Chart** Adds a chart to the report.

⑤ **NEW Insert Flash Object** Adds a Flash (SWF) file to the report.

⑥ **Remove All Vertical Guidelines** Hides (not delete) vertical guidelines (7).

⑦ **Remove All Horizontal Guidelines** Hides (not delete) horizontal guidelines (7).

Figure 4-28 Page header section with the Show Hidden Sections In Design option turned off

Chapter 4

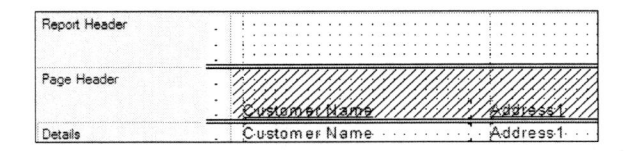

Figure 4-29 Page header section with slanted guidelines

> (7) These options are not the same as clearing the **GUIDELINES** option on the Layout tab of the Options dialog box.

Format Editor Number Tab Change

> In Crystal Reports 2008, the **CUSTOM STYLE** option illustrated in Figure 4-30 from Crystal Reports XI has been removed from the Style list as shown in Figure 4-31.

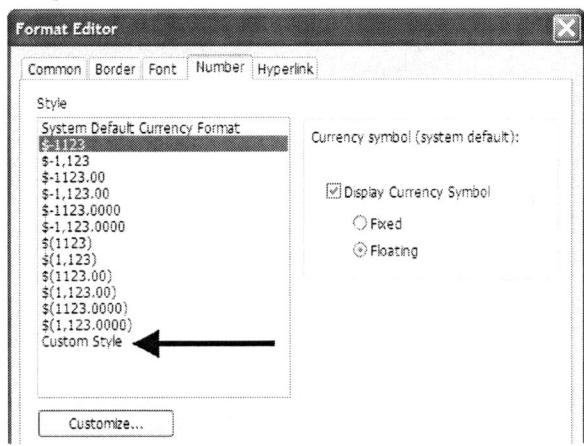

Figure 4-30 Crystal Reports XI Number tab options

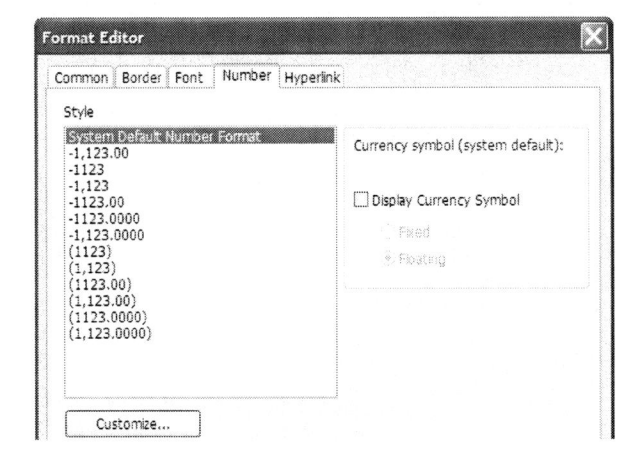

Figure 4-31 Crystal Reports 2008 Number tab options

4-25

What's New In Crystal Reports 2008

Special Fields

Crystal Reports now has 26 built-in fields that you can add to reports. You can drop and drag these fields from the Field Explorer to the report, just like you drop and drag fields from tables in the Field Explorer.

Figure 4-32 shows the Special Fields that you can add. Because these are system fields, the data can and often does change each time the report is run.

Table 4-10 explains the data that each of the Special Fields contains.

> Special fields, like the fields from a table that are added to the details section, have headings automatically created in the page header section.

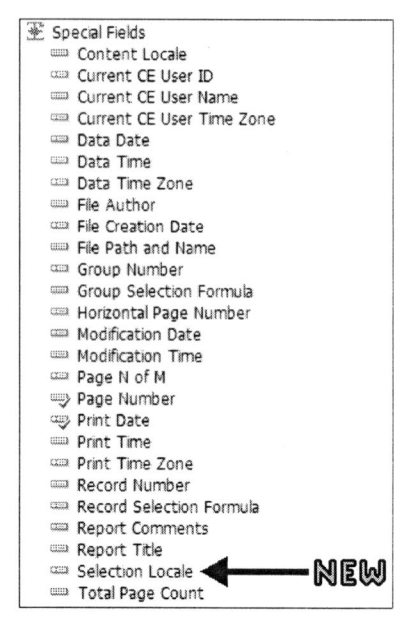

Figure 4-32 Special Fields

Special Field	The Field Will Print The . . .
Content Locale	Information in the **LOCATION** field. This data comes from the Regional & Language Options dialog box, which is part of Windows. (8)
Current CE User ID	ID number of the Business Objects user. (8)
Current CE User Name	Name of the Business Objects user. (8)
Current CE User Time Zone	Time zone that the Business Objects user is in. (8)
Data Date	Date the data was last refreshed in the report.
Data Time	Time the data was last refreshed in the report.
Data Time Zone	Time Zone that the data was last refreshed in the report.
File Author	Information in the **AUTHOR** field. (9)
File Creation Date	Date the report was first created.
File Path And Name	File path and name of the report. (The location on the hard drive or server). For example: C:\Crystal Reports Book\E3.2 Employee list.rpt.
Grouping Number	Number of each group in the group header or footer section. If the report does not have any groups, this field will print a "1".
Group Selection Formula	Group selection formula if applicable.

Table 4-10 Special Fields explained

4-26

Special Field	The Field Will Print The ...
Horizontal Page Number	Page number by objects like cross-tabs and OLAP grids that print on more than one page horizontally.
Modification Date	Date the report was last modified. This would be helpful during the report creation and modification process.
Modification Time	Time the report was last saved.
Page N of M	Page number and total number of pages in this format - Page 3 of 24. (10)
Page Number	Current page number.
Print Date	Date the report was printed. (8)
Print Time	Time the report was printed. (8)
Print Time Zone	Time zone the report was printed in. This data comes from the Date & Time Properties dialog box, which is part of Windows. (8)
Record Number	System generated number that is a counter for each detail record. It is based on the sort order in the report, not the order that the records are in the table.
Record Selection Formula	Record Selection formula that was created in the Record Selection Formula Editor.
Report Comments	Information in the COMMENTS field. (9)
Report Title	Information in the TITLE field. (9)
Selection Locale	NEW Contains the locale setting (the country) of the computer that the report is running on.
Total Page Count	Total number of pages in the report. (10)

Table 4-10 Special Fields explained (Continued)

(8) This data comes from the computer that the report is run from.
(9) This data comes from the Summary tab on the Document Properties dialog box.

> (10) The Page N of M and Total Page Count fields add to the processing time when the report is generated. If the report has hundreds of pages, you may notice a delay while the data is being processed, but it is bearable. If the report contains hundreds or thousands of pages, it is best to leave the Page N of M field off of the report while you are designing it because Crystal Reports has to generate the page numbers for the entire report prior to displaying or printing the report, which will take some time. Right before you put the report into production, add this field to the report.

The Select Expert

There are now three Select Expert options. For the most part, using the Select Expert is point and click. The only time that you have to type is if the value that you want to use is not in the drop-down list. This sometimes happens because the drop-down list only displays the first 500 unique values in a field. Any field that has multiple values that are identical will only display the value once in the drop-down list. An example of this would be a date field because it is possible that multiple records have the same date in the same field.

If you want to create a customer order report and only want to display records for the Wheels Company, this company name may not appear in the drop-down list because there could be more than 500 companies in the table and this company name is near the end of the alphabet. This is an example of when you would have to type something in the Select Expert.

The other time that you would need to type something in the Select Expert is if you are using a value that is not one of the values for the field. For example, if you want to select records that have an order amount greater than $600. You may have to type 600 in the field if the Order Amount field does not have that value in any of the first 500 values that are in the drop-down list.

> **NEW** The Select Expert now lets you create criteria by record, group or saved data as shown in Figure 4-33.

The **RECORD** option lets you create criteria for a field.

Select the **GROUP** option when you want the criteria based on a group name or summary field.

Figure 4-33 Select Expert submenu options

Select the **SAVED DATA** option when you want to filter data that has already been saved with the report. This option does not cause data to be refreshed.

There are three ways to open the Select Expert as discussed below:

① Right-click on the field that you want to create criteria for and select the **SELECT EXPERT** option that you need.
② Click the **SELECT EXPERT** button on the Expert Tools toolbar.
③ Report ⇒ Select Expert.

> In Crystal Reports 2008, the **RECORD** and **GROUP SELECTION** options have been removed from the Select Expert dialog box as shown in Figure 4-34. Figure 4-35 shows the Select Expert in Crystal Reports XI.

> In Crystal Reports 2008, the **PASTE DATA** button has been removed from the Browse Data dialog box shown in Figure 4-36 when it is opened from the Field Explorer. The Paste Data button is still available when the Browse Data toolbar button in the Formula Workshop is clicked. Figure 4-37 shows the button in Crystal Reports XI.

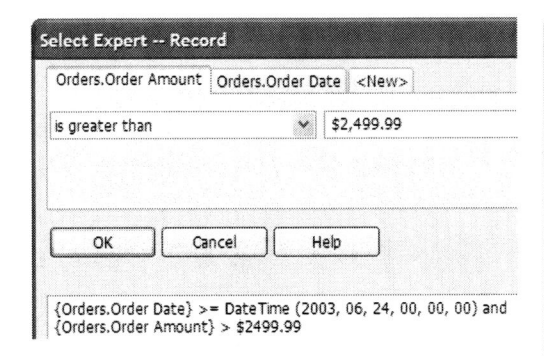

Figure 4-34 Select Expert dialog box in Crystal Reports 2008

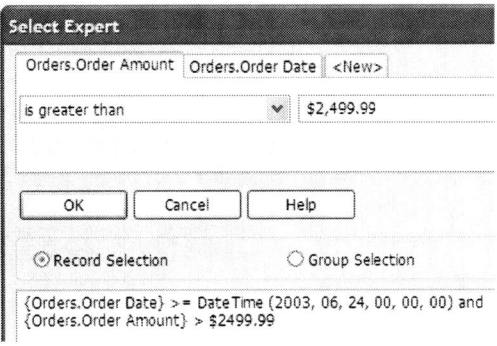

Figure 4-35 Select Expert dialog box in Crystal Reports XI

Figure 4-36 Browse Data dialog box in Crystal Reports 2008

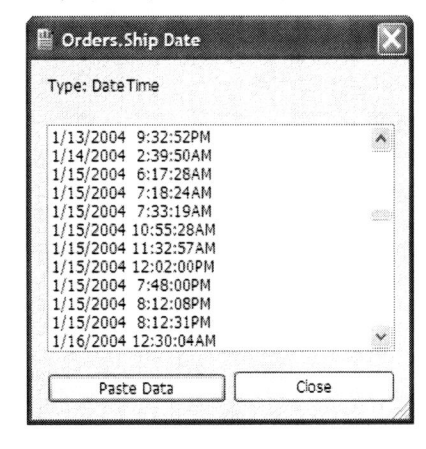

Figure 4-37 Browse Data dialog box in Crystal Reports XI

Printing Change

The Print Date special field now displays the entire date automatically as shown in Figure 4-38, opposed to cutting it off as it did in Crystal Reports XI, as illustrated in Figure 4-39.

Figure 4-38 Print date in Crystal Reports 2008

Figure 4-39 Print date illustrated in Crystal Reports XI

What's New In Crystal Reports 2008

Page Setup Options

As shown in Figure 4-40, there are several options that you can select from to change the printed page layout to what is best suited for the report. The options shown are the defaults that are set when Crystal Reports is installed. The graphic at the bottom of the dialog box will change as the options are changed.

The **MARGIN** fields now have Formula field buttons. This will allow formulas to control the margin sizes.

The biggest printing change is that the page orientation (landscape and portrait) can be applied to each section of the report.

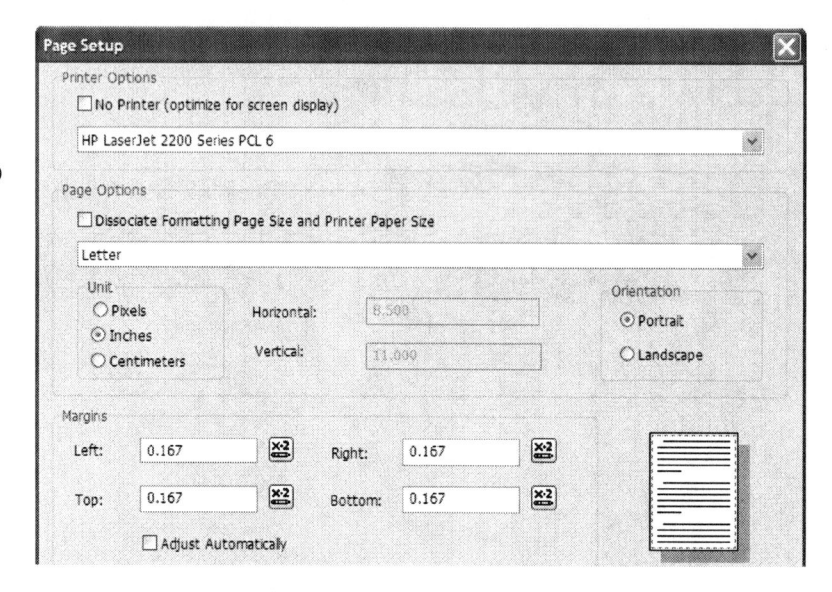

Figure 4-40 Page Setup dialog box

Table 4-11 explains the Page Setup options (File ⇒ Page Setup) that you may not be familiar with. Figure 4-41 shows the Page Setup dialog box in Crystal Reports XI.

Setup Option	Description
No Printer	If this option is not checked, the paper sizes for the default printer that the report is run from will be displayed in the **PAGE OPTIONS** drop-down list. Check this option if you do not want to use the default printer options. You should check this option if the report will not be printed. This option will optimize the report to be viewed on a screen or on the Internet. It can also be used to resolve printing problems, as you will learn later in this chapter.
Dissociate Formatting Page Size and Printer Paper Size	NEW Select this option if you need complete control over how the report will print on the page. This includes setting the horizontal and vertical dimensions which is helpful if the report will be displayed on the Internet.

Table 4-11 Page Setup dialog box options explained

Chapter 4

Setup Option	Description
Adjust Automatically	If checked, this option will cause the margins to change automatically when the paper size or orientation is changed. If selected, check the report to make sure that the margins that are automatically selected are appropriate. You may have to change the margins manually.

Table 4-11 Page Setup dialog box options explained (Continued)

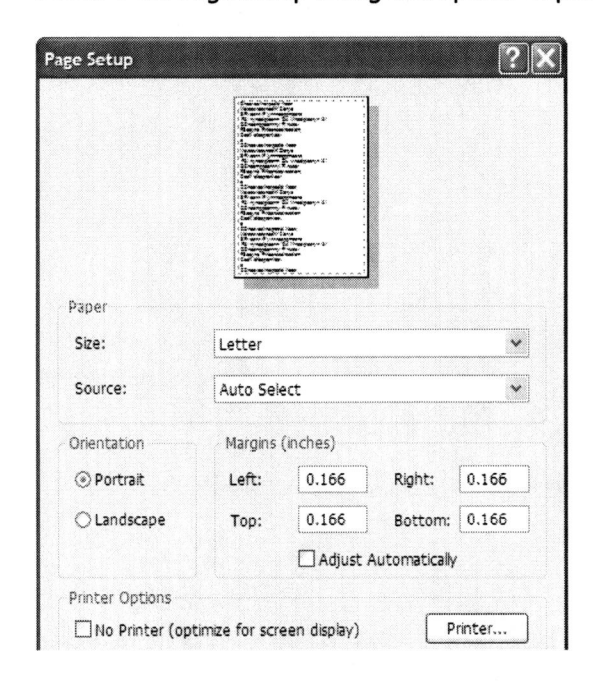

Figure 4-41 Page Setup dialog box in Crystal Reports XI

> The **PRINTER** button shown above in Figure 4-41 has been removed from the Page Setup dialog box.
>
> It opened another Page Setup dialog box, which is shown in Figure 4-42.

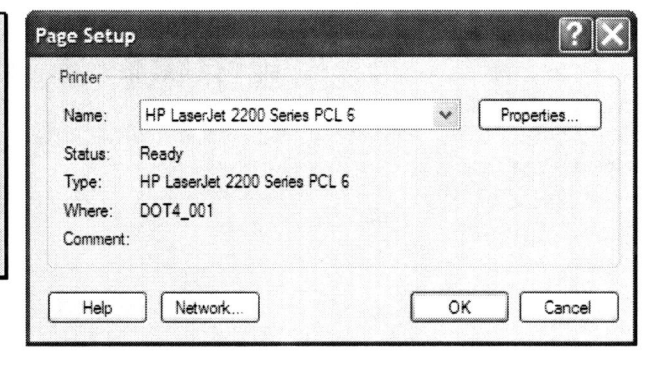

Figure 4-42 Page Setup dialog box that was removed from Crystal Reports 2008

4-31

What's New In Crystal Reports 2008

Change The Paper Size

As shown earlier in Figure 4-40, the default paper size is **LETTER**. Some reports, in particular, financial reports may need to be printed on legal paper.

To change the paper size, open the Page Setup dialog box, then select the paper, envelope or post card size that you need as shown in Figure 4-43.

The **PAPER SIZE** options in the drop-down list are in order by type. They are no longer in alphabetical order like they were in Crystal Reports XI, as shown in Figure 4-44.

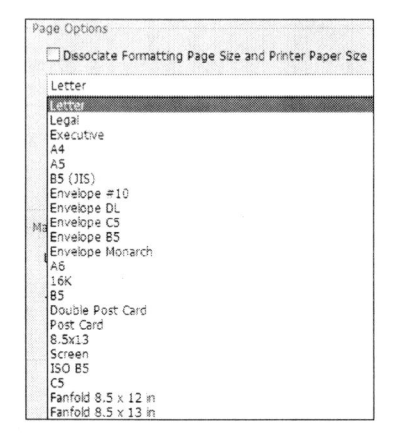

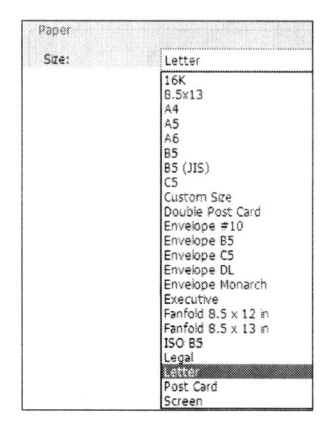

Figure 4-43 Page options in Crystal Reports 2008

Figure 4-44 Page options in Crystal Reports XI

The Section Expert

The Section Expert has been modified. The **PAGING** tab has been added and the page and orientation options from the Common tab were moved to the Paging tab. You can use the Section Expert to format a section of the report, similar to how the Format Editor lets you format fields.

You can also create formulas for many of the options on the Section Expert which is shown in Figure 4-45.

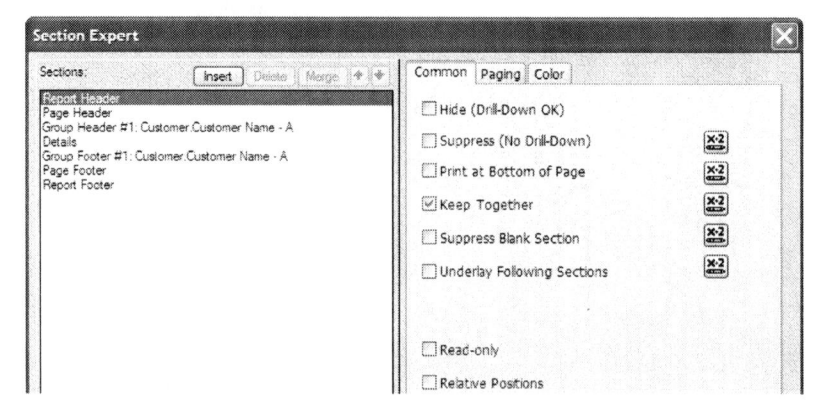

Figure 4-45 Section Expert in Crystal Reports 2008

Chapter 4

> 💣 The **FREE FORM PLACEMENT** option shown in Figure 4-46 on the Common tab has been removed in Crystal Reports 2008.

Figure 4-46 shows the Common tab in Crystal Reports XI.

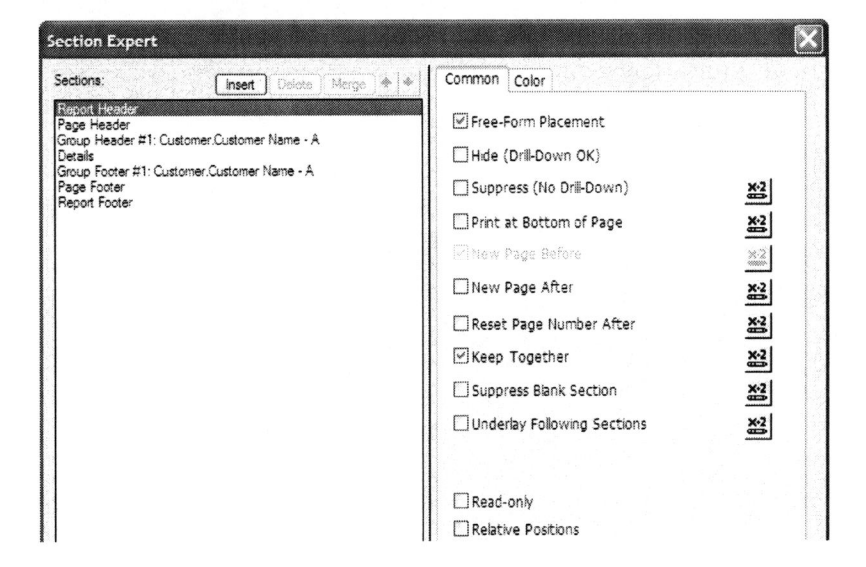

Figure 4-46 Section Expert in Crystal Reports XI

With section formatting, you can make the following types of changes to a report.

① Force each group to start at the top of a new page.
② Change the line spacing in the details section to something other than single spacing.
③ Create page breaks.
④ Conditionally suppress a section of the report.

There are three ways to open the Section Expert as discussed below.

① Right-click on the section name on the left side of the design window and select Section Expert.
② Click the Section Expert button on the Experts toolbar.
③ Report ⇒ Section Expert.

> 📝 The advantage to using the first option above to open the Section Expert is that the section that you want to modify will be highlighted on the left side of the Section Expert dialog box when it is opened. Table 4-12 explains the formatting section options on the Common tab. Table 4-13 explains the options on the Paging tab. Table 4-14 explains the section options that are only available for a specific section of the report.

Option	Description
Hide (Drill-Down OK)	Hides the objects in the section when the report is printed. The section can be viewed on the preview window. If the report section that this option is applied to is part of a higher level group and the group is drilled-down, the objects in the section will be visible on the drill-down tab. This option is not available for subsections.
Suppress (No Drill-Down)	The section that this option is applied to will not be printed, does not allow drill-down and cannot be viewed on the preview window, even if a higher level section is drilled-down. This option is also available for subsections.
Print at Bottom of Page	Forces the section to be printed as close to the bottom of the page as possible, even if the detail records stop printing half way down the page.
Keep Together	Keeps the section together on the same page when printed. This option is sometimes confused with the Keep Group Together option on the Group Expert dialog box. These options produce different results.
Suppress Blank Section	Prevents the section from printing when all of the objects in the section are blank.
Underlay Following Sections	Causes the section to print next to the section below it. This allows charts or images to print next to the data that it represents.
Read-Only	Suppresses formatting in the section and prevents any formatting to the section. This option is similar to the **LOCK FORMAT** and **LOCK SIZE/POSITION** options on the Format Editor and Formatting toolbar.
Relative Positions	Locks an object next to another object like a cross-tab or OLAP grid. For example, if the cross-tab grows, the object will be repositioned so that it remains aligned with the grid object.

Table 4-12 Common tab section formatting options explained

Option	Description
New Page Before	Forces a page break before the section prints. (11)
Reset Page Number After	Resets the page number back to one after the section has printed. This option also resets the Total Page Count special field.
New Page After	Forces a page break after the section prints. (11)
Orientation	**NEW** Lets you select how the report will print on the page as shown in Figure 4-47. Figure 4-48 shows the options on the Paging tab for the details section. The orientation options are not available in the page header and footer sections.

Table 4-13 Paging tab options

(11) This option is often used to force each group to start on a new page.

Formatting options that are not available for a section of the report are dimmed out.

For example, in Figure 4-47, the **NEW PAGE BEFORE** option is not available for the report header section.

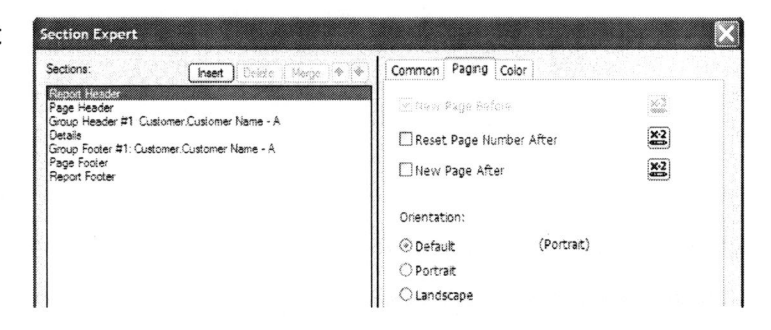

Figure 4-47 Paging tab options for the report header section

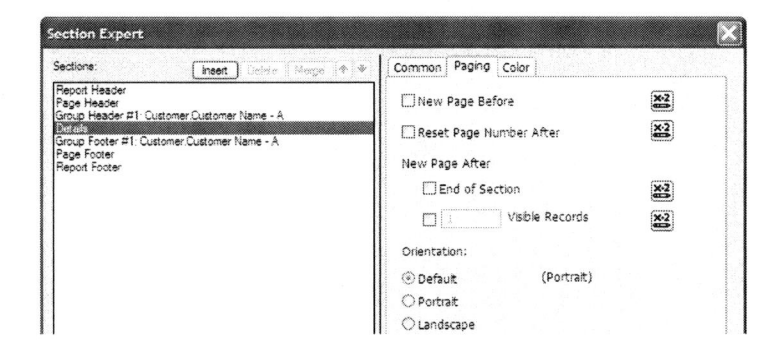

Figure 4-48 Paging tab options for the details section

Section	Option	Description
Page Footer	NEW Clamp Page Footer	If checked, this option shown in Figure 4-49 will remove white space starting after the last section that has data, down to the page footer section causing the page footer section to print further up on the page. This option is not best suited for reports that will not be printed on paper. It is also helpful when displaying the report on a web page. Figure 4-50 shows a report without this option selected. Figure 4-51 shows the same report with this option selected.
Page Footer	Reserve Minimum Page Footer	Select this option when you need to remove space in the page footer section to gain more space on the printed page.

Table 4-14 Section specific formatting options explained

What's New In Crystal Reports 2008

Section	Option	Description
Details	Format With Multiple Columns	Displays data in columns similar to a newspaper layout. When checked, the **LAYOUT** tab will be displayed, as illustrated in Figure 4-52. The options on the Layout tab let you set the size of the columns. These options let you change the page orientation of the section.

Table 4-14 Section specific formatting options explained (Continued)

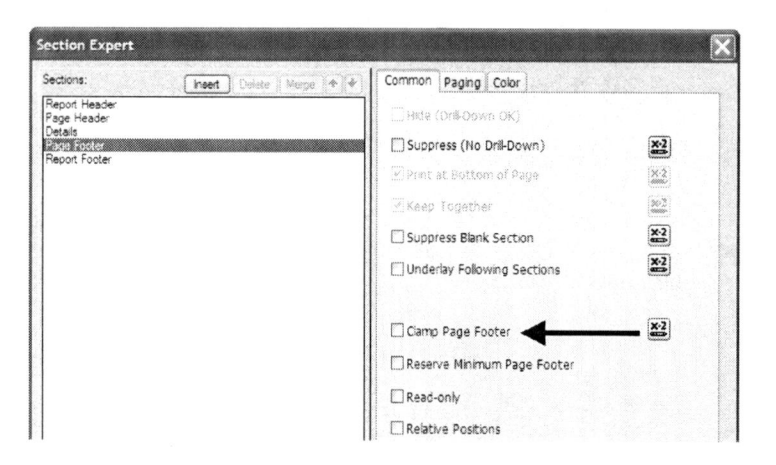

Figure 4-49 Common tab options for the page footer section

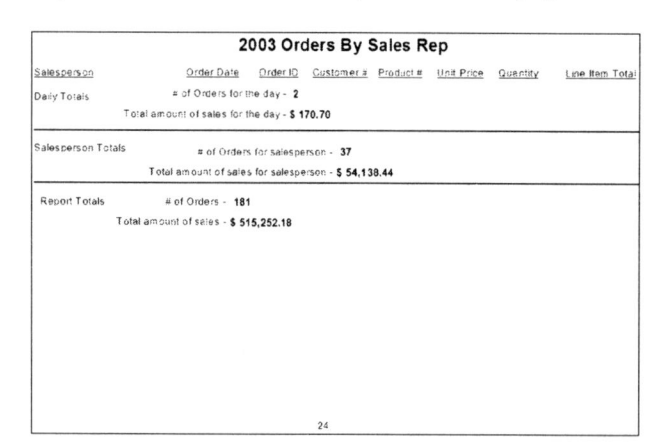

Figure 4-50 Report without the Clamp Page Footer option selected

Chapter 4

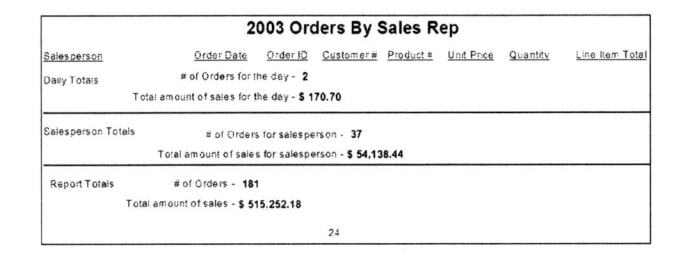

Figure 4-51 Report with the Clamp Page Footer option selected

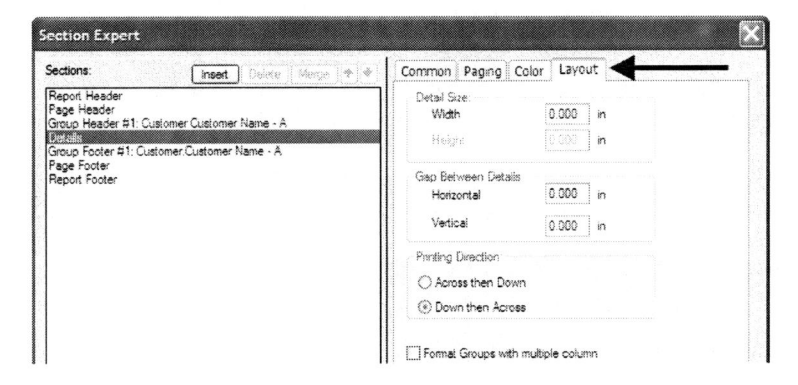

Figure 4-52 Layout tab illustrated

Formula Workshop Changes

There have been some changes and additions to different parts of the Formula Workshop shown in Figure 4-53, as discussed below. The changes are indicated with the "New" icon.

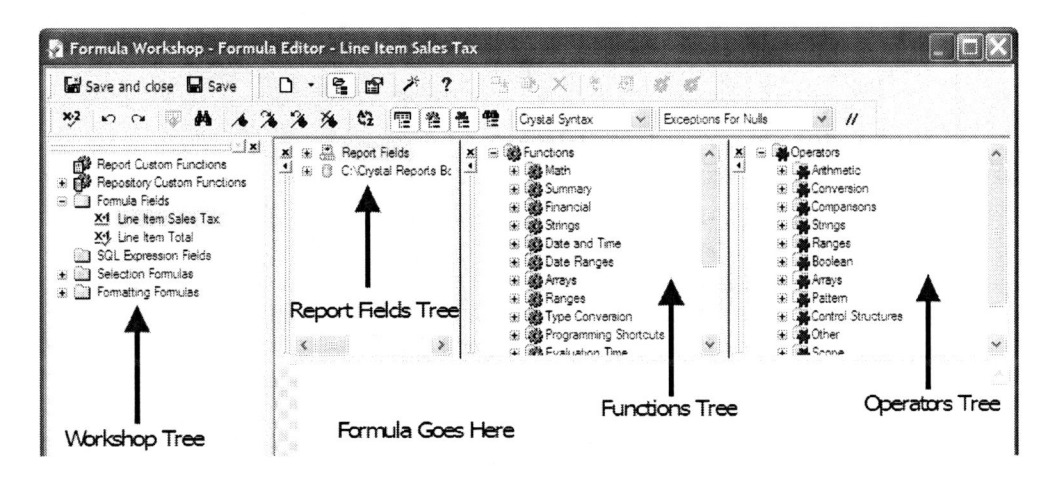

Figure 4-53 Formula Workshop

Workshop Tree

The new Selection Formula Editor in the Workshop Tree is explained below.

Selection Formulas The formulas in this category are created when you use the Select Expert or the selection formula options on the Report menu. You can also create selection formulas in the Formula Workshop. If you click on the Group Selection option, the **GROUP SELECTION FORMULA EDITOR** will open. If you click on the Record Selection option, the **RECORD SELECTION FORMULA EDITOR** will open.

NEW If you click on the Saved Data option, the **SAVED DATA SELECTION FORMULA EDITOR** will open. The only difference that you will notice with these editors is that the title bar of the Formula Workshop will change as shown in Figure 4-54. Compare this title bar to the one shown above in Figure 4-53.

Figure 4-54 Record Selection Formula Editor title bar

New Button Drop-Down List Options

The **SAVED DATA SELECTION FORMULA** option shown in Figure 4-55 is new and will let you create a formula to filter the data that has already been saved with the report.

The sections below discuss data that is saved with a report. The saved data options are on the File menu.

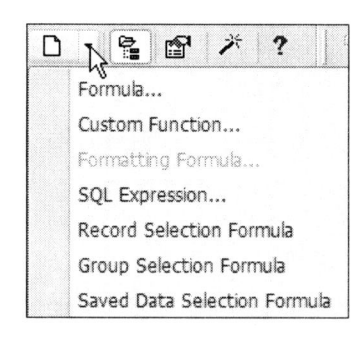

Figure 4-55 New formula options

Saving The Report With Data

This is the default save data option. You can preview and print reports faster with this option selected because the data does not have to be retrieved. This option is also useful if you need to send the report to someone that does not have access to the data. One downside to saving the data with the report is that the report requires more hard drive or server space. A second downside is that anyone that runs the report with saved data will not be using the most current data. A third downside occurs if the database has security. Unless the report has been published to a Crystal Reports Server, the security is bypassed and anyone that opens the report will have access to the data, whether they should or not.

Chapter 4

Fields in tables are indexed to reduce the time it takes to retrieve the records needed to create the report. Fields that are used in the record selection criteria are often used as an index.

> Indexes are not usually helpful in reports that use saved data. The exception to this is reports that have parameter fields that the person running the report can use to change the record selection formula. The **REPORT BURSTING INDEXES** command will let you create indexes in reports that are saved with data.

Saving The Report Without Data

Selecting this option requires less disk space. With this option you will be using live data each time the report is run. The downside is when you need to preview or print the report, it will take a little longer to process because the data has to be retrieved. Most of the time, you will not notice the delay.

> From a report developers perspective if you have the space it will save time, a considerable amount of time if there are thousands of records for the report, if you save the data with the report while you are creating and modifying it. The danger that some developers have <not us of course> is that they forget to change the save data option before putting the report into production. Another danger is not testing the report with live data. Remember that most data is volatile, meaning that it changes frequently, is deleted and added to on a regular basis. Not testing with live data before putting the report into production could be a bad career move, if you know what I mean. Testing with live data before putting the report into production, also means that the report will not go into production with the saved data.

Expression Editor Toolbar

Table 4-15 explains the Expression Editor toolbar buttons.

Button	Purpose
x•2	The Check button tests the syntax of the formula or custom function and identifies syntax errors.
↶	The Undo button undoes the last action made to the formula.
↷	The Redo button redoes the last action that was made to the formula.
🗐	The Browse Data button lets you view the data in a field in the Report Fields window. (12)

Table 4-15 Expression Editor toolbar buttons explained

What's New In Crystal Reports 2008

Button	Purpose
🔍	The Find or Replace dialog box shown in Figure 4-56 searches the formula, fields, functions or operators for words or expressions. You can also replace text in formulas using this dialog box. The **EDIT TEXT** option is where you type in the formula that you want to find.
🔖	The Bookmark button inserts a bookmark on the current line of the selected formula. Click the button again to remove the bookmark. Bookmarks let you mark a line of code as important. The bookmark feature is helpful in long formulas when you have to go from one part of the formula to another.
	The Next Bookmark button will place the cursor at the next bookmark in the formula.
	The Previous Bookmark button will place the cursor at the previous bookmark in the formula.
	The Clear All Bookmarks button deletes all bookmarks in the current formula.
A↕Z	Sorts the options in the Report Fields, Functions and Operators trees in alphabetical order or returns them to their original order.
	Displays or hides the Report Fields tree. (12)
	Displays or hides the Functions tree.
	Displays or hides the Operators tree.
	NEW Displays or hides the formula search results as shown in Figure 4-57.
Crystal Syntax ▼	Lets you to select **CRYSTAL SYNTAX** or **BASIC SYNTAX** as the formula syntax editor.
Exceptions For Nulls ▼	This option allows you to select **EXCEPTIONS FOR NULLS** or **DEFAULT VALUES FOR NULLS** as the method for dealing with null values in the data. Fields in a formula that have a null value will return invalid data or generate an error. Selecting the Default values for nulls option will replace data that has a null value with a default value for the field type. String fields are changed to an empty string. Number fields are changed to zero. If you don't know how or do not want to write code to test for nulls or check for errors, select this option.
//	Add comments to a formula. Commented lines are not evaluated as part of the formula. I type the // into the Formula section when writing the formula because I find it faster then clicking this button.

Table 4-15 Expression Editor toolbar buttons explained (Continued)

Chapter 4

(12) This button is not available for custom functions.

> The **SEARCH** options change depending on the field type or object that is selected prior to clicking the Find and Replace button.

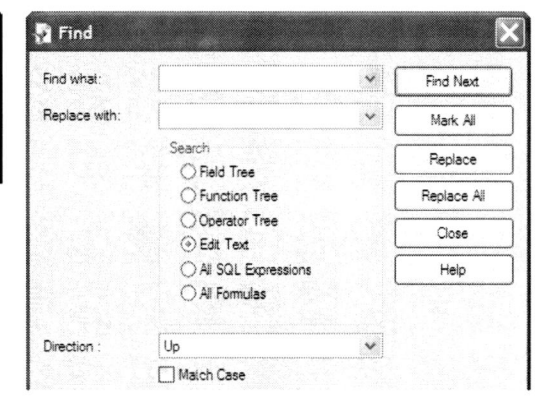

Figure 4-56 Find and Replace dialog box

The options on the shortcut menu provide more functionality.

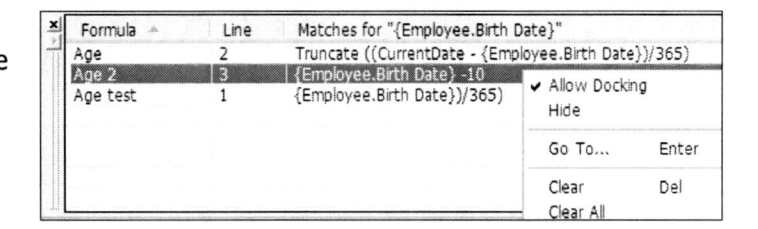

Figure 4-57 Find in formula search results window

4-41

REPORT DESIGN OPTION CHANGES IN CRYSTAL REPORTS 2008

Overview

In this chapter you will learn about the following report design option changes and new features in Crystal Reports 2008.

- ☑ Page breaks
- ☑ Create new parameter dialog box
- ☑ Parameters panel
- ☑ Predefined templates
- ☑ OLAP reports
- ☑ XML Export
- ☑ Bar codes
- ☑ Bind sort control
- ☑ Flash & Xcelsius integration
- ☑ Export an Xcelsius file to a PDF file

Report Design Option Changes In Crystal Reports 2008

Exercise 5.1: Create Page Breaks

Page breaks are one of the most used section formatting techniques. While the concept appears straight forward, it can be tricky and can produce unexpected results. In this exercise you will add a page break to a report that prints orders by month. The objective is to force a page break when the month of the order date changes in the group header section of the report.

1. Save the CH5.1 report as `E5.1 Report with a page break`.

2. Open the Section Expert and click on the group header section. On the Paging tab check the **NEW PAGE BEFORE** option.

3. Preview the report. You should notice that the first page of the report is blank. More than likely, having the first page break occur before the detail records for the first group are printed on the report, is not what you had in mind. Save the changes.

Exercise 5.2: Use The Change Group Dialog Box Options

If you look at the second page for any group in the report that you just modified, you will notice that the group header information (the Salespersons name) only prints on the first page of each group. The report would look better if the group name printed on every page. Options on the **CHANGE GROUP** dialog box will let you force the group header information to print on every page.

1. Save the CH5.2 report as `E5.2 Repeat group header option`.

2. Right-click on the group header section on the left side of the design window and select **CHANGE GROUP**.

3. On the Options tab, check the **REPEAT GROUP HEADER ON EACH PAGE** option shown in Figure 5-1.

    This option will cause the information in the group header section to print on every page of the report that the group prints on.

    Click OK. If you go to any page after the first page of a group, you will see the group header information, just like it is on the first page of each group. Save the changes.

Figure 5-1 Change Group Options dialog box

NEW The **NEW PAGE AFTER VISIBLE GROUPS** option will force a page break after a specific number of groups have printed on a page.

Chart Expert

The **AUTO-ARRANGE** layout option illustrated in Figure 5-2 resets the chart to its original size and position.

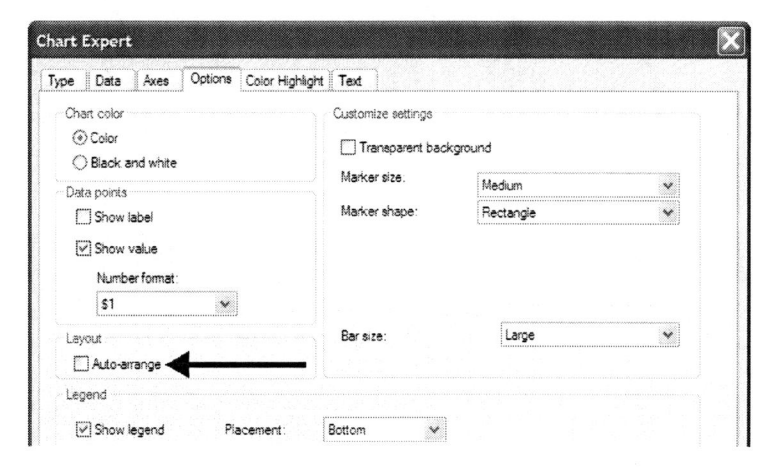

Figure 5-2 Options tab for a bar chart

The Create New Parameter Dialog Box

The layout of the options on the Create New Parameter dialog box has been modified as shown in Figure 5-3.

Reports can and often do have more than one parameter field.

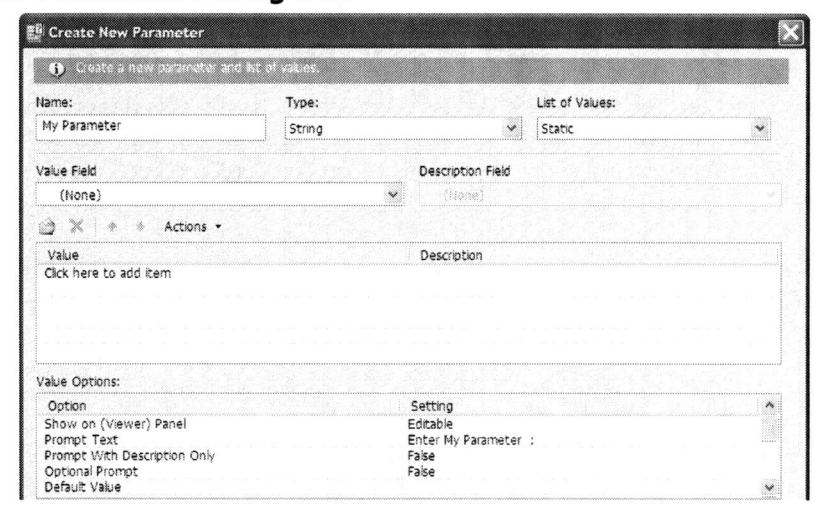

Figure 5-3 Create New Parameter dialog box

> **NEW** The **SHOW ON (VIEWER) PANEL** option shown above in Figure 5-3 has the following three settings which effect how the parameter panel on the preview tab can be used:
> ① The **DO NOT SHOW** setting hides the parameter section in the preview panel.
> ② The **EDITABLE** setting lets the person running the report change the parameter values in the preview panel.
> ③ The **READ ONLY** setting allows the parameter values to be viewed in the preview panel, but not changed.

Report Design Option Changes In Crystal Reports 2008

> **NEW** When creating a parameter field, you no longer have to press F5 after selecting the parameter field on the Select Expert. The Enter Values dialog box will open automatically.

The **LIST OF VALUES** drop-down list shown above in Figure 5-3 in Crystal Reports 2008 replaces the Static and Dynamic options that are in Crystal Reports XI, as illustrated in Figure 5-4.

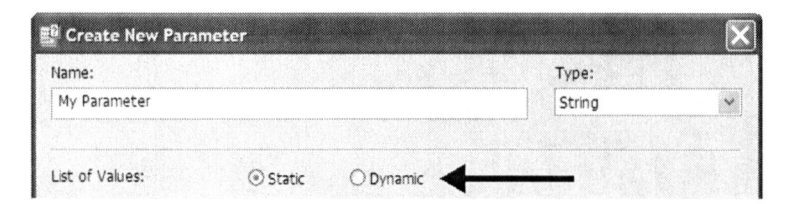

Figure 5-4 List of Values options in Crystal Reports XI

The updates to parameter fields in Crystal Reports XI provided a lot of useful new interactive functionality for reports. As you may have discovered, depending on the number of records retrieved by the parameter fields, it could take a while to refresh. This happened whether or not the parameter field was used as record selection criteria.

Now, the parameter field refreshing process had been modified to determine whether or not each parameter field in the report needs to have the data refreshed. If a parameter field is used for record selection and the report is not using the saved data option, the data will be refreshed. Otherwise, the data will not be refreshed.

If knowing whether or not the data will be refreshed is important to you, look at the icon next to each parameter field in the Field Explorer. If the parameter field has a question mark, the data is forced to be refreshed.

Parameter Panel

The Parameter Panel is new. It is part of the preview panel that was discussed in Chapter 4.

The options shown in Figure 5-5 make it easier for people to run reports that have parameter fields. The options are on the left side of the preview window and are activated by default when a report is run or refreshed that has a parameter field. The Parameter Panel toolbar buttons are explained in Table 5-1.

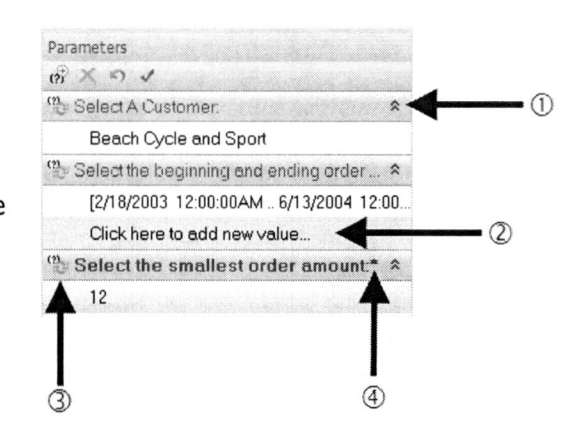

Figure 5-5 Parameter Panel options

Chapter 5

Button	Description
Prompt for parameters	Opens the Enter Values dialog box.
Remove value	Deletes the last value that was added to the parameter panel.
Revert all changes	Deletes all of the parameter changes since the last time the report was run.
Apply changes	Runs the report with the current parameter options.

Table 5-1 Parameter Panel toolbar buttons explained

You can change the parameter options by double-clicking in the space below the parameter that you want to change. For example, if you wanted to change the date range, double-click on the 2/18/2003 date shown above in Figure 5-5. The Enter Values dialog box would open with the prompt to change the date range.

Table 5-2 explains the Parameter Panel interface options illustrated in Figure 5-5. You can open the CH5 Cascading prompts report to see how this feature works.

Option	Description
1	Clicking on the arrow displays or hides the parameter values for the field.
2	Double-click on this section to add or change the parameter value.
3	When visible, the question mark means that the data will be forced to be refreshed for the parameter field.
4	The asterisk indicates that the value for the parameter field has changed, but has not been used to filter the data in the report.

Table 5-2 Parameter Panel interface options explained

Long List Of Values Options

Parameter field drop-down lists that have a lot of values are now separated into groups of 200 records.

If the value that you are looking for is not in the first group of values, open the drop-down list shown in Figure 5-6 and select another level or click on the navigation buttons on either side of the drop-down list.

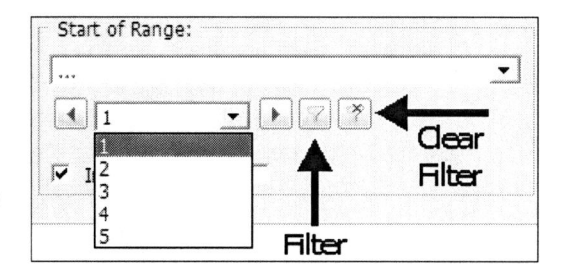

Figure 5-6 Parameter field long list of values options

The **FILTER** button lets you create a filter for the values in the entire list. The **CLEAR FILTER** button removes the filter.

You can use the CH5 Cascading prompts report to see how this option works.

5-5

Report Design Option Changes In Crystal Reports 2008

Predefined Templates

One thing that I found interesting about templates is that if there is an object in the template that is not in the report that the template is being applied to, the template adds the object to the report. There are two ways to open the Template Expert as discussed below.

① Click the **TEMPLATE EXPERT** button on the Expert Tools toolbar.
② Report ⇒ Template Expert.

> The **CONFIDENTIAL UNDERLAY** template in Crystal Reports XI, which is illustrated in Figure 5-7 has been removed in Crystal Reports 2008.

Figure 5-7 Confidential Underlay option in Crystal Reports XI

OLAP Reports

OLAP reports look similar to cross-tab reports because they present the data in a summarized format in rows and columns. OLAP reports use an OLAP cube as the data source. The difference between OLAP data and the data that a cross-tab report uses is that OLAP data has already been summarized before it is placed in the cube structure that is used as the data source for a report. OLAP data must be on a server. The OLAP Cube does not have to be on a server, but it usually is. You should only use the OLAP wizard if the OLAP data is the only object on the report.

> The **OLAP CUBE** contains the data. The **OLAP** grid is where the data is placed.

Exercise 5.3: Create An OLAP Report

The process of creating an OLAP report is basically the same in Crystal Reports 2008 as it was in Crystal Reports XI, but some options have changed. In this exercise you will create an OLAP report that will display product order totals by measure levels, by week and by year. This information has already been summarized in the OLAP cube. If you selected the default options, a lot of data would be displayed. A benefit of OLAP data is that you can select which products, measures and weeks you want to display on the report.

Chapter 5

There are three basic steps to creating an OLAP report. The steps are: create an OLAP connection, select options on the Rows/Columns screen and modify the report.

The requirements for this report are:

① Display totals for four weeks.
② Include all three measures: In this data set, measures are the sales, (production) costs and (profit) margins for the companies.
③ Include the following product (categories) levels; Bakery, Fruit and Vegetable, Wine and Spirits.

Step 1: Create An OLAP Connection

1. Click on the OLAP Cube Report Wizard link on the Start Page. You will see the screen shown in Figure 5-8.

   The **OLAP Data** screen lets you select the data source for the report. There are two types of data sources that you can select from, as discussed below.

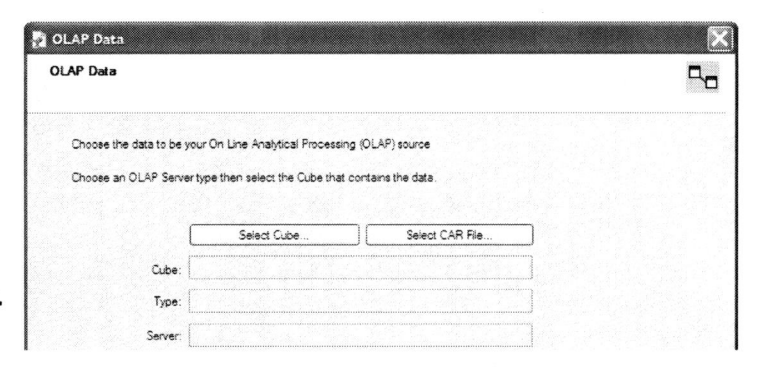

   Figure 5-8 OLAP Data screen

   ① **Select Cube** This option lets you select an OLAP Cube to use as the data source.
   ② **Select CAR File** This option will let you select a CAR file, which will use a Crystal Analysis application file as the data source.

2. Click the **SELECT CUBE** button.

   You will see the dialog box shown in Figure 5-9.

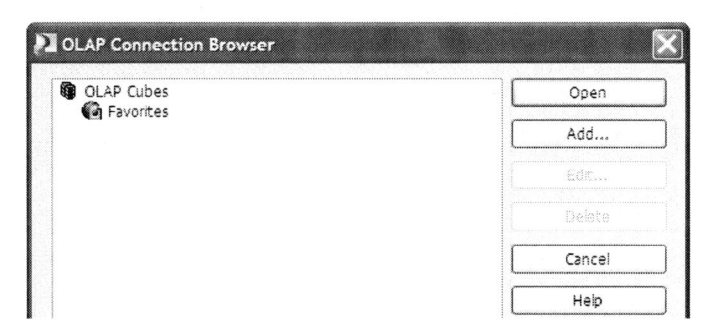

   Figure 5-9 OLAP Connection Browser dialog box

Report Design Option Changes In Crystal Reports 2008

If you see the OLAP Connection that you need on this dialog box, you would click on it, then click **OPEN**. If not, you have to create a connection for the OLAP cube that you need, which is what you will do now.

3. Click the **ADD** button.

   You will see the dialog box shown in Figure 5-10.

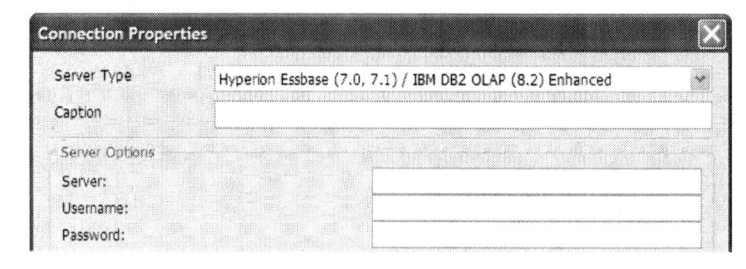

Figure 5-10 Connection Properties dialog box

The **CONNECTION PROPERTIES** dialog box lets you create OLAP connections. The **SERVER OPTIONS** will vary depending on the server type option that is selected.

> You have to select a server type and create a caption for every connection type.

4. Open the Server Type drop-down list and select **MICROSOFT OLE DB PROVIDER FOR OLAP SERVICES 8.0**, then type `OLAP Report` in the **CAPTION** field.

5. Select the **LOCAL CUBE FILE (.CUB)** option, then click the Browse button. Navigate to the folder that you saved the sample files in, then double-click on the Sales Reports.cub file.

> If you can't find the file, you can use the Search tool in Windows and search for the Sales Reports.cub file.

6. Click the **TEST CONNECTION** button on the Connection Properties dialog box to confirm that your connection is working.

   Click OK when you see the "Connected Successfully" message.

   Your Connection Properties dialog box should have the options shown in Figure 5-11.

   Click OK to close the dialog box.

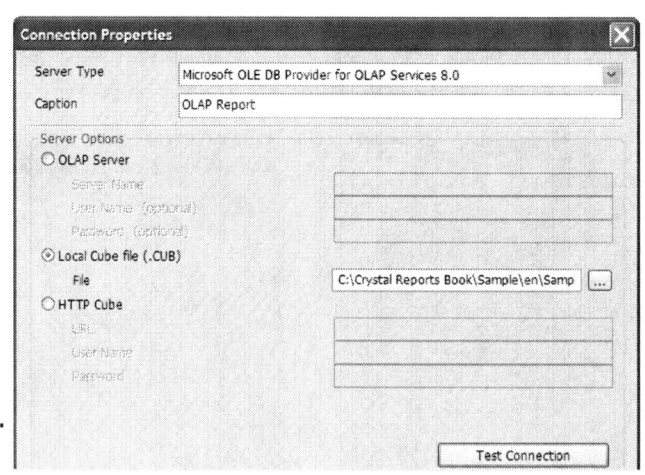

Figure 5-11 Connection Properties options

5-8

Chapter 5

The Connection Properties options have changed. Figure 5-12 shows the options in Crystal Reports XI.

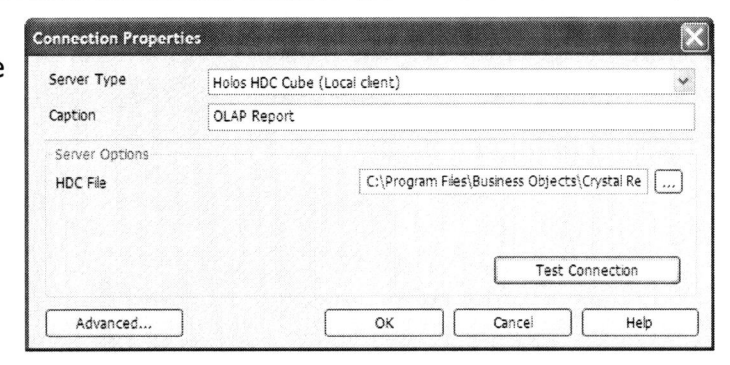

Figure 5-12 Connection Properties options in Crystal Reports XI

7. Click on the plus sign in front of the OLAP Report option, then click on the plus sign in front of the Sales Reports folder. You should see the connection to the Sales Reports cube as illustrated in Figure 5-13.

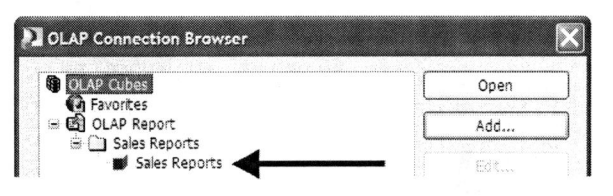

Figure 5-13 Sales Reports cube connection

Click on the Sales Reports cube connection, then click the **OPEN** button. Your OLAP Data screen should have the options similar to those shown in Figure 5-14.
The server path is probably different.

Click Next.

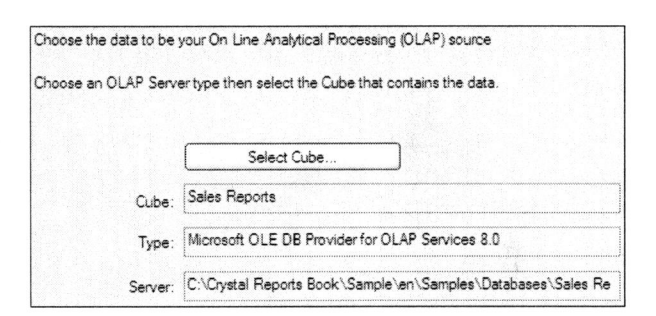

Figure 5-14 OLAP Data screen options

Report Design Option Changes In Crystal Reports 2008

Step 2: Select Options On The Rows/Columns Screen

In this part of the exercise you will select the dimensions, rows and columns for the report. Figure 5-15 shows the Rows/Columns screen.

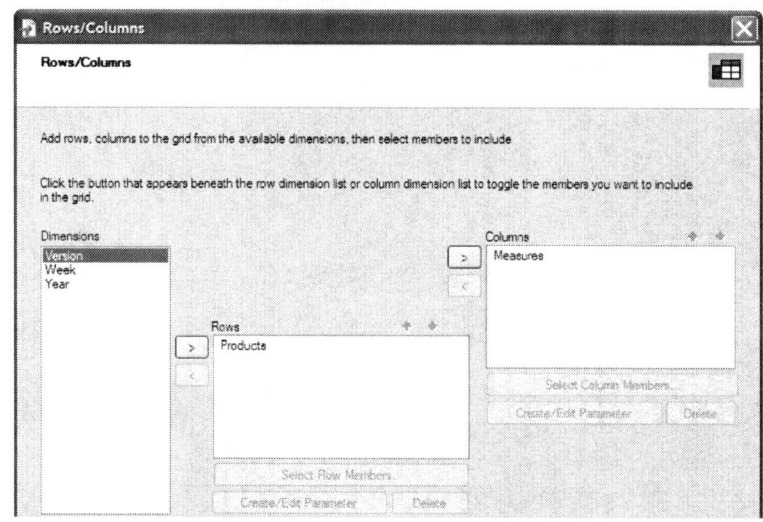

Figure 5-15 Rows/Columns screen

The **DIMENSIONS** section determines how the data will be grouped on the report. The dimensions listed are all of the ones that have not already been added to the rows or columns sections.

In this OLAP cube, the available dimensions that you can select from are Version, Week and Year. If you added the week dimension to the rows section, the report would be grouped by products.

If you wanted the product data grouped by week, the week dimension would have to be the first item in the Rows section.

The **ROWS** and **COLUMNS** sections basically work the same as they do on the Cross-Tab wizard. Like cross-tabs, you should put the item that has the most data down the left side (rows) of the OLAP grid and the item with the least data, across the top (columns) of the OLAP grid.

With OLAP data, I find it easier to figure out the layout order by working from the inside of the grid (the cells) out. The goal of this report is to show product totals by measures (sales, costs and margin), by week and by year. The data in this OLAP cube have the totals at the week level.

The way that you select the weeks, measures and products that will appear on the report is by clicking on the **SELECT ROW MEMBERS** or **SELECT COLUMN MEMBERS** buttons. These buttons let you select the specific year, measures and products that will appear on the report. For example, if you want two baking products, two fruit products and one wine product, that is what you would select for the Product row options. If you want to

Chapter 5

only show the activity for the products just mentioned for the first month of the year, you would select the first four weeks. Each of these options is known as a **MEMBER**.

Select The Row Dimension Options

1. Add the Week dimension to the **ROWS** section, then move the Products field below the Week dimension by clicking on the down arrow button.

2. Click on the Week dimension, then click the **SELECT ROW MEMBERS** button.
   The Member Selector dialog box is how you select which weeks (in this exercise) that you want totals for.

3. Click on the plus sign in front of the **ALL WEEKS** option, then check the first four weeks as shown in Figure 5-16. Click OK.

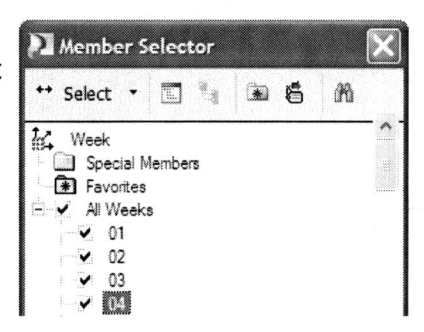

Figure 5-16 Weeks selected for the report

4. Click on the Products row option, then click the Select Row Members button.

5. Click on the plus sign in front of All Products.

   This report needs to include all products in three regions: Bakery, Fruit and Vegetable and Wine and Spirits.

   Click on each of these categories, then check each product under each of these three categories as shown in Figure 5-17.

   Click OK to close the Member Selector dialog box.

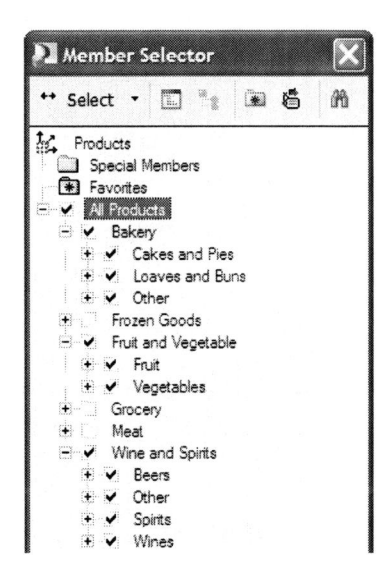

Figure 5-17 Three product categories selected

5-11

Report Design Option Changes In Crystal Reports 2008

Select The Column Dimension Options

In this part of the exercise you will select the measures that you want to appear on the report.

1. Click on the Measures field, then click the Select Column Members button.

2. As shown in Figure 5-18 all of the measures are already selected. Click OK to close the Member Selector dialog box.

   Click Finish. Your report should look like the one shown in Figure 5-19. The report needs to be modified.

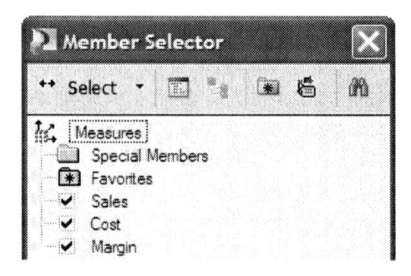

Figure 5-18 Measures selected

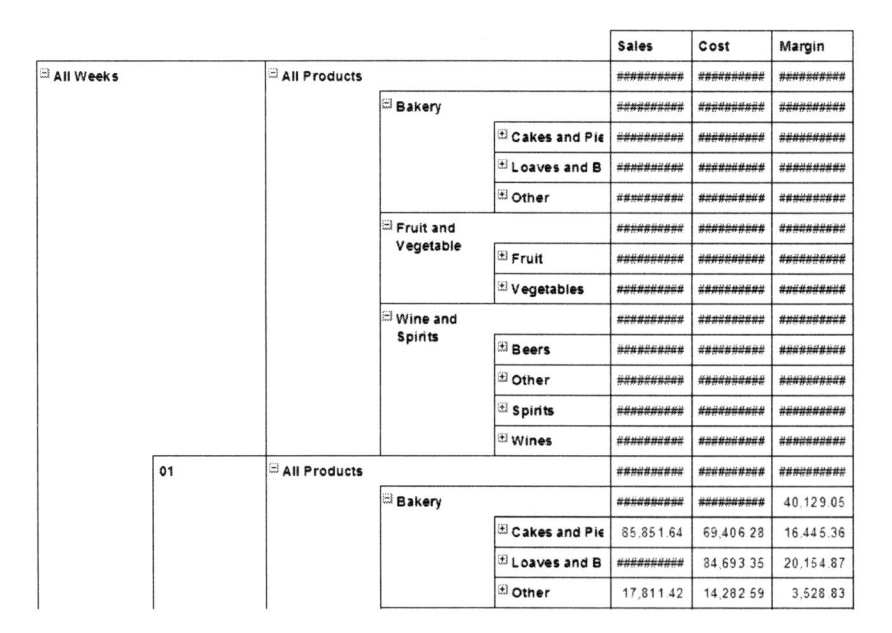

Figure 5-19 E5.3 OLAP report (before formatting)

3. Save the report as `E5.3 OLAP`, then click on the Design tab.

Step 3: Modify The OLAP Report

The following changes need to be made to the report:

① The All Weeks, Month and All Products columns need to be made smaller.
② The Product section needs to be made larger.
③ All of the columns with numeric values need to be wider.

5-12

Chapter 5

1. Select the two week level fields and make them smaller.

2. Select the first two product level fields and make them smaller. Make the third product level field wider. This is the Product Name field.

3. Select the three **VALUE** fields and make them wider. Save the changes.
   The first page of the report should look like the one shown in Figure 5-20.

Actual	All Years			Sales	Cost	Margin
All Weeks	All Products			170,888,357.64	139,298,880.85	31,589,476.80
		Bakery		10,510,721.83	8,505,040.99	2,005,680.83
			Cakes and Pies	4,334,286.74	3,509,385.38	824,901.35
			Loaves and Buns	5,277,895.03	4,268,379.24	1,009,515.79
			Other	898,540.06	727,276.36	171,263.69
		Fruit and Vegetable		33,436,399.40	26,261,723.40	7,174,676.02
			Fruit	17,756,355.16	14,107,593.93	3,648,761.22
			Vegetables	15,680,044.24	12,154,129.48	3,525,914.80
		Wine and Spirits		12,853,800.35	9,575,611.58	3,278,188.77
			Beers	1,970,447.35	1,467,980.13	502,467.19
			Other	889,367.01	663,250.62	226,116.40
			Spirits	2,578,580.17	1,921,461.19	657,118.99
			Wines	7,415,405.81	5,522,919.65	1,892,486.18
01	All Products			4,606,543.80	3,748,960.80	857,582.99
		Bakery		208,511.29	168,382.23	40,129.05
			Cakes and Pies	85,851.64	69,406.28	16,445.36
			Loaves and Buns	104,848.22	84,693.35	20,154.87

Figure 5-20 Page 1 of the OLAP report

XML Export Format

The XML export options have been modified. This export format is similar to the HTML export format because it is also creates web pages. XML stands for Extensible Markup Language.

By default, XML uses a built-in schema that will format the data or content for the report. Figure 5-21 shows the XML export options.

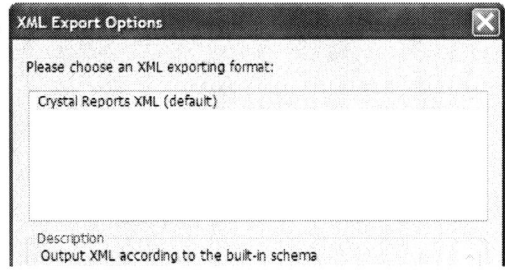

Figure 5-21 XML export options

If you have already created an XML export using a different schema, you should see it in the dialog box.

Report Design Option Changes In Crystal Reports 2008

If you need to customize or add an XML schema, you can use the Manage XML Exporting Formats dialog box (File ⇒ Export ⇒ Manage XML Exporting Formats) shown in Figure 5-22.

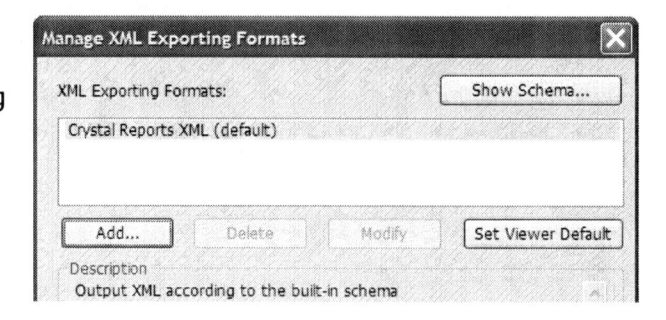

Figure 5-22 XML Export Formats

The people that will view a report in XML format will need software that recognizes XML files.

Figures 5-23 and 5-24 show the XML Export options in Crystal Reports XI, so that you can see the differences.

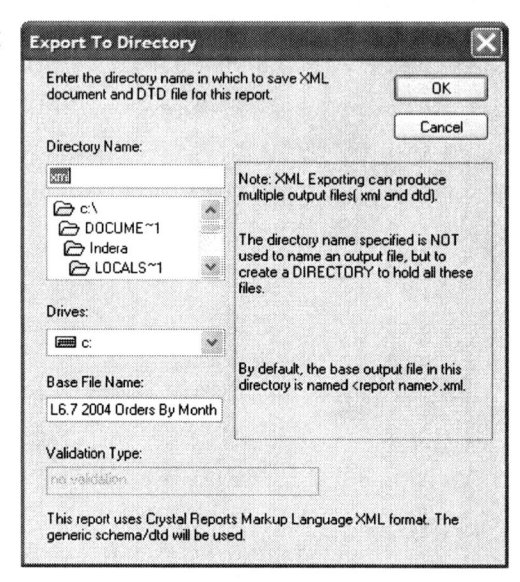

Figure 5-23 Crystal Reports XI XML Export options

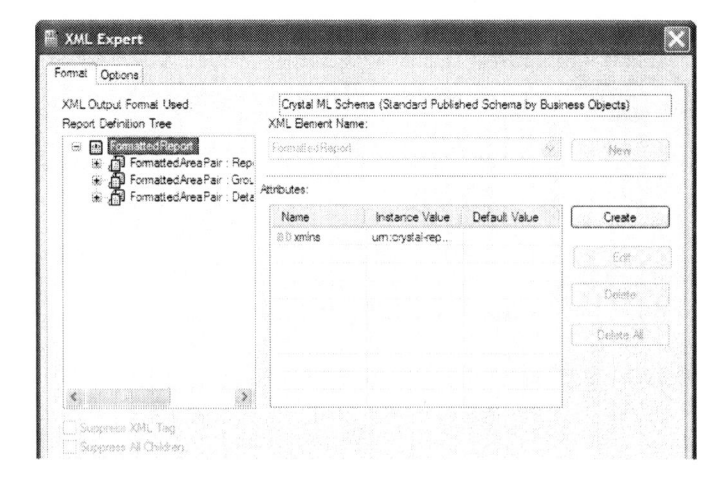

Figure 5-24 Crystal Reports XI XML Expert

5-14

Chapter 5

Basic XML Export

The steps below will show you how to export the data from a report to a file that can be used as the XML source file. An XML style sheet needs to be applied to the source file. XML is beyond the scope of this book.

1. Open the CH2.6 file, then File ⇒ Export ⇒ Export Report.

2. Open the Format drop-down list and select XML.

3. Open the Destination drop-down list and select Disk File.

4. Click OK. You will see the dialog box shown earlier in Figure 5-21.

5. Click OK. Save the file as `CH5 Basic XML Export`.

6. If you double-click on the file, it should open in your browser and should look similar to the one shown in Figure 5-25.

```
<?xml version="1.0" encoding="UTF-8" ?>
- <CrystalReport xmlns="urn:crystal-reports:schemas:report-detail" xmlns:xsi="http://www.w3.org/2001/XMLSchema-
    instance" xsi:schemaLocation="urn:crystal-reports:schemas:report-detail
    http://www.businessobjects.com/products/xml/CR2008Schema.xsd">
  - <ReportHeader>
      <Section SectionNumber="0" />
    </ReportHeader>
  - <Group Level="1">
    - <GroupHeader>
      - <Section SectionNumber="0">
        - <Field Name="GroupNameOrderDatemonthly1" FieldName="GroupName ({Orders.Order Date},
            "monthly")">
            <FormattedValue>January</FormattedValue>
            <Value>January</Value>
          </Field>
        </Section>
      </GroupHeader>
    - <Details Level="2">
      - <Section SectionNumber="0">
        - <Field Name="FirstName1" FieldName="{Employee.First Name}">
            <FormattedValue>Anne</FormattedValue>
            <Value>Anne</Value>
          </Field>
        - <Field Name="LastName1" FieldName="{Employee.Last Name}">
            <FormattedValue>Dodsworth</FormattedValue>
            <Value>Dodsworth</Value>
          </Field>
        - <Field Name="OrderDate1" FieldName="{Orders.Order Date}">
            <FormattedValue>01/01/2004</FormattedValue>
            <Value>2004-01-01T00:00:00</Value>
          </Field>
```

Figure 5-25 XML export source file

NEW   Find In Field Explorer Option

If selected, this option will highlight the field in the Field Explorer window. I'm not sure of the benefit of this feature because if you have the tool tips option turned on, you can see which table the field is in by holding the mouse pointer over the field on the design window. This option is on the shortcut menu when you select a field, as shown in Figure 5-26.

5-15

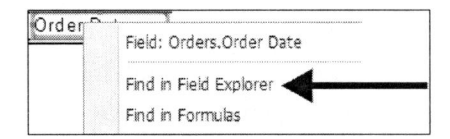

Report Design Option Changes In Crystal Reports 2008

(image: context menu showing Field: Orders.Order Date, Find in Field Explorer (indicated by arrow), Find in Formulas)

Figure 5-26 Find In Field Explorer option illustrated

Bar Codes

Crystal Reports now supports basic bar code creation and printing. Currently, the bar codes that can be produced are very basic. Usually bar codes print a UPC or ISBN code. The two formats currently supported, do not have all of the functionality that other bar code software has. To access the bar code utility, follow the steps below.

1. Right-click on the field that has the data that you want converted to a bar code and select **CHANGE TO BAR CODE**.

   You will see the dialog box shown in Figure 5-27.

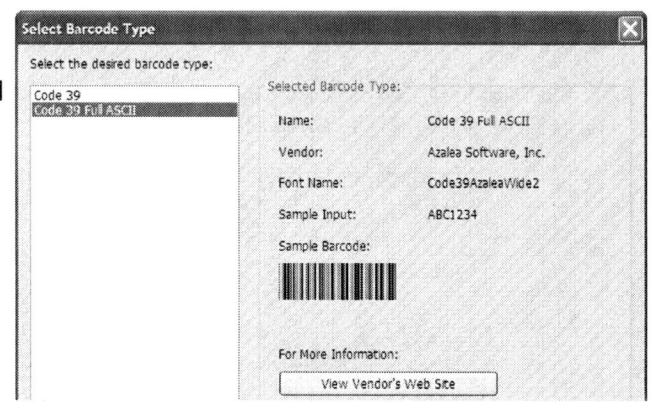

(image: Select Barcode Type dialog box showing Code 39 and Code 39 Full ASCII options, with Selected Barcode Type details: Name: Code 39 Full ASCII, Vendor: Azalea Software, Inc., Font Name: Code39AzaleaWide2, Sample Input: ABC1234, Sample Barcode, and View Vendor's Web Site button)

Figure 5-27 Select Barcode Type dialog box

2. Select the type of bar code that you want and click OK. The data in the field will be changed to a bar code as shown in Figure 5-28.

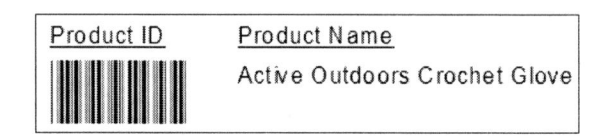

(image: Product ID field displayed as barcode next to Product Name "Active Outdoors Crochet Glove")

Figure 5-28 Product ID field changed to a bar code

Exercise 5.4: Bind Sort Control

The bind sort control will allow the person viewing the report to be able to sort the report on their own. Sorting the records will handle a lot of the users requirement of needing a report sorted more than one way. You could create parameter fields that will allow the user to select a sort order. The advantage of using bind controls instead of parameter fields for sorting data is that the data does not have to be refreshed.

In this exercise you will add two bind controls to a report to allow the user to sort the report on more than one field. Bind controls can only be used on fields that are sorted or grouped on.

Chapter 5

1. Save the CH5.3 report as `E5.4 Bind Control`.

2. Sort the report on the Region and Postal Code fields.

3. Insert ⇒ Sort Control.

   You will see the dialog box shown in Figure 5-29.

   Select the Region field, then click OK.

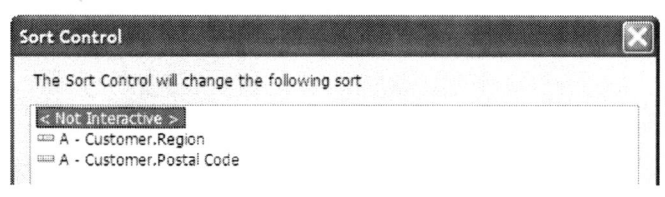

   Figure 5-29 Sort Control dialog box

4. The mouse pointer will change to a cross-hair. Draw a box over the Region heading, then click on a blank space on the report. Resize the text object so that it is smaller.

5. Right-click on the Postal Code heading and select Bind Control. Select the Postal Code option, then resize the control. Save the changes. The report should look like the one shown in Figure 5-30.

Address1	Region	Country	Postal Code
Post Box: 278	Abu Dhabi	United Arab Emirates	3453
8287 Scott Road	AL	USA	35818
1922 Beach Crescent	AL	USA	35857

Figure 5-30 Bind controls added to the report

6. Click on the down arrow for the Region field. The report should be sorted in descending order by region. Click on the up arrow on the Postal Code field. The report should be sorted in ascending order by Postal Code.

It is not a requirement that the control be placed on a field heading, that is just my preference. You can place the control any place on the report. The reason that I place them there is so that there are no extra fields on the report when it is printed.

If you placed the controls in the report header, they would be visible on the first page of the report as shown in Figure 5-31 unless you suppress the section.

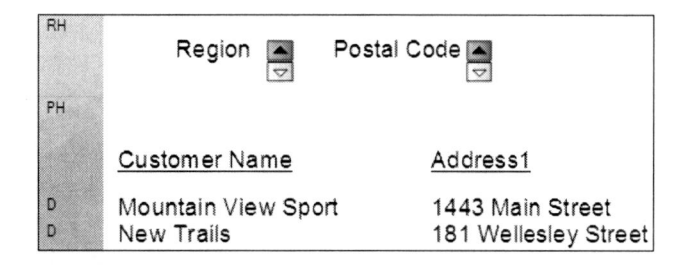

Figure 5-31 Bind controls in the report header section

Bind controls can also be used on reports that are embedded in an application, viewed in the Business Objects Enterprise or Crystal Reports Server.

Report Design Option Changes In Crystal Reports 2008

How To Remove A Bind Control From A Report

If you need to remove a bind control from a report, follow the steps below.

1. Right-click on the Bind Control in the report and select **BIND SORT CONTROL**.

2. Select **<NOT INTERACTIVE>** on the Sort Control dialog box shown earlier in Figure 5-29, then click OK.

3. Open the record Sort Expert dialog box to confirm that the report will be sorted as needed. Bind controls change the sort order that is on the Record Sort Expert dialog box, each time they are used.

> If the report needs to be sorted by fields other than the ones that have a bind control, those fields should be sorted on after the field(s) with bind controls. Not doing so may confuse the person viewing the report because the way that the report is primarily sorted will not be based on the bind control field that the person selected, which will be confusing.

Adding A Flash File To A Report

> The process to add a Flash (SWF) file to a report that was created with Adobe Flash or with Crystal Xcelsius is the same.

This new feature allows a standard Flash file (For example, a Flash file that displays graphics or video) to be added to a report in any of the following ways:

① Embedded directly in the report.
② Via a URL.
③ Link to the file name.

> **Viewing Flash Files**
>
> You need to have the current version of the free Flash player installed to view Flash files in a report. You can download the latest version from http://www.adobe.com.
>
> Some Flash files are designed to start immediately and others require interaction from the user, like a mouse click or clicking a button. If the Flash file that you are adding to the report is the latter, it is a good idea to put an indication of this on the report, if the Flash file does not indicate what needs to be done to start playing the file.

Chapter 5

To open the **INSERT FLASH OBJECT** dialog box shown in Figure 5-32, select one of the options listed below.

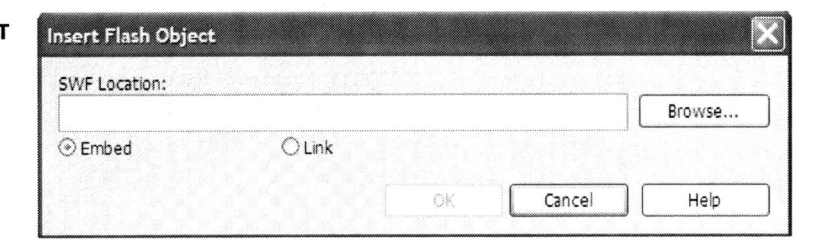

Figure 5-32 Insert Flash Object dialog box

① Click the Insert Flash Object button on the Insert Tools toolbar.
② Right-click on a blank space in the report and select Insert Flash Object.
③ Insert ⇒ Flash.

1. Click the Browse button on dialog box shown above in Figure 5-32, then navigate to and double-click on the Flash file.

2. Select one of the options below.

   ① Select the **EMBED** option if you want to save a copy of the Flash file in the report. Selecting this option will greatly increase the size of the report. The reasons that I can think of to select this option is if there is a chance that the Flash file will be modified, moved or deleted. The other reason is because you need to include the Flash file in a PDF document.
   ② Select the **LINK** option if you want to keep the report size small, know that the Flash file will be modified and you want the changes to the Flash file to be included in the report.

> Embedded Flash files cannot be exported to Excel. They can be exported to a PDF file.

3. When you see the outline of the Flash file, click in the section of the report where you want to place the Flash file, then preview the report.

Report Design Option Changes In Crystal Reports 2008

Formatting A Flash File

Formatting a Flash file will remind you of formatting an image file because you can resize the file.

Right-click on the Flash file in the report and select Format Flash. You will see the Flash tab shown in Figure 5-33.

The **SWF LOCATION** field lets you select a new location for the current Flash file or a different Flash file, by clicking on the button at the end of the field.

The **IMAGE FOR PRINTING AND EXPORTING** option is used to select an image that will be used to represent the Flash file when the report is printed or exported. Flash files cannot be printed.

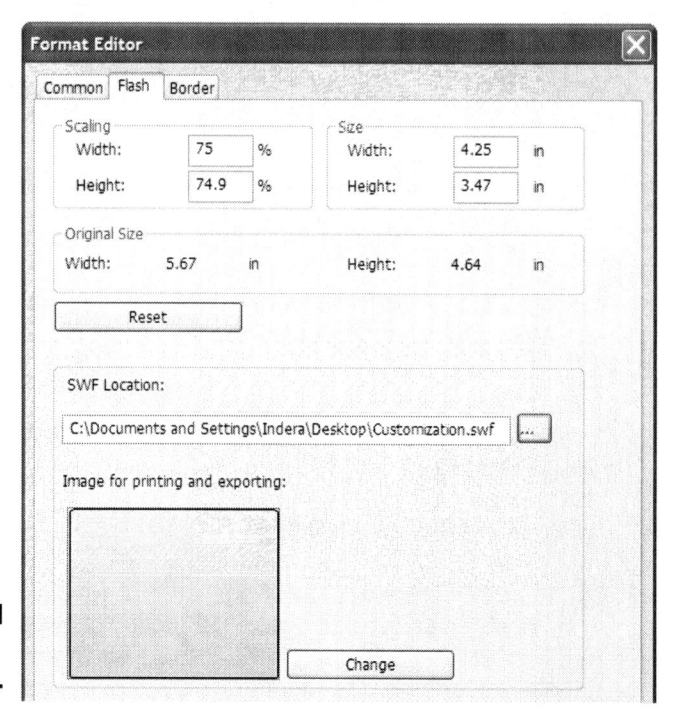

Figure 5-33 Flash tab on the Format Editor

Exporting A Report With An Xcelsius File To A PDF File

In the prior section you learned how to add a Flash or Xcelsius Flash file to a report. PDF files do the best job of retaining the look and feel of the report. In addition to incorporating the groups, which can be turned into bookmarks, as you learned about in Chapter 3, Flash files created in Xcelsius that are embedded in the report will retain their functionality in the PDF file.

INDEX

.car file, 4-16, 4-19, 5-7
<Not Interactive>, 5-18

A

Add to all group levels option, 3-7
Adobe Acrobat PDF export, 3-10, 5-20
Adobe Flash & Flex integration, 4-3, 5-18
Allow multiple values option, 2-36
Allow range values option, 2-36
Array, 2-37
Auto Complete option for functions, 3-9
Auto Complete option for tables & fields, 3-10
Auto-arrange layout option, 5-3

B

Bar codes, 4-2, 5-16
Bind sort control, 4-2, 5-16
Blank report option, 1-9
Bookmarks, 3-11
Built-in bar code support, 4-2, 5-16
Business Objects Enterprise Log on dialog box, 1-21

C

Cascading prompts, 2-33
Category folders, 1-24
Change group Options dialog box, 5-2
Chart Expert, 2-7
Chart layout options, 2-8
Clamp page footer, 4-35
Confidential underlay template, 5-6
Copying a formula, 3-4
crAscendingOrder function, 2-44
crDescendingOrder function, 2-44
Create bookmarks from group tree option, 3-11
Create new parameter dialog box, 2-26, 5-3
Cross-Tab Expert, 2-13
Cross-Tab layout options, 2-9
Cross-Tab printing issues, 2-21
Cross-Tab reports, 2-2

Cross-Tab shortcut menu, 2-22
Crystal Reports 2008 workspace, 4-2
Crystal Reports XI edition differences, 1-6
Crystal Reports XI Release 2 overview, 3-2
Crystal Reports XI workspace, 1-9
Crystal Xcelsius integration, 4-3, 5-18
CrystalReports.com, 1-34, 4-2
CSV export options, 3-12
CurrentFieldValue function, 2-18
Custom colors, 3-5
Custom function, 1-26
Custom style option, 4-25

D

Data source connections, 4-19
Database menu options, 4-11
Database server is case-insensitive option, 1-34
Default export options, 2-23
Default values for nulls option, 4-40
DefaultAttribute function, 2-18
Deleting projects & reports, 1-20
Dependency checker, 1-5, 1-19, 1-31
Dissociate formatting page size & printer paper size, 4-30
Drop and drag charts & cross-tabs, 1-6
Duplicating a formula, 3-3
Dynamic & cascading prompts, 1-6, 2-32
Dynamic graphic location, 1-6, 1-30
Dynamic list of values, 2-31

E

Embed flash file option, 5-19
Enable HTML preview option, 1-17
Enhanced Cross-Tabs, 4-2
Enhanced report viewer, 1-5
Error message help, 1-32
Excel 2003 viewer, 2-22
Excel data only export, 3-14
Excel spreadsheet - connect to, 4-22
Exceptions for nulls option, 4-40
Expert tools toolbar, 4-16
Export Flash file to PDF, 5-20

Export mode options, 3-13
Export options, 3-10
Expression Editor toolbar, 4-39
External Command toolbar, 4-17
Extract to here option, 1-8

F

Field explorer, 3-3
Find and Replace dialog box, 4-41
Find in Field Explorer option, 5-15
Find in formula results window, 4-41
Find in formulas option, 3-8
Find section on the preview panel, 4-7
Flash file, 5-18
Flexible pagination, 4-3
Format menu options, 4-10
Formatting formulas, 1-25, 2-18
Formula Editor, 1-23
Formula Expert, 1-25
Formula fields, 1-25
Formula fields in charts, 2-9
Formula Workshop, 3-9
Free form placement option, 4-33
Functions tree, 1-23

G

GridRowColumnValue function, 2-18
Group section on the preview panel, 4-7
Group selection formula editor, 4-38
Group selection formula option, 1-24
Group selection option, 4-28
Group sort parameter field, 2-43

H

Help menu options, 4-12
Hierarchical group reports, 1-4, 2-47
Histogram chart, 2-24
HTML preview, 1-5, 1-16

I

Importing values, 2-25
Include this value option, 2-36
Include ties, 2-38
Insert Flash object menu option, 4-24, 5-19
Insert menu options, 4-9
Insert sort control menu option, 4-24

Insert Summary dialog box, 3-6
Insert tools toolbar, 4-15
Interactive messages, 1-4
Isolate group sections, 3-13
Isolate report/page sections, 3-13

J

Join function, 2-46

L

Legacy mode, 3-13
Line height option, 4-10
Link Flash file option, 5-19
Locale settings, 4-2
Lock format option, 4-34
Lock size/position option, 4-34
Long list of values options, 5-5

M

Maintain column alignment option, 3-17
Maximum() function, 2-45
Minimum() function, 2-45
My recent reports, 4-4

N

Navigation tools toolbar, 1-14
New page after visible groups option, 5-2
New patch installation, 1-4
No lower value option, 2-45
No upper value option, 2-45
Nodes, 1-24

O

Object package, 1-18, 4-7
Object size & position dialog box, 3-4
OLAP connection properties dialog box, 5-8
OLAP cube, 5-6
OLAP reports, 5-6
Operators tree, 1-23
Orientation, 4-34

P

Page breaks, 5-2
Page indicator, 1-15
Page orientation, 4-34
Page setup options, 4-30
Paging tab options, 4-34
Paper size, 4-32
Parameter fields, 2-25
Parameter panel, 4-2, 4-7, 5-4
Paste data button, 4-28
PDF Export options, 3-10
Picture tab options, 1-30
Pivot Cross-Tab option, 2-22
Predefined templates, 5-6
Preferred viewing locale option, 4-9
Preview panel, 4-7
Printing parameter range fields, 2-45
Product Locale option, 4-9
Projectexplorer.xml, 1-21
Projects, 1-18
Prompt group, 2-33

Q

Query panel, 4-11

R

Recent reports, 1-10
Record selection formula editor, 4-38
Record selection formula option, 1-24
Record selection option, 4-28
Recursive join, 2-47
Reduced installation file size, 4-2
Remove all horizontal guidelines
    menu option, 4-24
Remove all vertical guidelines
    menu option, 4-24
Remove toolbar buttons, 4-17
Report bursting indexes, 4-39
Report custom functions, 1-24
Report export configuration, 1-5, 2-23
Report fields tree, 1-23
Report menu options, 4-12
Report navigation toolbar, 1-15, 4-6
Report options dialog box, 1-33
Report Packages, 1-19
Report viewers, 2-22
Report wizard change, 4-4
Repository, 1-22

Repository custom functions, 1-25
Repository Explorer, 1-21
Repository Explorer toolbar buttons, 1-22
Resources online, 1-10
Respect keep group together on
    first page option, 1-34
RTF export format, 1-5, 2-22

S

Sample reports, 1-14
Save reports to CrystalReports.com, 4-2
Saved data option, 4-17
Saved data selection formula editor, 4-38
Saved data selection formula option, 4-38
Saving the report with data, 4-38
Search options, 4-41
Section Expert, 4-32
Select Expert, 4-27
Selection formulas, 1-25, 4-37
Selection locale special field, 4-27
Separated values (CSV) export, 3-12
Shortcut menus, 4-24
Show group outlines option, 3-17
Show hidden sections in design
    menu option, 4-24
Show on (viewer) panel option, 5-3
Show online resources, 1-10
Single edition, 4-2
Single sign-on, 1-4
Smart tag & HTML preview options, 1-17
Software updates, 1-10
Sort control, 4-2, 4-9, 5-16
Sort fields in the Field Explorer, 3-4
Sorting a list of values, 2-30
Special fields, 4-26
Spell checker, 1-8
SQL expression fields, 1-25
Standard mode, 3-13
Standard toolbar, 4-13
Start.html, 1-8
Start Page, 1-8, 4-3
Static list of values, 2-28
Status bar, 4-6
Swapping fields, 3-8

T

Template Expert, 5-6
Toggle preview panel button, 4-7
Top N reports, 1-5, 2-37

U

Updated data drivers, 1-6
Updated repository explorer, 1-5
Use a formula as group sort order, 2-44
Use worksheet functions for summaries
 option, 3-17

V

View menu options, 1-16, 4-8
Visual theme option, 4-18

W

What's new in Crystal Reports 2008, 4-2
What's new in Crystal Reports XI, 1-4
Word 2003 viewer, 2-22
Word editable (RTF) export, 2-22
Workbench, 1-5, 1-21, 3-2, 4-7
Workbench toolbar, 1-18, 3-2, 4-7
Workshop tree, 1-24
Workshop tree toolbar, 3-9
Workspace, 1-9, 4-2

X

Xcelsius Flash file, 5-18
Xcelsius integration, 4-3, 5-18
XML Expert option, 4-12
XML Export options, 5-13

Z

Zoom options on status bar, 4-6

No Stress Tech Guides

What's New In Crystal Reports 2008
ISBN-10: 1-935208-01-2
ISBN-13: 978-1-935208-01-3

Business Objects Crystal Reports 2008 For Beginners
ISBN-10: 0977391299
ISBN-13: 978-0-9773912-9-5

Crystal Reports Basic for Visual Studio 2008 For Beginners
ISBN-10: 0977391280
ISBN-13: 978-0-9773912-8-8

Crystal Reports XI For Beginners, Second Edition
ISBN-10: 1-935208-00-4
ISBN-13: 978-1-935208-00-6

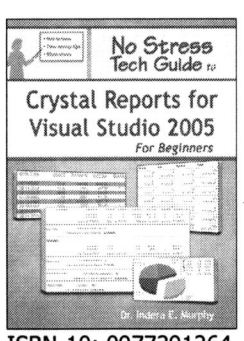

Crystal Reports for Visual Studio 2005 For Beginners
ISBN-10: 0977391264
ISBN-13: 978-0-9773912-6-4

ACT! 2007
ISBN-10: 0977391256
ISBN-13: 978-0-9773912-5-7

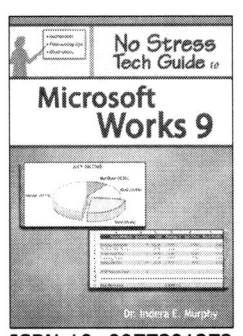

Microsoft Works 9
ISBN-10: 0977391272
ISBN-13: 978-0-9773912-7-1

Microsoft Works 8 & 8.5
ISBN-10: 0977391213
ISBN-13: 978-0-9773912-1-9

OpenOffice.org Writer 2
ISBN-10: 0977391248
ISBN-13: 978-0-9773912-4-0

Other Titles	ISBN-10:	ISBN-13:
Microsoft Works 7	0977391221	978-0-9773912-2-6
Windows XP	0977391205	978-0-9773912-0-2

Visit us on the web at www.tolanapublishing.com